Exemplary Traits

Exemplary Traits

Reading Characterization in Roman Poetry

J. MIRA SEO

OXFORD
UNIVERSITY PRESS

Oxford University Press is a department of the University of Oxford.
It furthers the University's objective of excellence in research, scholarship,
and education by publishing worldwide.

Oxford New York
Auckland Cape Town Dar es Salaam Hong Kong Karachi
Kuala Lumpur Madrid Melbourne Mexico City Nairobi
New Delhi Shanghai Taipei Toronto

With offices in
Argentina Austria Brazil Chile Czech Republic France Greece
Guatemala Hungary Italy Japan Poland Portugal Singapore
South Korea Switzerland Thailand Turkey Ukraine Vietnam

Oxford is a registered trade mark of Oxford University Press
in the UK and certain other countries.

Published in the United States of America by
Oxford University Press
198 Madison Avenue, New York, NY 10016

© Oxford University Press 2013

All rights reserved. No part of this publication may be reproduced, stored in a
retrieval system, or transmitted, in any form or by any means, without the prior
permission in writing of Oxford University Press, or as expressly permitted by law,
by license, or under terms agreed with the appropriate reproduction rights organization.
Inquiries concerning reproduction outside the scope of the above should be sent to the
Rights Department, Oxford University Press, at the address above.

You must not circulate this work in any other form
and you must impose this same condition on any acquirer.

Library of Congress Cataloging-in-Publication Data
Seo, Joanne Mira, 1973–
Exemplary traits: reading characterization in Roman poetry / J. Mira Seo.
pages. cm.
Includes bibliographical references and index.
ISBN 978–0–19–973428–3 (alk. paper)
1. Latin poetry—History and criticism. I. Title.
PA6047.S556 2013
871'.0109–dc23
2012033892

1 3 5 7 9 8 6 4 2
Printed in the United States of America
on acid-free paper

DM Matris Optimae

CONTENTS

Preface ix
Abbreviations and Texts xi

Introduction 1

1. We'll Always Have Paris: Aeneas and the Trojan Legacy 32

2. Lucan's Cato and the Poetics of Exemplarity 66

3. Seneca's *Oedipus*, Characterization and *decorum* 94

4. Parthenopaeus and *mors immatura* in Statius' *Thebaid* 122

5. Amphiaraus, Predestined Prophet, Didactic *Vates* 146

Conclusions 185

Appendix: Seneca's Hippolytus and Fatal Attraction 189
Works Cited 201
Index Locorum 211
Index 217

PREFACE

The main inquiry of this book emerged from a hunch: what if Roman readers did not read literary character the same way we do? What did Roman audiences expect from the figures that populate their texts? This book begins by posing these questions and presenting the cultural and intellectual background to this thought experiment: in the introduction, my aim is to uncover the patterns of thought that shape Roman ideas of character in philosophy, rhetoric, and literature. These formalized verbal practices all share modes of transmission through education, audience (elite Romans), concepts, and terminology. Matthew Roller's brilliant investigation of exemplarity in Roman culture provided further insight into Roman habits of replication and emulation that helped me to understand the function of literary character more deeply. Literary characters, like figures of Roman myth and history, accrete and embody multiple associations. Roman poetry assumes characters' communicative function as semiotic and referential, with less interest in psychological "roundness." My readings of individual literary characters explore this semiotic and referential potential and their function within the poetics of each work. The implicit allusiveness of character effectively transmits poetic genealogy, a lesson I suggest Roman poets may have first observed in Apollonius' epic. Each of the chapters presents a study of an individual character and demonstrates a way to read that figure. The techniques of characterization can range from the forensic (Vergil's Aeneas and his alter ego, Paris) to the philosophical (Stoic exemplarity and Lucan's Cato), and characterization can have surprisingly powerful effects on narrative, as I argue in the analyses of Statius' Parthenopaeus and Amphiaraus. I hope that these readings will stimulate further reassessment and appreciation of Roman literary characterization.

I am grateful to all of my exemplary teachers, friends, and colleagues (with much overlap in those three categories!) who have supported me and my work in its long progress from dissertation to book. Very little of the original dissertation in which this study began remains, though its principles of inquiry are still clearly marked by the influence of my invaluable advisors, Elaine Fantham, Denis Feeney, and Bob Kaster. It is a richer work because of their continued guidance. My thanks also to my wonderful teachers at Swarthmore College, Gil Rose, Rosaria Munson, William Turpin, and Grace Ledbetter, who began my scholarly career in so many ways. My generous colleagues at the University of Michigan in Classical Studies and in Comparative Literature guided me through the growing pains of the manuscript, and their comments and suggestions were crucial to the final shape of the project. My thanks also to diligent and insightful research assistants: from University of Michigan, Alan Itkin, good friend, and now Ph.D. in Comparative Literature, and Curtis Tate, an undergraduate major in Classical Studies; from Yale University, Spencer Klavan, a Classics major (and my first Whiffenpoof), who provided invaluable assistance with indexing. I also owe a great professional debt to my kindly editor, Stefan Vranka, and to the anonymous readers from the press and from my tenure review at Michigan. Skip Gates and the W. E. B. Du Bois Institute at Harvard University generously supported my work on incredibly stimulating research leaves. Very warm thanks to dear friends from Princeton and beyond for their interest and intellects, especially Sean Corner and the stellar Katharina Volk. All my love to my family, and most of all to my husband, Nick Tolwinski, who always helps.

JMS
New Haven, CT

ABBREVIATIONS AND TEXTS

Abbreviations of the names of classical authors and texts typically follow or expand those of *The Oxford Classical Dictionary*. Periodical titles are abbreviated as in *L'Année philologique*. The editions used for the major works discussed are listed below; exceptions to these editions are noted. All translations are my own unless otherwise specified.

Apollonius: F. Vian, ed. (1996) *Apollonios de Rhodes Argonautiques*. Paris.
Vergil: R. A. B. Mynors, ed. (1972) *P. Vergili Maronis Opera*. Oxford.
Lucan: A. E. Housman, ed. (1927) *M. Annaei Lucani Belli Civilis Libri Decem*. Oxford.
Seneca: O. Zwierlein, ed. (1987) *L. Annaei Senecae Tragoediae*. Oxford.
Statius: D. R. Shackleton Bailey, ed., trans. (2003) *Statius Thebaid*, vols. 1 and 2. Cambridge (MA).
—*Statius Silvae*. Cambridge (MA).

Introduction

I. Exemplary Traits

Since the title of the book is *Exemplary Traits: Reading Characterization in Roman Poetry*, I should begin by defining each of the elements in turn. The first phrase, *"Exemplary Traits,"* indicates a methodology and a metaphor that are both active throughout the work: while the phrase may simply signify positive or distinctive aspects of conduct or character, "exemplary" in a Roman context also suggests the phenomenon of exemplarity, that peculiarly Roman emphasis upon models and emulation in ethics and poetics. Exemplarity as a cultural practice in Rome features prominently in the methodology of my literary readings (on which far more below in this introduction). "Traits," as a term associated with genetics, conveys a metaphor of heredity that also emerges throughout my readings of texts and their interrelation: just as poetic texts express their own "immanent genealogies" (to use Barchiesi's phrase), literary characters may also demonstrate heredity and genealogical affiliation through allusion. The next phrase, *"Reading Characterization,"* proposes the composition of character (*"Characterization"*) as a literary technique to be interpreted and analyzed (through *"Reading"*) in its own right, not taken for granted as a simple object of identification. Furthermore, "characterization" in place of "personality" or "individuality"; here we might see a subtly polemical insistence on the formal, poetic quality of literary character that seems to take issue with an unexplored assumption that fictional characters are or should be as much like "real people" as possible, as in Auerbach's tremendous discussion of Odysseus' scar. Finally, *"Roman Poetry,"* which seems very self-evident but is perhaps the most complicated term of all: how "Roman" literature written in Latin by Romans is and how Roman-ness is defined by this tradition so influenced by Greek models is very much under pressure in recent scholarship.[1] And finally, how can we understand characterization in *"Poetry"* as parallel to other formalized and marked forms of Roman discourse that represent character, such as historiography, rhetoric, or philosophy?[2]

The central question of this work may be formulated as follows: what reading practices open up if critics regard characterization in Roman poetry as intimately connected to presentations of the self in other areas, in particular, rhetoric and philosophy?

Poetic Rules for Composing the "Self"

Though important work has been done in ancient characterization, the dominant models depend heavily on analysis of literary characters as personalities who are psychologically analyzable within their cultural contexts.[3] What possibilities might open up for the texts, however, if we read characterization as a mode of communication, a process of becoming over the course of the work, if we track the pieces as they fit together, and tease apart the elements of composition—that is, if we regard characters themselves as functional elements of composition? Some aspects of Roman fictional characters have been much criticized, as in the dissatisfaction with Vergil's vague Aeneas and Livy's distinctly two-dimensional and almost painfully edifying exemplary figures.[4] What analytic approaches might help us to contextualize and defamiliarize our readings of Roman character, especially in extended mythological narratives like epic?

This literary study explores characterization as a poetic device that communicates a view of character as performative, aemulatory, conditioned by the Roman practices of rhetoric, discourses of exemplarity, and Stoic notions of the

---

[1] Feeney (2005), Hunter (2006).

[2] See the ambitious and insightful definition of "poetry" and its limits that introduces Volk's discussion of "the self-conscious poem" in Volk (2002) 6–12 and accompanying bibliography.

[3] Greek literature has inspired more study along these lines, especially in Pelling (1990); Christopher Gill in particular has done very significant and provocative work in both Greek and recently in Latin: Gill (1984); Gill (1986); Gill (1990); Gill (2006). See also in the Pelling volume, Halliwell (1990).

[4] The Aeneas problem explored but unresolved in Braund (1998) and Feeney (1990b); There is much overlap in my account below with the subtle and lucid Levene (2010) 164–87, which unfortunately I did not have a chance to see before much of this introduction was written. Paralleling my approach, Levene also attempts to locate Livy's "inadequate" characterization by contextualizing Livy's authorial practice in historiographical conventions, rhetorical practice, and Gill's philosophical analyses. In particular, Levene relies heavily on Gill's distinction between the psychologically focused (i.e., interior) "personality viewpoints" and "character viewpoints" that depend on social (i.e., exterior) assessment (173). Emphasis on this particular point enables Levene to address the issue of Livy's marked inconsistency of character, as characters may be portrayed inconsistently depending on the social judgment at stake, that is, for the sake of the didactic exemplum desired (183).

self. Referentiality, broadly defined, will be the common thread that links these literary texts to a larger Roman discourse of the self. In a recent reassessment of persona theory in Horace's self-presentation, Kirk Freudenburg similarly emphasizes an "intertextualist" approach to the self, suggesting that positing a binary between a literary, artificial mask in opposition to some unrecoverable, "real historical person" may be insufficient as a reading of both text and biographical "fact."[5] Freudenburg's readings locate Horatian self-construction in the larger cultural and "discursive systems" available for self-fashioning, and define this dynamic "intertextualist" approach to the self in adapted Fowlerian terms, replacing Fowler's "text/s" with "self/selves" in bold:

> We do not read a **self** in isolation, but within a matrix of possibilities constituted by earlier **selves**, which functions as a *langue* to the *parole* of individual **self**-production: without this background, the **self** would be literally unreadable, as there would be no way in which it could have meaning.[6]

Reading even first-person "autobiographical" texts in this light places the audience in a very different position vis-à-vis the figure on the page. Freudenburg describes it as becoming the "authors of Horace"; we readers of epic or tragic characters similarly find ourselves "authoring" these referential figures through our recognition and familiarity with broader cultural modes, referents, and identities.

Freudenburg's analysis thus assimilates the creation of referential, constructed, rhetorical selves to the process of literary intertextuality. The Saussurean concepts of *langue* and *parole* Freudenburg adduces similarly inform Conte's articulation of the larger mechanisms of referentiality: Conte distinguishes between specific points of contact (text to text), as well as larger structures of reference. As in Saussure's linguistic model, any individual moment of correspondence (textual repetition = the metaphorical *parole*) will be meaningless without the larger system or network of references (*langue*).[7]

---

[5] Freudenburg (2010) 272.

[6] Freudenburg (2010) 273. The quote is of course from one of Fowler's most seminal works, "On the Shoulders of Giants: Intertextuality and Classical Studies," Fowler (1997) 14 = Fowler (2000) 117.

[7] Conte brilliantly expands Pasquali's more delimited *arte allusiva* to explore literary genealogy and specifically the definition of genres. Stephen Hinds well articulates Gian Biagio Conte's view of these levels of intertextuality: "In the defining illustration of Conte's powerful double vision of literary imitation, Homer functions for Virgil in the *Aeneid* as the 'modello-esemplare,' i.e. 'as the model constituted by the accretion of a series of individual imitations'; but he also functions as the 'modello-codice,' i.e. as 'the representative of the institution of epic poetry itself.' The former kind of imitation involves the 'reproduc[tion of] single *loci*,' the latter involves the 'assimilat[ion of] rules and codifications,'" Hinds (1998) 41.

Conte contends that the rules and codifications that emerge from a pattern of reference can be used to define genre; poets use models to declare their work's legitimacy within a genre, but these genres are defined through the version of the model a poet wishes to transmit. As Hinds has importantly observed, authors produce "tendentious," partial versions of their models through selective reference.[8] The image of the model used to validate a poet's own work is always only an idiosyncratic version, put to an instrumental use. These uses are as diverse as the poets, and even within a single work, many different functions may emerge, from constructing literary history, to making scholarly comment or correction on an earlier tradition, or even to misguiding the reader's expectations in a familiar narrative.

Therefore character, like genres, can be established through reference to literary models. A character synthesizes many different sources to create a whole. The composite character, like the codes of genre, has its own logic and consistency that the audience's familiarity validates. The audience's recognition takes many forms: we may recognize patterns of allusion that direct us to a singular model, such as the eponymous goddess from the Homeric *Hymn to Demeter* in the case of Apollonius' Thetis, or to a multiplicity of sources, like Vergil's Dido, but what is the effect of this imitation? Traditional scholarship often elucidated the textual sources for various literary characters, but rarely asked the question "What does this do?"[9] Individual moments of reference can create meaning through the relationship between specific texts, but what about large-scale patterning? This question can only be answered through careful study of the character: what rules shape the identity of a particular character, and where they come from. Characters draw on nonliterary as well as literary models, and any identity that has cultural meaning, be it Homer's Paris, the historical Antony in Alexandria, or a beautiful ephebe in Domitian's Rome, can contribute.

If we accept that characters exhibit codes that draw on broad fields of reference, we are able to read them as nodes of intertextuality. The portrayal of character may provoke an emotional response, as when Augustine weeps for Dido, but our emotional responses are only a part of the information we receive from a character. Reading book 4 of the *Aeneid* or Catullus' Lesbia poems may engage the audience emotionally, but it seems that scholars have been reluctant to take on the issue of characterization as a poetic technique

---

[8] Hinds (1998) 100–104.

[9] Pease's (1935) magisterial commentary on *Aeneid* 4 lists a dozen sources for Vergil's Dido, ranging from Homer's Circe to Euripides' Medea. Similarly, Bruère (1951) argues that Lucan based Cornelia, the wife of Pompey, on Catullus' Ariadne and Ovid's Alcyone, and concludes that incongruities with historical fact and inconsistencies of internal narrative can be explained in places by Lucan's adherence to a poetic model.

because they have not been able to escape the idea that characters are mimetic of real people, and that we should respond to them as such. In identifying how Livy's characters are unsatisfactory by modern expectations, David Levene suggests, "the ancients had different criteria for what makes effective characterization than we do, and . . . Livy's characters work well in those terms even if they may not always do so in ours" (172). I emphasize the literary construction of character precisely to resist prioritizing psychology as the exclusive aim of characterization. If we study literary characters divorced from the narrative and formal structures that constitute them, the *technai* of literary artifice, we encounter the problem stated so pungently by Rawdon Wilson in his criticism of Auerbach, "Characters are, so far as I can tell from reading *Mimesis*, simply actual persons who happen to inhabit books rather than the streets of Istanbul."[10] On the other hand, literary analysis of characters in ancient texts still involves cultural and psychological factors, and these factors are located as much in the audiences of the texts as in the author, as Freudenburg has asserted.

Authors and their audiences constitute a cultural community with literary and social expectations. If an individual is portrayed in a certain way by an author, there should be, in a text that succeeds in communication, a recoverable response from the audience who share the author's literary and cultural knowledge. The literary aspect of recognizing characterization as a form of allusion is prima facie not too problematic since we can accept that characters have essential literary functions. Naturally it follows that Roman poets created characters with attention to literary artifice, and it is therefore further conceivable that Roman poets would use the same compositional devices (such as allusion) they have recourse to elsewhere in their poetry.

But defining characterization as a literary technique with its own rules is important because it potentially conflicts with the assumption that Roman poets are aiming for psychological "roundness" in their characters.[11] If psychological roundness in literature—the portrayal of a convincingly autonomous, psychologically full character that reflects our own Cartesian sense of a self-conscious and interior subject—if this expectation simply did not exist for Roman authors or their readers, then we must confront some serious implications for current interpretive models. Addressing these implications will, I hope, explain why defining characterization as an allusive technique may improve our understanding of Roman poetic compositional and reading practices of the first century CE. Three factors will require brief analysis: (1) the function of poetry in the Roman context, (2) "interiority" in Roman

[10] Wilson (1975) 192.
[11] Forster (1927) 43–64.

literature, and (3) the proper location of "inadequacies" in Roman literary characterization.

(1) The function of poetry: perhaps Romans did not read texts to "identify" with characters in some subjective, Flaubertian mode. So why did Romans read poetry? Although the question is so vast as to seem rhetorical, the various, well-defined genres established in Latin literature by the first century CE may provide the beginnings of an answer. As Conte has demonstrated in numerous cases, every Roman text embodies a set of codified expectations both for formal aspects of a work (the "rules" of the genre), and for the author-audience alignment, that is, each text presents a poet-persona appropriate to the chosen genre and constructs its "ideal" audience.[12] Therefore, although we may not be able to recover why a particular reader chose to read a love elegy by Propertius instead of a didactic epic on Epicurean philosophy *on some singular occasion*, the prescriptively codified nature of Roman genres does give some indication as to what the author and the audience expected of each other when immersed in an elegiac text: for instance, if the reader happened to pick up Propertius' *Monobiblos*, she would find the subversively immoderate poet-lover "Propertius" titillating and flattering her in assuming that she shared his urbane, nonconformist attitudes to sex and adultery as well as his prodigious literary sophistication.[13] These expectations for genre and roles may be modified, renegotiated, and even parodied (as in Ovid's reception and transformation of Roman elegy), and transgression of these expectations often constitutes Roman poetic innovation and the audience's literary pleasure.[14] Most significant to this discussion, however, is the strongly prescriptive nature of the Roman reading experience.[15] Both the author and the reader have an ideal role to play in the reading relationship, roles that are constructed by the text, even

---

[12] Conte (1986); Conte (1994); see Volk (2002) 37ff. on the "intra-textual drama" of didactic poetry in which the speaker teaches a student through the text, what she calls the "teacher-student constellation" and one of her necessary criteria for the didactic.

[13] In Prop. 3.3.19–20, Apollo seems to suggest that the *libellus* might substitute for an absent lover, perhaps even provide a kind of textual foreplay for a lonely young woman (*quem legat expectans sola puella virum*).

[14] Ginsberg (1983) 25 stresses the rhetorical origins of the poet's stance in the *Amores* as a kind of *captatio benevolentiae*. As he states, "In the *Amores*, the thoughts, emotions, indeed the character of the audience are not only presumed, but are to a certain extent prefabricated." This is the extreme version of the model presented here.

[15] The fictionality of authorial persona has long been assumed and in contemporary scholarship has been well analyzed as adhering to generic codes, especially in first-person genres such as love elegy and satire. My discussion emphasizes the structured nature of the reader's role as a way of escaping the subjective assumptions of the audience's identification with characters demanded by analogies to the novel.

if an individual reader, say, a stern Cato, is always free to reject Martial's facetious epigrams.[16]

This emphasis on preconceived roles for author and audience in Roman literary production may illuminate another aspect in the case against psychological roundness: (2) "interiority" in Roman literature. Did Romans prefer "flat" or overtly "constructed" characters? Or is psychological roundness some kind of technical issue, like perspective and the discovery of the vanishing point in Italian Renaissance painting?[17] This seems unlikely given that there are arguable examples of interiority and psychological realism in epistolary writing (e.g., Cicero) or philosophical writing (e.g., Seneca).[18] Prose written in the first person still constructs an authorial persona in relation to an ideal audience (Cicero's and Pliny's letters were clearly written to establish their reputations for posterity; Seneca's philosophical letters to Lucilius exhibit a teacher-student relationship),[19] but the prose authors do not, on the whole, suffer the critiques of Vergil's Aeneas, or Ovid's heroines of the *Heroides*, that the fictional characters do not sustain an impression of psychological realism. Even poetry written in the first person largely escapes censure on this topic, since focus on the first-person poetic persona is essential to avoid committing an unfashionable biographical fallacy in literary scholarship.[20] To summarize: if psychological roundness and especially an impression of interiority does exist to an extent in first-person prose genres like letters, then the "problem" with Roman characters

---

[16] In fact, the disapproving or inappropriate reader is the one most explicitly evoked in Latin poetry, apart from specifically named addressees, as in *Ars Amatoria* 1.31–4 (*este procul* . . .), or the programmatic epigram in the prologue to Martial book 1:

> Nosses iocosae dulce cum sacrum Florae
> festosque lusus et licentiam volgi,
> cur in theatrum, Cato severe, venisti?
> an ideo tantum veneras, ut exires?

> If you knew about the ritual pleasant to laughing Flora, and the entertainments they celebrate and the ribaldry of the audience, why did you come to the theater, grim Cato? Or was it for that very reason, only to make your departure?

[17] See Gombrich (1969) on Renaissance painting and the "discovery" of the vanishing point; as he argues, the difference in Renaissance painting is not a technical discovery, but rather results from a change in the cultural needs and expectations of representation in Renaissance Italy.

[18] This may depend on what is meant by "realism" in both epistolarity and Stoic philosophy: on the problematics of defining the formal elements of ancient epistolarity, see Gibson and Morrison (2007). Seneca's version of Stoicism may seem impossibly idealized, but it does indicate a broad variety of emotional experiences and responses. Nussbaum (1994) provides the most sympathetic view of Stoic beliefs on the attainment of true wisdom, though criticized by Gill (2006) 359–401 for misrepresenting Stoicism as being more Cartesian than the evidence would indicate.

[19] Riggsby (1995).

[20] Hardie (1990); Oliensis (1998).

is not a technical issue. Furthermore, constructed authorial personas are critically assumed in first-person genres such as satire or love elegy, but characters in mythological narratives such as epic or tragedy are often condemned as excessively rhetorical or psychologically implausible. This is paradoxical and indicates an inconsistency in contemporary scholarly response, since Roman literary techniques and expectations show a remarkably consistent awareness of "constructed" character from first to third person, even arguably in the second person, if we accept the notion of an ideal reader as inherent to every text.

It appears that contemporary and ancient expectations of literary character come into particular conflict surrounding the characters of mythological, that is, fictional narrative. This is perhaps unsurprising considering that traditional epic may be assimilated to other extended fictional narratives told in the third person like the novel. Which brings us to the final problem: (3) locating the critique. If these characters seem flat, contrived, or "unbelievable" to us, then rather than critiquing Roman authors for their insufficiencies, perhaps it would be more fruitful to consider why characters in Roman mythological poetry seem so markedly constructed, and what the audience understood from these representations.

Defining the Roman Self and Audience Expectations

We might be able to approach an answer through an investigation of audience expectations of character beyond the literary. If literature does reflect cultural norms and beliefs, the presentation of character in Roman poetry may reflect ideas about psychology and the individual. What cultural and/or social beliefs, then, might be able to explain the perceived lack of psychological roundness in Roman poetic characterization? Further, how might these factors be traced and concretely linked to the process of poetic composition? It would clearly be inadequate and unconvincing to say that characters in Roman poetry seem "flat" and "artificial" because the Romans were stilted, psychologically undeveloped people. As important recent work on ancient Greek and Roman emotions has shown, Roman accounts of emotions are highly sophisticated but also in some ways fundamentally at odds with Western post-Enlightenment belief in that there seems to be a stronger emphasis on the external context to emotions as caused or defined by others or circumscribed by social reactions rather than as an exclusively internal, psychological phenomenon.[21] For example, Christopher Gill's 2006 *The Structured Self in Hellenistic and Roman Thought* argues strongly that the Cartesian ideal of the self-conscious, uniquely individual subject does not correspond to ancient ideas of the self.[22]

---

[21] Braund and Gill (1997); Sorabji (2000); Braund and Most (2003); Kaster (2005a).
[22] Gill (2006).

The radically individual and especially subjective ideal of Romantic and post-Romantic literature therefore might also be an inappropriate expectation for ancient literature.[23] In the following overview, I connect the use of exempla in the writing of history and the working of Roman cultural memory to the exercise and inculcation of a persona in rhetoric, finally concluding with the overlap between the philosophical works of Panaetius and the connections between his persona theory as transmitted by Cicero's *De Officiis* and ancient literary criticism.[24] Much of this discussion engages with the work of specialists in fields other than literature; the complex nuances of other scholars' work will have to be sacrificed in order to draw out the as yet unacknowledged implications their analyses have for Roman literary characterization.

Is there a distinctly Roman network of concepts and principles that constitutes their understanding of the self? Matthew Roller demonstrates a peculiarly Roman "habit" of thought through a diachronic survey of Roman historical myths, commemoration through visual images, and historical writings. The broad social injunction to ethical *imitatio* (as in the ancestor masks of the Roman *pompa funebris*) reveals a "discourse of exemplarity."[25] Roller demonstrates that Romans had a strong cultural tendency to establish models of ethical behavior via specific exemplary individuals. As Roller articulates, these exemplary individuals became templates of behavior used by the Romans to embody particular characteristics with an ethically normative force. Just as Horatius Cocles could come to stand as a kind of shorthand for *virtus*, so too could a figure like Appius Claudius Caecus embody characteristics to avoid. According to Roller, exempla themselves are fairly schematic in their elements. The individuals themselves are not endowed with long personal histories. A single representative deed defines who and what the individual will become for Romans both in the immediate moment and for later generations.

Roller defines the "discourse" as the interplay between the exemplary actor and audience acceptance of the deed both in the moment and beyond (primary and secondary audiences); audience reception may change over time, but the figure remains singularly associated with both the significant deed and the ethical message. While the role "exemplary discourse" played in Roman

---

[23] See Kaster (2005b) on the parallels between rhetorical and literary evocations of the passions. As he establishes in his premise, "Along the way we shall see how both rhetoric and literature start from much the same understanding of how the passions work—especially the passions' grounding in certain kinds of judgment and evaluation—and how both rhetoric and literature can create, through their appeals to the passions, the sense of shared understanding and sentiment that is integral to a common culture" (319).

[24] A recent important contribution to the study of exemplarity in historical epic is Tipping (2010) on Silius Italicus; although our texts do not overlap, Tipping's sensitivity to the ambiguity of literary exempla is a critical model for reading Roman epic.

[25] Flower (1996); Roller (2004).

historical memory and cultural identity was, as Roller argues, directed toward transmitting and perpetuating Roman ethical norms and values for individuals, conflict and appropriation were always part of the reception of these models. Roller also notes the genealogical aspect of characteristics in the Roman historical imagination: a Brutus must always be a tyrant-expeller, and the Claudii were consistently known for their arrogance and cruelty, as Suetonius and Tacitus explicitly state in their accounts of Tiberius.[26] If, as Roller claims, "the socioethical dynamics of exemplarity are fundamental to Roman historical consciousness itself," this historical consciousness should apply equally convincingly to the strongly historical and genealogical consciousness of the Roman literary tradition.[27] In other words, the contemporary focus on unique individuality seems to be less of an ideal in ancient Roman conceptions of the self; Roman historical consciousness narrativized individuals as characters in an ongoing functional discourse of ethical value that regarded historical figures as "flexible ethical touchstones," in Roller's terms.

Schematized models, the tendency to conceive of characteristics as genealogical as well as mimetically reproducible, and the relative flexibility of reception as demonstrated by Roller have their counterparts in Roman literary discourse. In Roman poetry, earlier texts furnished models for later authors, who often explicitly defined their relations to antecedents in genealogical terms, as Ovid in the *Tristia* lists names of his predecessors in elegy.[28] Poetic characters too can embody literary affiliation through mythological genealogy and, on another level, through literary allusion (a poetic form of imitation). Each successive author serves as a "secondary audience," providing an implicit comment on the functions of characters from earlier texts, as well as other types of figures available in the Roman cultural environment.

Roller's observations on the relatively schematic and instrumental constructions of exempla have affinities with rhetorical theory and philosophical discussions of the persona. Recent scholarship has emphasized rhetorical education as a critical institution in the transmission of social values and ideals.[29] While training may have been restricted to the aristocratic members of Roman society (despite the marginal status of grammarians and teachers), the idealized roles practiced and performed by speakers in public must have found acceptance across a broad class spectrum of the audience to be effective. Although rhetorical handbooks and the declamatory exercises found therein

---

[26] Roller (2004) 24.

[27] Roller (2004) 7. On literary genealogy in Latin literature, see crucially Barchiesi (2001a); Hinds (2001).

[28] Ovid *Tr.* 4.10.41–56; on Horace's self-conscious creation of a lyric genealogy, see Feeney (2002).

[29] Gleason (1995); Bloomer (1997); Corbeill (2007).

may represent a theoretical abstraction of courtroom or political speech, they represent valuable evidence for the concerns and expectations of the literate class from which the Roman poets and the majority of their audience would have been drawn. Martin Bloomer's 1997 article in particular strongly delineates the idealized hierarchical roles assigned to students of rhetoric. Bloomer argues that the specific rhetorical exercises of declamatory training, far from being fantastical and therefore irrelevant fictions, represent a fundamental "technology of the self," as the student practiced taking on the voice and sentiments appropriate to different members of society. Students enacted and reinforced the roles established by social codes. As Bloomer states, "Persona writing is a kind of ritualized composition where stereotypes are called out for new service or renewed service in a conflict which itself is a remanifestation of a familiar problem."[30] Preestablished and familiarly understood social roles and types had to be in place in order to be deployed effectively.

In techniques such as the *fictio personae*, derived from the Greek *prosōpopoiia*, adolescents engaged in fitting words to characters; Quintilian's account of the technique stresses the importance of appropriateness for the purposes of plausibility:

> His [sc. fictiones personarum] et adversariorum cogitationes velut secum loquentium protrahimus (qui tamen ita demum a fide non abhorrent si ea locutos finxerimus quae cogitasse eos non sit absurdum) et nostros cum aliis sermones et aliorum inter se credibiliter introducimus, et suadendo, obiurgando, querendo, laudando, miserando personas idoneas damus.
>
> We use them to display the inner thoughts of our opponents as though they were talking to themselves (but they are credible only if we imagine them saying what it is not absurd for them to have thought!), to introduce conversations between ourselves and others, or of others among themselves, in a credible manner, and to provide appropriate characters for words of advice, reproach, complaint, praise, or pity.[31]

Character, both for the speaker and for any additional personas the speaker might choose to represent, was carefully circumscribed and relied upon adherence to preconceived notions of appropriateness to gender, station, and circumstance. Just as individual words and sentiments had to conform to the rules imposed by the character in use, so too, Bloomer argues, did the orator

---

[30] Bloomer (1997) 59.
[31] Quintilian 9.2.30, translation from Russell (2001); cf. Ps. Quintilian *Decl. Min.* 260.

in training practice a variety of personas while shaping his identity to suit the role of elite Roman paterfamilias he was to play upon maturity.[32] As in Roller's account of exemplarity, analyses of Roman rhetoric also reflect the Roman cultural "habit" of thinking in terms of highly structured patterns of social identity or roles; rhetoric articulates these roles through attention to language, and in particular, to style and appropriateness of expression.

This concern with appropriateness in language extends beyond oratory and, as one might expect, takes on a marked significance in the literary sphere. As Roy Gibson's recent book well demonstrates, Roman poetry frequently serves as the medium through which the overlap between literary critical terms and philosophical concepts could be explored.[33] By analyzing the definition and application of the Latin term *decorum* from its programmatic origins in Panaetian thought as articulated in Cicero's *De Officiis*, through Horace's philosophical poetry and finally in Ovid's *Ars Amatoria*, Gibson provides an illuminating intellectual history of this concept. As Gibson defines the "language of *decorum*":

> Ideas of the appropriate and the seemly are typically expressed in Latin by a range of terms including *decet, decens, decor, decorum, accommodatus, aptus, congruens,* and *conveniens* (and in Greek by, for example, *prepō, prepon, harmottō, oikeios*). As a rough guide, *aptus, conveniens, congruens* and *accommodatus* express the idea of appropriateness in a more neutral fashion, placing emphasis on aspects such as close fit or harmony; while *decet, decens, decor,* and *decorum* place greater emphasis on the aesthetic aspect of pleasing appearance. The two sets of terms are often intermingled, on the apparent assumption that what is appropriate or proper will also—perhaps "therefore"—be seemly or becoming, and are found alike in contexts of ethical and aesthetic discussion in the 1st century BCE.[34]

Gibson's argument establishes *decorum* as an inherently aesthetic term whose ethical applications in Cicero are explored at different extremes by Propertius and Horace, and finally appropriated for ethically subversive purposes by Ovid. Gibson's main interest, however, lies in the poets' adaptations of this fungible concept as markers of their engagement and response to each other, and as a testament to a common intellectual milieu in the first century BC.

---

[32] Much recent scholarship has focused on rhetorical handbooks and declamatory texts as sources for normative constructions of gender and masculinity following the lead of Gleason (1995), in particular, Richlin (1997); Gunderson (2000); Gunderson (2003); Connolly (2007).

[33] Gibson (2007).

[34] Gibson (2007) 116.

Gibson's valuable study documents the broad interaction between the fields of poetry and philosophy beyond individual philosophical poets such as Lucretius or Horace. His work does not address, however, except in passing, the significance of locating Cicero's *De Officiis* as a central and influential expression of *decorum* and the Panaetian four-personae theory for literary characterization.

In Cicero's *De Officiis* 1.93–151, *decorum*, the "fitting" or "seemly," a Latin translation of the Greek *to prepon*, is the prescriptive criterion on which humans should base their ethical behavior, according to the Panaetian four-personae theory of ethics. The Panaetian four-personae theory of the self as transmitted in the *De Officiis* has traditionally been regarded as an innovation in Stoic thought that represents a new Hellenistic interest in a unique individuality. In Christopher Gill's words, "there seems to be an increased interest in actual, differentiated human beings and a reduced interest in the normative 'sage.'"[35] Nonetheless, Gill convincingly demonstrates that quite the opposite is true: Cicero's account of Panaetius reflects a socially constructed view of individuals, whose behavior, comportment, and even manner of dress are held to a standard of what is *appropriate* for their status and position in life. Although the four personae seem to allow for a novel degree of individuality in that only the first persona (Greek *prosōpon*) contains an essential human quality of rationality, while the second, third, and fourth personae all relate to the specific and individual qualities and circumstances of persons, Gill argues that the overall ethical goal of this theory is to harmonize the four personae so that the individual conforms to a lifestyle that exhibits *decorum*, or moral beauty.[36] This four-personae theory of ethics consistently posits conventional wisdom and social norms as the standards of *decorum*; according to this theory, standards for correct ethical behavior do not permit Socratean or Cynical radical nonconformity, since the appropriateness of behavior is always judged according to the socially determined expectations of class, gender, and status.

Gill reads Cicero's prescriptions for correct comportment in *De Officiis* 1.93–151 as reflecting an ancient emphasis on externalized social roles. In his reading of Cicero's renderings of Panaetius, Gill highlights the aesthetic cast of Panaetian ethical theory and explains it with recourse to the cultural norms and preconceptions of Greco-Roman society.[37] Cicero's discussion in the *De Officiis* uses extensive analogies from theater and poetry to illustrate how

---

[35] Gill (1988) 170.

[36] Gill (1988) 173.

[37] Gill (1988) 194: "In his *decorum* theory, then, Panaetius articulated a widely held assumption: that if a person was to 'play' his social role well, and in a way that would enable him to 'shine' in his society, he had to adhere to certain accepted patterns of speech, movement, and style of life in general."

individuals should "play" their roles, and the social expectations that define them.[38] Gibson states the importance of these analogies:

> But note first that much of the following treatment proper of *decorum* (1.105–25), owing to its foundation in the theory of the *persona* (*prosōpon*), sustains the analogy between dramatic actors and ethical agents. Furthermore, the next part of Cicero's treatment (1.126–49) is concerned with a match between that *persona* and one's words, deeds, and bodily movements. The items announced for treatment here— *facta, dicta, corporis motus et status* (1.126)—are common alike to stage actors and moral agents in everyday life. In retrospect it thus becomes clear that "the simile of the playwright really controls the whole presentation of *decorum*."[39]

Gibson observes that the discourse of *decorum* in Cicero's *De Officiis* consistently refers to externalized, observable deeds and actions, thus constituting a performance of self that is aptly expressed in theatrical metaphor. This idea of identity as performance seems to have strong affinities with Bloomer's analysis of declamatory exercise as a "technology of the self"; the moral agent, much like the student of rhetoric, must practice playing his role according to the script written for him by the combination of his four personae.

Furthermore, just as in Roller's account of exemplarity, we see again an attention to stereotyped categories quite opposed to contemporary notions of self-actualization or radical individualism. Cicero's writings on both philosophy and rhetoric stress *decorum* as an aesthetic quality that emerges from appropriate adherence to expected norms, as in *De Officiis* 1.97, where he presents poetic characterization as an illustration of the concept:

> We are able to infer that it is grasped in this way from that seemliness [*decorum*] to which poets aspire. (This is often discussed more fully in a different context.) We say that poets "observe what is seemly" when what is said and done is worthy of the role. If Aeacus or Minos were to say, "Let them hate provided that they fear," or "The father himself is his children's tomb," it would seem unseemly, because we believe them to have been just men. When Atreus says it, however, there is loud applause: the words are worthy of his role. The poets, though,

---

[38] This overlap between literary and philosophical conceptions may even have been influenced by some direct cross-fertilization, as suggested by Georg Luck (1975), who posits the influence of Menander's *Misoumenos* on Zeno's Stoic advice on love, and the subsequent transmission of Menandrian conceptions through Panaetius to Cicero's *De Officiis*.

[39] Gibson (2007) 119.

will judge what is seemly for each by his role; but nature has imposed on us a role that greatly excels and surpasses that of other creatures.[40]

Much like Quintilian's description of *fictio personae*, Cicero's analogy stresses the plausibility of the characterization; its success depends upon the degree to which it corresponds to the audience's notion of what a certain type of figure (a just or villainous character) ought to do or say. *Decorum* always contains an element of reflexivity; in order to achieve *decorum*, the moral agent, like the poet, must take into account the expectations established by earlier models in the tradition. *Decorum* as a concept translated from aesthetics into the realm of ethics reveals the parallels between the circumscribed performance of social roles and the aesthetically determined boundaries of characterization. This referential and aemulatory notion of individuals furthermore should be taken in the larger context of Roller's observations on the Roman cultural discourse of exemplarity.

As I hope to have shown in this brief overview, the common language and concepts used of the self as persona in rhetorical theory, philosophy, and literary criticism when contextualized within a larger "habit" of Roman exemplary thinking seem to reveal a distinctively Roman approach to the self. This Roman self, understood here as aemulatory, referential, and circumscribed by traditional expectations of society, may in turn define the rules and referentiality of Roman characterization. Roman literary characterization's frequent reference to models, both literary and historical, takes place within a matrix of cultural beliefs about the self that may be reconstructed, however incompletely, from the intellectual tradition derived mostly from elite texts. Nonetheless, these texts likely represent the level of education and conventional beliefs of the literate class who wrote poetry in early imperial Rome. As I have argued above, the novelistic expectation that Roman literary characters should reflect subjective interiority seems to be both damaging and anachronistic: damaging because this approach presumes a *lack* in the creativity or capacity of the authors, from which no productive analysis can issue; anachronistic because the underlying assumption of a Cartesian radical subjectivity for ancient Rome should be questioned in light of ongoing research by scholars such as Christopher Gill. Nonetheless, I do not intend to demonstrate that all Roman literary characterization consists of stereotypes and cookie-cutter schemata. Rather, I suggest that reading Roman literary characterization as a form of literary allusion allows us to appreciate that the numerous possibilities and ingenious variations Roman poets perform in lexical allusion are present in literary characterization

---

[40] Translation from Griffin and Atkins (1991). Cf. Cicero also *Orator* 70–4 on appropriateness in rhetoric, and Horace *AP* 119–30.

as well.[41] All of the sources these poets use are familiar, but the characters are always new and in the process of being formed by the audience's reception.

The Ovid Code

Ovidian texts and discussions of his poetics appear explicitly many times throughout these case studies, but there is no single chapter devoted to a paradigmatic Ovidian character. If one had to choose a single character to embody Ovid's version of allusive characterization, the consensus of contemporary scholarship has already granted Medea that palm despite the regrettable loss of Ovid's tragedy (followed by Persephone in second, with Ariadne very closely behind in third).[42] Self-conscious artist surrogates naturally abound,[43] and the vast range of genres and personae Ovid creates in his diverse oeuvre makes it impossible to cover the topic of characterization in Ovid in a single chapter here.[44] In some sense, Ovid's overtly rhetorical and exuberantly allusive poetics could be considered a watershed in the representation of character, inasmuch as his *Heroides* had traditionally been critiqued as *suasoriae* in verse.[45] And yet, as recent discussions of even the earliest periods of Latin literature have shown, framing the literary tradition, immanent literary histories, and tendentious essentializations of poetic predecessors have been part of the Roman literary tradition from the very beginning.[46] Ovid certainly has no monopoly on referentiality among the Roman poets, as the history of scholarship on Latin literature can attest, nor was his education any more steeped in rhetorical training than other elite Romans of the early empire. Ovid's distinctive presence in this study

---

[41] As Richard Hunter illustrates in his discussion on New Comedy and its Roman imitators, stock characters and stereotyped situations contribute to rather than detract from creatively humorous possibilities, Hunter (1985) 59–82; this phenomenon is not limited to Roman comedy, however, as the following discussions will attempt to show.

[42] Medea: Hinds (1993), Newlands (1997); Persephone: Heinze (1919), Hinds (1987); Ariadne: Conte (1986) 60–64.

[43] Of a vast bibliography, Leach (1974) on Arachne and others; Rosati (1983), Hardie (2002b) on Orpheus and others as surrogates; Rimell (2006) for a female, Medusan counterpart to Orpheus and Pygmalion as male creators; recently on the Ulysses of the *armorum iudicium* (*Met.* 13.1–398) as a poetic surrogate, Pavlock (2009) 110–31.

[44] Although Ginsberg (1983) chapters 1 and 2 attempts to establish an account.

[45] A classic discussion of Ovid's rhetoric and Seneca the Elder's testimonia is Higham (1958), now supplemented by a proliferation of companion articles, among which Kenney (2002) and Auhagen (2007) provide both overviews and close readings; on the *Heroides* specifically and their rhetorical background, see Jacobson (1974) 322–30.

[46] Hinds (1998) 52–83 on uses and abuses of Ennius to construct the "archaic"; Feeney (2005); on contingent literary genealogies, Barchiesi (2001a). To suggest that Ovid's intervention in the tradition represents *the* decisive factor in Roman poetic characterization would seem to affirm the pejorative reading of decline espoused in Williams (1978).

is as a paradigm of Latin poetics, a super-trope that lays bare the backgrounds, assumptions, and strategies of Roman poetry most explicitly. My readings take contemporary Anglo-Italophone Latinists' conceptions of Ovidian poetics (what we might call an "Ovid code") as fundamental to the understanding of all the authors under discussion, not only those who reference Ovid directly.

What does the "Ovid code" look like? Alessandro Schiesaro's sophisticated rebuttal of the "excessive" rhetoricity of the *Heroides* offers an important starting place:

> Precisely because they almost obsessively repeat a familiar theme, the *Heroides* produce a peculiar aesthetic effect and meaning. They bring to an extreme a fundamental quality of poetry based on mythical plots—their predictability—and by so doing force the reader to confront the implicit conventions of that form of poetry. *Omnia iam vulgata* (Virg. *Georg.* 3.4 "all is trite") was felt to be an appropriate comment already in Virgil's times. Ovid takes his illustrious predecessor at his word, and proceeds to explore the expressive potential of repetition and predictability, of viewing the world without any illusion that a direct take is possible, but with the belief that artificiality can, paradoxically, heighten original perception.[47]

While the *Heroides* are the work most transparently related to rhetorical practice, Schiesaro goes beyond previous discussions to observe that Ovid's poetry thematizes convention and repetition and thus proposes artificiality as a condition of reality. Similarly, Katharina Volk has noted on Ovid's rhetorical quality, "What has become clear is the poet's willingness and ability to represent different perspectives on the same situation, tell different versions of the same story, and repeatedly change his mind and suddenly espouse a position opposite to the one he held before. As a result, reality appears elusive, all but disappearing behind the shifting linguistic structures through which it is represented."[48] Ovid reveals the fundamentally constructed nature of the world through his foregrounding of rhetoric's sophistic potential; his generic self-consciousness molds the literary tradition into a series of tendentious codes and genealogies (most of which teleologically end with himself and his own times);[49] these qualities reveal the constructedness and contingency of Augustan ideological structures while simultaneously reveling in the benefits that the Augustan peace enabled. As he naughtily states in the *Ars Amatoria*, "Rome will offer you so many and such gorgeous girls, you'll declare,

---

[47] Schiesaro (2002) 72.
[48] An admirably lucid and suggestive few pages in the excellent Volk (2010) 67–70.
[49] Harrison (2002).

'This city contains whatever there is in the world!'"[50] The traditional label "subversive" does not quite do justice to the Ovidian position; even in exile, Augustan Rome, the city of Venus, remained his ideal, as his exile poetry reveals.[51]

To sum up the "Ovid code" in my readings of Roman poetry: (1) rhetorical (broadly defined) presentation; (2) consistent (self-)interest in generic codes and their potential to construct literary genealogies; (3) inquiry into contemporary cultural norms and engagement with the present. This articulation of Ovidian poetics is in itself a tendentious simplification, but I hope it will provide a shorthand guide to the poetic qualities shared by all the texts under discussion to greater and lesser extents. Where relevant, Ovid's works are (frequently) adduced as model texts in the discussions of Seneca and Statius, but equally important are the pre-"Ovidian" affinities seen in Vergil's explicit essentialization of the Homeric tradition in book 1 of the *Aeneid* and the sustained, almost Ciceronian implication of Aeneas with Paris throughout the epic.[52] Similarly, Lucan's explicit meditation on exemplarity and rhetorical practice through a Cato trope shares the stamp of the rhetorical schools without alluding directly to any specific Ovidian model. In many cases, *post Ovidium ergo propter Ovidium*, but while Ovid's poetry magnifies and thus makes visible the possible range of allusive techniques and traditions that preceded him, not every rhetorical or essentialized literary trope need be attributed directly back to an Ovidian precedent. And far from becoming more simplistic, vulgar, and stereotypical, Ovid's successors exhibit a bolder palette of audience responses based on a heightened awareness of textual referentiality, as we shall see.

Case Studies

Each of the chapters discusses an individual text and its characters, and though the assumptions we make about poetic practice and cultural background may be similar in each case, each poet's treatment produces different outcomes and demonstrates a variety of triangulated relationships with the audience. The studies are presented in the chronological order of the texts as an evocation of the accretive and responsive nature of authors to the tradition, rather than out of commitment to a formal periodization. Each of the works analyzed here provides a snapshot of poets dynamically rearranging their models and the genealogies implicit in their antecedents, and therefore reflect a contingent rather than teleological development.

---

[50] *Ars* 1.55–6: *tot tibi tamque dabit formosas Roma puellas,* / *"haec habit" ut dicas "quicquid in orbe fuit."*

[51] On Ovid's depiction of Rome as "Venus' own place," see Barchiesi (1999), especially 122.

[52] Ovid's importance to Statius can hardly be overestimated, particularly in his characters; see especially Keith (2002).

The first poetic case under discussion, though not a Roman author, presents a Greek model for poetic reception and imitation through character that proved fundamental for later Roman poets who similarly wrote under the shadow of the Greek corpus of mythological poetry. Apollonius' allusive Thetis embodies a literary genealogy that renders his epigonic *Argonautica* a necessary prequel to the *Iliad*: her characteristics will be passed on to her son Achilles. In his version of Thetis, Apollonius deftly draws together the similarities between the characters of two Homeric texts, the Iliadic Achilles and Demeter of the Homeric hymn, to locate the hereditary sources of Thetis' son's rage. In doing so, the Hellenistic poet illustrates the Alexandrian scholarly dictum, "to explain Homer from Homer," by using his own idiosyncratic canon of Homeric texts to validate his allusive epic.

All of the subsequent studies feature what might be termed "problem characters" in Roman literature. Whereas Greek epic and tragedy seem to be more amenable to successful psychological interpretation—naturally because their strong ethical content overlaps effectively with the rich philosophical tradition[53]—there are some Roman literary characters that attract scholarly hostility for their perceived flaws, Aeneas primary among them, Lucan's Cato certainly, and the others have their own detractors that these readings hope to refute.

Chapter 1 begins the Roman investigation proper with a study of Vergil's Aeneas, a figure with his own ambiguous maternal inheritance. This chapter outlines the character's dynamic process of becoming visible, beginning with the indistinct picture of new hero at the opening of the poem. The mechanisms of *fama* bring Aeneas' character into being as he is defined by repute, *kleos*, and his own self-identification through speech. But the Vergilian *Fama*'s identification with agents of slander, rumor, and invective equally generates plausible, competing versions of Aeneas to take form; these coalesce into a Trojan doppelgänger, Paris. Vergil floats an unflattering image of Phrygian Paris behind Aeneas, deriving a problematic alter ego based in the eastern adulterer Paris of Greek mythological tradition, and further imbued with erotic characteristics derived from the recently dominant genre of Roman love elegy. While garnering audience assent through this pattern of allusions, the text further leaves a trail of topographical clues about their parallel lives. This suspect doppelgänger therefore embodies a myriad of conflicts and contradictions about the ambiguous origins of Roman identity. Within the sensitive historical context of a newly developing Augustan discourse on *Romanitas* and through the unlikely

---

[53] A primary example of such successful analysis being Williams (1993), one of the most insightful studies of Greek literature and the self, and also Christopher Gill's work on literary characters.

medium of patriotic ktistic epic, Vergil's problematic founder seems to reflect the ambiguities of *Romanitas* under the recently founded monarchy.[54]

Chapter 2 on Lucan's Cato, yet another distinctly unpopular figure of Roman epic, similarly examines the dynamics of characterization over the course of the epic. Whereas the figure of Aeneas had to become visible, Cato's characterization is based in his conspicuousness. Lucan highlights Cato Uticensis' constructedness as an object of imitation in Stoic hagiography and oratory through a process of lethal "Cato imitation" by other characters. These figures (Brutus, Vulteius, Scaeva, Pompey, and Cato's own men in Libya) imitate Cato's paradigmatic suicide in a formalized schema that itself replicates Seneca's frequent depictions of Cato's suicide as the greatest act of virtue. Exempla inspire imitation, but by their very nature require comparison with a model, and ultimately, assessment. The surprise here is that not even Lucan's Cato himself is exempt from comparison with his own ideal.

Chapter 3 on Seneca's *Oedipus* traces the pressure of literary tradition on the representation of character.[55] Although both plays cover roughly the same mythological events, the character of Seneca's Oedipus differs greatly from that of Sophocles in the *Oedipus Tyrannus*. Seneca's Oedipus fairly cringes with fear from the opening monologue, and his dread and foreboding persist until his ecstatic self-mutilation at the end of the play. This chapter examines Oedipus' fear as a metaliterary awareness of Thebes as metonymic of tragedy, especially as defined by Ovid in his Theban narrative of the *Metamorphoses*. This unusually cowardly Oedipus may therefore be understood through his location in a post-Ovidian Thebes. This Ovidian construction of Thebes as a paradigmatic locus of tragedy for Roman literature is later confirmed in Statius' proem to the *Thebaid*.

The final two chapters present character studies from Statius' *Thebaid*. The *Thebaid* provides a rich synthesis of allusive, generic, and literary historical concerns, and these individual character studies will continue the reappraisal of Statius and his epic that has been at the heart of revived interest in Flavian literature.[56] Statius' self-conscious conventionality in characterization enables particularly original epic effects within the venerable tradition of mythological hexameter poetry. The essentialized character types of the *Thebaid* impose their own narratives and seem to distort or even hijack the plot of the poem; at times these character-driven narratives trade on their very familiarity to

---

[54] On Roman identity as an ongoing question in the *Aeneid*, see Quint (1993); Gurval (1995); Toll (1997); Reed (2007).

[55] Perhaps an alternative to the predominantly psychoanalytic readings of recent scholarship such as Schiesaro (2003), Littlewood (2004); my approach finds more affinity with Hinds (2011) on Seneca's use of Ovid in the *Thyestes* and other plays.

[56] E.g., Heslin (2005); Ganiban (2007); McNelis (2007).

mislead and surprise. These narrative effects reveal the poet's collusion with the audience in allusive characterization. In yet another sense, these allusions provide a record of the scholarly poet's intellectual environment and that of his ideal audience: Statius' reception of earlier poets and his engagement with Neapolitan philosophical schools provide invaluable evidence for an intellectual history of the Flavian period.

Chapter 4 explicates the literary genealogy of Statius' Parthenopaeus to argue that the densely allusive characterization of this figure represents a significant codification of generic conventions. The litany of ill-fated youths in Ovid's *Metamorphoses* 10 may be the immediate epic predecessor for a strong association between ephebic male beauty and death, but Statius' thorough development of the theme offers a compelling homoerotic revision of the epic tradition as far back as Homer. The visual and literary cultures of Domitian's court also provide an essential context for Statius' unwarlike young hero. The compellingly pathetic trajectory of this untimely death creates a homoerotic "swerve" in the poem's narrative that reverberates backward through the tradition.

Chapter 5 traces the functions of Amphiaraus from exemplar of epic delay, to figure of divine enlightenment informed by antecedents in philosophical epos, to his katabasis and the novel representation of a prophet in the underworld. Locating the literary models and paradigmatic prophet representations that inform the characterization of this critical figure provides an insight into the innovative treatment of Amphiaraus' encounter with Dis in the underworld. In Statius' narrative, the prophet embodies the inevitability of the mythological tradition, yet paradoxically provokes the most surprising narrative effects of the poem.

Each of these studies represents a moment of generic "self-fashioning," the establishment of a set of idealized rules for Roman mythological poetry that each poem reverses, challenges, or transgresses on various levels. As Hinds and Barchiesi affirm, Roman epic like other types of poetry defines itself by dramatizing its purity against potential subversive elements, such as women and femininity, or by displaying an "exaggerated alias" that contains an account of untainted origins.[57] These idealizations and their failures also appear on the level of character as reversals of poetic primacy (Apollonius' epic precedes the *Iliad*), or disturbing inadequacies for an elevated figure (Aeneas the founder), or narrative surprise (Amphiaraus, a prophet in Hades). The violations these characters embody further represent the idea that the literary tradition is constantly being negotiated and reformed, both by the poets and by their audiences. There are few studies of characterization as a form of allusion, and those

[57] Hinds (1997) 223; Barchiesi (2001a) 357.

that exist do not adequately relate the subject of character to the larger issue of literary tradition.[58] Characterization brings together questions of intertextuality, literary history, and the cultures of reading that our texts ask as much as they answer.

II. Hellenistic Origins, Epic Genealogies: Thetis in the *Argonautica*

This case study focuses on a relatively underanalyzed encounter between characters that represents a critical moment of the Argo's journey in book 4. While I have thus far emphasized the particularly Roman cultural and intellectual conditions for poetic production, this example from Alexandria is intended to illustrate the origin of a peculiarly literary approach to characterization that will later prove fundamental to Roman poets. The *Argonautica* was translated into Latin by Varro of Atax and known intimately by Vergil, as evidenced by the *Aeneid*.[59] The *Argonautica*'s treatment of character displays in microcosm the same attention to literary genealogy through allusion that has been observed so extensively in the epic's broader narrative. Apollonius' characters exemplify the epic's synthesis of scholarly comment and generic innovation, as has been well discussed in the case of the major figures, Jason and Medea.[60] In this limited episode Apollonius confronts the mythological future of the *Iliad* explicitly by assimilating the chain of his generic affiliations to Thetis' bloodline.

As the Argonauts continue their journey back to Pelias with the fleece, they must confront the infamous Planktai, the Clashing Rocks, which even their magical vessel might not survive without immediate divine intervention. Hera observes the impending danger to the Argonauts and imperiously directs Thetis to lead the other sea nymphs to their aid. Given the less than harmonious relations between Thetis and her estranged husband, the Argonaut Peleus—a situation made all the more awkward by the fact that Hera herself orchestrated the unfortunate match—Hera's augmenting her request with

---

[58] Clauss (1997b); Keith (2002); Hinds (1993).

[59] Richard Hunter, as with all topics Apollonian, is indispensable on the reception of the *Argonautica* at Rome; see Hunter (2004). Nelis (2001) details Vergil's extensive use of the *Argonautica* and provides important discussion of the intertextual relationship between the two poems.

[60] Hunter (2004) 104–17 explores various "rewritings" of Homeric heroes in the *Argonautica* as studies of heroic anger; see also Clauss (1993); Goldhill (1991) 313–21 also treats the problematic exemplarity of Homeric heroes as a marker of the literary past in Apollonius. On the Argonautic Medea as an intertextual character, see Clauss (1997b), which has some overlap with Clauss (1997a).

flattery and specious claims to Thetis' obligation for past favors highlights Hera's manipulative disingenuousness. This deceitful portrait of Hera derives from the Iliadic *Dios apatē* episode (*Il.* 14) in which Hera requests the magical *kistis* from Aphrodite under equally false pretenses.

Thetis' execution of Hera's wishes leads to another charged encounter overlaid heavily with Homeric reworking; as Thetis meets with Peleus to inform him of the divine rescue to come, her resentment and anger, held in check in her conversation with Hera, erupts in an acrimonious reunion with her mortal husband. Apollonius' wrathful Thetis evokes the complex, bitter mother of Achilles in the *Iliad*, especially in her complaints to Hephaistos in book 18 about the painful outcome of her broken marriage to Peleus. This exchange between Thetis and Peleus further shares many narrative and lexical elements with another Homeric text, the *Hymn to Demeter*, a poem in which the bereaved mother, Demeter, expresses her rage in a distinctly Achillean mode. These references to the hymn, and in particular the similarities between Thetis and Demeter, seem to point to the "future" story of the Trojan War. The hymn's portrayal of Demeter evokes both Thetis and Achilles in the *Iliad*; this composite Demeter is the direct model (*modello esemplare*) for Apollonius' Thetis. By evoking the hymnic Demeter as a primary model for the sea nymph, Apollonius transfers this maternal grief and heroic rage onto his Thetis. Thetis, as the mother of the infant Achilles, already has much to be angry about (the loss of her child's immortality, a fact she will confront more pressingly in the *Iliad*), but the quality and nature of her *mēnis* anticipates a legacy that will lead to the deaths of countless Greeks and Trojans.

Both representations of Hera and Thetis exemplify Apollonius' characterization through a pattern of recurrent allusion to a primary model text; in the case of Hera, the *Iliad*, in the case of Thetis, a two-tier or so-called "window" allusion to the *Iliad* as mediated by the Homeric *Hymn to Demeter*.[61] Characterization enables the reader to recognize a dominant model text, since features or qualities of a single character in the *Iliad* or a Homeric hymn possess a certain consistency and unity that recalls a particular text. When these consistent features are reproduced in individual characters in similar situations, the reader recognizes the model text and can evaluate the applicability or inappropriateness of the reference. This process of recognition is an essential part of how the reader perceives character in the *Argonautica*. At the same time, the different types of reference embodied by these two characters

---

[61] Thomas (1986) 188 defines "window reference" as follows: "It consists of the very close adaptation of a model, noticeably interrupted in order to allow reference back to the source of that model: the intermediate model thus serves as a sort of window onto the ultimate source, whose version is otherwise not visible. In the process, the immediate, or chief, model is in some fashion 'corrected.'"

reveal the complexity of poetic reading. Apollonius' use of the hymn seems to suggest that hymnic Demeter is herself a composite of the *Iliad*'s Thetis and Achilles. The hymn's characterization of Demeter, therefore, provides a venerable model for Apollonius' own richly allusive characterization in the epic. Apollonius thus rewrites literary history to push Homeric imitation back to the earliest texts of the Homeric corpus.[62]

Thetis-Demeter-Achilles

The favor that Hera is so strenuously trying to extract from Thetis is not a difficult one—not for a sea nymph, anyway. Saving a boatload of sailors from marine peril? Since Leucothoe handed a drowning Odysseus her enchanted scarf in *Odyssey* 5, Nereids seem to have had little to do other than rescuing the unfortunate mortals who suffer setbacks at sea. And yet, as the example of the indignant Calypso reminds us, more intimate relations between sea goddesses and humans have rarely been great successes. The marriage of Peleus and Thetis, the very marriage that Hera claims the credit for in her speech to Thetis, is one of the worst. Its very badness lies not in the eternal bickering of immortal spouses, but in the heartbreak visited upon a divine mother, whose splendid offspring, despite his superior gifts, must face human indignities, emotional suffering, and finally, untimely death in the Trojan War. This is the unspeakable subtext that keeps bubbling up yeastily under Hera's disingenuous claims to Thetis' gratitude. The more Hera asserts her own benefactions, the more she seems to flounder as she attempts to avoid the *Iliad*'s narrative.

Wisely, Hera leaves something out of the temporal scheme of her speech. Given that the *Iliad*, as noted above, pervades Apollonius' text here as elsewhere, how could the goddess (and the poet) resist mentioning, epitomizing, or otherwise alluding to the great epic of Achilles' *kleos*? The swiftly edited ellipse between Achilles' current and graphically evoked infancy and his future marriage to Medea in Hades (*A.* 4.811–5) begs this question. Hera, as a calculating rhetorician, could hardly mention so unfortunate a result of the marriage she claims the credit for arranging: the mortality of Thetis' son. Hera's narrative, so detailed in its temporal scope, elides a significant period between Achilles' infancy and eventual future on the Isle of the Blessed. In other words, we're missing an *Iliad*.

---

[62] Very little has been written about the Alexandrian reception of the *Homeric Hymns* as epigonic and thus potentially imitative of Homer's epics; while a scholarly consensus seems to have been established that the hymns were not written by Homer, the frequent rewriting of the hymns by Callimachus, Theocritus, and Apollonius is suggestive; as Hunter (2006) 25 notes, Callimachus alone reworked the Homeric *Hymn to Apollo* in three different versions in his hymns to Apollo, Artemis, and Delos.

The audience's awareness of the *Iliad* is essential to understanding the circumstances of the meeting. Why does Hera so desperately overcompensate in her request to Thetis? The presumption seems to be that Thetis prima facie will be unwilling to help the Argonauts, and especially her husband, Peleus. Hera herself urges Thetis to forgive her husband, only drawing further attention to their estrangement and thus introducing the question: why does Thetis hate Peleus so much? After all, this is hardly the pitiable Peleus of the *Iliad*, whom Thetis describes scornfully as "broken with age" (*Il*. 18.434–5); he is one of the doughtiest warriors of the mission, as Hera has stated (*A*. 4.792). Apollonius explains Thetis' anger in two ways: first, through the narrative itself. After encountering Thetis, Peleus has a flashback to the acrimonious end to their marriage, when he mistakenly interrupted Thetis' attempt to immortalize the baby Achilles. Thetis' anger at his ignorant intrusion causes her to abandon her husband and her son. The sustained resentment, however, must surely be due to her constant awareness of her son's resulting vulnerability: to insult, to suffering, and to mortality (that is, to the narrative of the *Iliad*). Rather than reprising Thetis' Iliadic sorrow, however, Apollonius represents this maternal concern as Thetis' anger. This wrathful mother emerges through another, perhaps surprising model: lexical similarities lead us to the bereaved Demeter of the Homeric *Hymn to Demeter*.

The hymn's Demeter and Apollonius' Thetis share similarly disastrous maternal experiences. Both goddesses experience the death of a child through a plan of Zeus; although the child ultimately survives in the underworld, this provides scant comfort. Both goddesses also endeavor to immortalize human infants through the same fiery supernatural ritual, with less than total success. Hera initiates the extra-Homeric references to Achilles' lost invulnerability by tactlessly mentioning Thetis' children in the plural (*A*. 4.807). Alternative mythological versions of Achilles' failed procedure mention some collateral damage: Thetis killed several of their children before Peleus prevented her from completing Achilles' treatment.[63] The suggestive similarity between this implicit reference to Thetis' immortalization of Achilles, and Demeter's care of the baby Demophoön emerges through echoes of the Homeric *Hymn to Demeter* in Hera's speech and in the meeting between Peleus and Thetis that follows. In Thetis' encounters with Hera and Peleus, Apollonius reproduces the hymn's wording more precisely than in the Homeric references discussed above; when adapting Homer's language, Apollonius often substitutes synonyms or varies the syntactical structure.[64] The markedly stricter adherence to the hymn's locutions suggests a significance that requires explanation.

---

[63] See Vian (1996) *ad loc.* for sources, also Hunter (1993) 98.
[64] Cf. discussions of Knight (1995), and Nelis (2001), especially chapter 1.

The Homeric *Hymn to Demeter* emerges as a prominent subtext that explains the characterization of Thetis. Demeter's bereavement and her subsequent rage are appropriate analogues to Thetis' own prescient concerns about her child's fate; Thetis herself exhibits these characteristics both in the *Argonautica* and in the *Iliad*. Alexandrian scholars had already determined that the Homeric Hymns were not written by Homer, although the *Hymn to Demeter* was one of the best known and frequently referenced in later poetry.[65] Why, therefore, does Apollonius use the hymn so explicitly here if the real target is the story of the *Iliad*? Investigating the hymn in relation to the *Iliad* presents a surprising possibility: what if the Homeric *Hymn to Demeter* is a kind of *Iliad*? What if Thetis' imitation of Demeter isolates and reproduces an essentialized Iliadic narrative that exists within the hymn, an *Iliad* driven by the *achos* of a bereaved mother instead of a disgruntled warrior? If we read the hymn in this way, as I suggest Apollonius does, we enter the realm of what Alessandro Barchiesi has called the "future reflexive": a later work's allusive reflections of an earlier text creates an awareness of "future" events. As Barchiesi describes the *Heroides*, "The text sees its future reflected in the mirror of its model, and at the same time sends its reader backwards to that model."[66] This dynamic is even further complicated by using an intermediary text (the hymn) to evoke the Iliadic "future"; Homer's *Iliad* is potentially available, but the Homeric hymn is lexically privileged. But before discussing the implications of this additional complicating factor, it may be useful to examine the links between the Thetis-Peleus episode and the Homeric *Hymn to Demeter* in detail.

Just as the *Iliad* begins with the rage inspired by Agamemnon's blundering, in the *Argonautica* the affinities between Thetis and Demeter also privilege anger as a prime motive. As she attempts to dispel Thetis' grudge against her husband, Hera hypocritically makes the excuse that Peleus made a mistake, ἀάσθη, but that even gods are subject to *atē* (A. 4.817—this advice sounds especially disingenuous coming from this most infamously vengeful of divinities). Although we are not yet told why Thetis is so angry with Peleus (the explanation

---

[65] As Allen et al. (1936) lxxix explain, the *Homeric Hymns* are rarely cited in scholia to the *Iliad* where discussions of Homeric language and usage are in question, thus implying that the hymns were not considered relevant to discussion of Homer qua author. *Vita* V gives the only explicit statement on authorship of the hymns and a justification: οὐδὲν δ' αὐτοῦ θετέον ἔξω τῆς Ἰλιάδος καὶ τῆς Ὀδυσσείας, ἀλλὰ καὶ τοὺς ὕμνους καὶ τὰ λοιπὰ τῶν εἰς αὐτὸν ἀναφερομένων ποιημάτων ἡγητέον ἀλλότρια καὶ τῆς φύσεως καὶ τῆς δυνάμεως ἕνεκα ("Nothing should be regarded as his outside of the Iliad and the Odyssey, but rather even the hymns and the rest of the poems attributed to him should be considered of another on account of their nature and vigor") (*Vita* V.19–22). Richardson (1974) 68–73 makes a case for the *h.Cer.* as one of the most popular Homeric hymns in Hellenistic and later poetry in his commentary.

[66] Barchiesi (2001b) 112.

to follow in a rueful flashback), a significant echo of the Homeric hymn provides a proleptic clue. The placement of the verb in its line-initial position is all the more emphatic in this written epic; the aorist form ἀάσθη appears twice in the Homeric hymn, both times referring to Metaneira as she interrupts the goddess' immortalization of Demophoön (*h.Cer.* 246, 258). Metaneira's error causes Demeter to erupt in anger; from this precedent it seems clear that Thetis will not forgive her mortal husband's foolishness. The implacable anger (χόλος *A.* 4.816) Hera seeks to dispel increasingly becomes a major part of Thetis' characterization as exhibited in her reluctant meeting with Peleus.

The interaction between the estranged couple that follows is exquisitely awkward. Thetis expresses herself bluntly to her husband. After making it abundantly clear that she and the Nereids lend their aid as a service to Hera (4.858-9), Thetis concludes her message by warning Peleus (4.863-4):

ἀλλὰ σὺ μή τῳ ἐμὸν δείξῃς δέμας, εὖτ' ἂν ἴδηαι
ἀντομένην σὺν τῇσι, νόῳ δ' ἔχε, μή με χολώσῃς
πλεῖον ἔτ' ἢ τὸ πάροιθεν ἀπηλεγέως ἐχόλωσας.

As for you, do not point out my form, when you see me coming with them [the other Nereids]. Bear this in mind, and do not anger me any more than you already have so neglectfully done before.

Her lack of affection could not be more painfully obvious. Not surprisingly, Peleus takes this rather hard, τὸν δ' ἄχος αἰνὸν ἔτυψεν (4.866), and a flashback to the precipitating incident follows. Extensive lexical and structural similarities suggest that Peleus' memory of their last marital moment is essentially a textual memory of the Homeric *Hymn to Demeter* (*h.Cer.* 212–55): Thetis was holding the baby in the fire and anointing him with ambrosia, just as Demeter hides the baby in the fire like a brand and feeds him nectar. Peleus, like Demophoön's mother, saw his son in the fire, cried out, and was condemned for his stupidity. As a final gesture, both goddesses cast the infant on the ground and stalk out.[67] Intertextual echoes with the hymn emphasize Thetis' fury: after their difficult encounter, Peleus remembers Thetis' earlier rage when Achilles was still a baby (χωσαμένη *A.* 4.868). This line-initial participle is a variation on *h.Cer.* 251, χολωσαμένη, describing the goddess' anger and subsequent abandonment of Demophoön (the verb χολόω has already been used twice by Thetis in the passage above). Peleus' regretful reminiscence is a reflexive marker of allusivity

---

[67] Vian (1996) 178 gives a list of verbal correspondences, as does Richardson's commentary on the Homeric hymn, Richardson (1974) 237ff.

that underscores the Homeric *Hymn to Demeter* as an important model text that explains Thetis' anger and its causes.[68]

Thetis' anger echoes Demeter's bereaved responses in the hymn. Peleus' flashback evokes the Demophoön episode as an immediate model for Thetis' behavior, but Thetis' anger also mirrors Demeter's greater cause for resentment, the loss of her daughter, Persephone. The participle expressing Thetis' rage in the flashback, χωσαμένη (A. 4.868), is also applied to Demeter upon discovering her daughter's abduction. Once Demeter hears from Helios what has happened to her daughter, she becomes enraged (χωσαμένη 91) and withdraws from all contact, human and divine. Just as Demeter performs this sequence twice (once for Persephone and once for Demophoön), so too does Thetis: once in the past, when she was enraged with Peleus and abandoned him and their child, and again in the present, when she leaves him with strict instructions not even to point out the Naiads. Through Peleus' flashback, Apollonius replicates the hymn's own intratextual doubling. Thetis reminds Peleus of the earlier event (πάροιθεν A. 4.864) and then summarily departs in another barely suppressed rage. Thetis' reminder to Peleus, like the flashback that significantly disrupts the temporal progress of the narrative, signals a return to the literary past (it seems that Thetis exhibits a proleptic, Achilles-like anger from the beginning of their encounter). Thetis' warning to heed past events and Peleus' flashback of that painful moment employ memory to frame an episode drawn from the hymnic Demeter's experience. Thetis recalls and replays the pattern of behavior (anger and abandonment) that echoes Demeter's own doubled bereavements and enraged responses in the Hymn.

Telescoping Demeter's double loss (her abandonment of Demophoön and the kidnapping of Persephone into Hades) into the Thetis narrative fits the chronological moment of the *Argonautica* (Achilles' infancy) while subtly introducing intimations of Achilles' doomed adult future. Recognizing the hymn's presence as a subtext reveals the logic behind Thetis' characterization as an angry mother by bringing together two different moments of Thetis' loss: her botched immortalization of the infant Achilles and her anticipation of the young warrior's death in the *Iliad*. The hymn itself presents the Demophoön incident as a doublet of the Persephone narrative, since both stories center on the loss of a child's immortality, which is then compensated by the granting of honors and ritual on the etiological level of the hymn.[69] While the Demophoön

---

[68] Peleus' flashback operates much as Conte (1986) 57–69 argues poetic memory can, signaling allusion in Latin poetry; Conte stresses formal, lexical correspondences framed by a context of remembrance as a significant indicator of self-conscious allusivity. On integrating reflexive signals into the "dramatic" texture of a narrative, see Hinds (1998) 3–4.

[69] On the structural and lexical similarities between the portrayal of Persephone and the baby Demophoön, see Felson-Rubin and Deal (1980).

episode complements the themes of the Persephone narrative, it also draws explicit parallels between the baby Demophoön and the Iliadic Achilles. Both are divinely nurtured and associated with vegetal imagery: Demophoön experiences miraculous, early flourishing growth (*h.Cer.* 235–41, esp. προθαλὴς 241), while Thetis compares Achilles to a sapling in an orchard (*Il.* 18.56–7, esp. ἔρνεϊ ἶσος 18.56).[70] Both Demophoön and Achilles are promised immortal honor in highly suggestive terms: Demeter ensures the infant τιμὴ δ' ἄφθιτος αἰὲν ἐπέσσεται (*h.Cer.* 263), while Achilles describes his future glory as κλέος ἄφθιτον (*Il.* 9.413).[71] Both Demeter and Thetis lose their children's immortality but gain honor for them in return. While it may be impossible to ascertain definitively whether these correspondences are a result of a common Indo-European origin or represent lexical borrowing on the part of the hymnic poet, the affinities between Achilles in the *Iliad* and Demophoön in the *h.Cer.* allow Apollonius to reach back to the *Iliad* via the hymn. Apollonius thus seems to reapply the hymn's borrowings of Achilles' attributes back to their original subject. We might regard this character-based allusion as "correction," a typical function of the "Alexandrian footnote." By registering the similarities between Demeter and Thetis, we come to recognize further connections between their children.

The narrative of the Iliadic Achilles ultimately becomes the target of Apollonius' references to the Homeric *Hymn to Demeter*. As the audience (already primed for a version of the *Iliad* by Hera's speech) encounters the explicit borrowings from the hymn, further similarities between the hymn and the *Iliad* come into focus. Thetis' behavior toward Peleus reflects a familiar myth pattern shared by the *Iliad* and the Homeric *Hymn to Demeter*: pain inflicted on the subject causes anger, leading to a withdrawal, which then occasions further disastrous results for others.[72] Through her encounter with Peleus, Apollonius sketches out a mini-*Iliad* with Thetis as the wrathful protagonist. Apollonius presents this mini-*Iliad* by demonstrating how the hymn has already translated this plot into a story of maternal grief. By taking Demeter's "version" of the *Iliad* as his primary model for the Thetis episode, Apollonius underscores the similarity between the pained, angry mother and her son's future behavior. Hunter correctly notes the family resemblance between Apollonius' Thetis and Homer's Achilles: "this anger is a characteristic of the Homeric Achilles which

---

[70] Nagy (1999) 181–4.

[71] Cf. *h.Cer.* 261, ἄφθιτον ὤπασα τιμήν; According to Nagy (1999), the term *aphthitos*, "unwithering," represents the ritual concept of immortality translated into the epic terms of poetic *kleos*, chapter 10 *passim*.

[72] A simplification for the purposes of this argument of Lord (1967). Laura Slatkin argues for a submerged theme of Thetis' anger in the *Iliad* through extensive correspondence between the Iliadic Thetis and the Demeter of the hymn, Slatkin (1986) 17–20; cf. Slatkin (1991).

Apollonius has transferred to his mother in the previous generation," but we should note that direct lexical correspondences between Thetis and Homer's Achilles are nonexistent.[73] Rather, this heredity emerges through extensive reference to the Homeric *Hymn to Demeter*, a mediating text that recasts the *Iliad* with a vengeful mother as its protagonist. As the example of Demeter's devastating fury shows, bereaved mothers can be just as destructive as powerful warriors; Thetis' anger at the bungling Peleus anticipates in microcosm the results of Achilles' wrath against the Greeks.

In the character of Thetis, Apollonius establishes a literary history embedded in character descending from the *Iliad* to the Homeric *Hymn to Demeter* to his own *Argonautica*. This character-based literary history parallels a "biological" genealogy, in which a mother's traits foreshadow the distinctive attributes of her son. Here, as elsewhere in the *Argonautica*, Apollonius demonstrates an Alexandrian concern for origins and an affinity for prequels; while most critical attention has been taken up with Apollonius' adolescent Medea, I hope to have shown that even relatively marginal figures like Hera and Thetis embody the poet's distinctive use of character as a vehicle for literary history.[74] Apollonius' Alexandrian epic consistently stages its temporal distance from the Homeric past by presenting elaborate literary histories, sometimes, as in this example, embedded in recognizable character patterns. By interposing the goddess of the Homeric *Hymn to Demeter* as the proximate model for his wrathful Thetis, Apollonius creates a literary genealogy that takes the *Hymn to Demeter* as an early model for imitating the *Iliad*. In doing so, Apollonius reveals how his own imitations of Homer have their own antecedents, even within the "Homeric" corpus itself. As readers, our own expectations of how a character like Thetis should behave are inevitably colored by certain primary representations, like the Iliadic Thetis. So we may not be that surprised at her bitterness and rage. But Apollonius creates a literary history that explains both her current state and its future implications.

Apollonius recalls the main characteristics of the Iliadic Thetis, proleptic grief and rage, by introducing the Homeric *Hymn to Demeter* as a pronounced intertext throughout this part of the narrative. This two-tiered allusion centers on the hymn's assimilation of Demeter to Achilles, and in performing this maneuver, Apollonius elucidates the essential similarities between Thetis and her son in the *Iliad*. Apollonius uses the hymn to triangulate certain essentialized characteristics of the Homeric Thetis that in turn affirm his own portrayal

---

[73] Hunter (1993) 99.

[74] Clauss (1997b) analyzes how the troubled, conflicted Medea of book 3 queasily incorporates Nausicaa's innocence and ominous intimations of Medea's Euripidean future; Hunter (1989) 18–19 well develops the temporal tension developed in Medea's portrayal through intertextual cues to Euripides' *Medea*.

of Thetis as the origin of Homer's Iliadic narrative. By sending the reader back to the source, Apollonius exposes Hera's false identity and manipulative motivations. Hera's version of Thetis' history and her future leave out certain critical details (namely, the crisis of the *Iliad*) that Thetis' allusive characterization fills with the maternal suffering that is to come. In the following chapters we will explore how Apollonius' palimpsestically layered characterization and presentations of literary heredity were passed down to Roman poets.

1

We'll Always Have Paris: Aeneas and the Trojan Legacy

In her threats against the Trojans in Italy, Juno wrathfully declares that Venus' offspring will be another Paris (*Aen.* 7.319–22):

> […] nec face tantum
> Cisseis praegnas ignis enixa iugalis;
> quin idem Veneri partus suus et Paris alter,
> funestaeque iterum recidiva in Pergama taedae.

> The daughter of Cisseus was not the only one who coneived a torch and gave birth to nuptial flames; yes, Venus' offspring will be the same, another Paris, and again there will be funereal torches in Pergamum reborn.

Juno proposes a cyclic view of history, where the events of the past return with different actors; Aeneas, like Paris, will bring his own (as yet unfounded) city to ruin through his marriage with Lavinia. You can take the man out of Troy, she suggests, but you can't take Troy out of the man.[1] The poem provides good evidence for this view: though the geographical movement of the poem is essentially westward, away from Troy, relics, phantasms, and ghosts of the ruined city constantly return, through objects, persons, and situations.[2] The inescapability of the past is equally affirmed by the poem's constant return to the literary works that chronicle Troy's fall. Trojanness, the very ethnicity of Aeneas and his fellow survivors, seems to indicate a form of problematic entanglement with the past.[3]

---

[1] Feeney (1991) 126–7, 147–9 emphasizes the consistently anti-Trojan tendencies of Juno from Homer to Ennius, Naevius, and Vergil.

[2] Ghosts and revenants in Bettini (1997); on regression and return as a theme in the *Aeneid*, see chapter 2 *passim*; Quint (1993).

[3] On the persistence of Oriental Trojanness, see Reed (2007).

The successful voyage from Troy to Latium does not guarantee that the survivors will be transformed by the touch of Italian soil into the ideal forebears of a great nation.[4] While the Trojans sail pointedly past the supernatural monsters encountered by Odysseus before them, the greatest challenge they must face seems to be the heritage they bear within. Aeneas' heritage, both literal (*Veneri partus suus*, 7.321) and literary, is a critical and ongoing topic in the poem; such genealogical interest befits a poem of national origins with a Julian ancestor of the *princeps* at its center.[5]

The thematics of transmission—genealogical, literary, ethnic—as related through *fama* and embodied in relics of the past, dramatically define Aeneas, for good or ill. This chapter traces the dynamics of creating character in the poem, that is, how the poem dramatizes the process of creating "Aeneas" out of multiple traditions and narratives. This process does not culminate in a single, fixed character, however, for the unstable multiplicity of sources and the explicitly unreliable nature of poetic fiction also generates competing figures within the text. Vergil's personification of *Fama* embodies this dynamic, and she asserts her creative potential in the convincing Paris who emerges as Aeneas' double from the multiple mouths of his enemies. As Philip Hardie has recently argued, "Fame and blame are opposites, but also Siamese twins: praise-poetry and blame-poetry, oratorical *laudatio* and *vituperatio*, are two sides of the same coin."[6] His observations on the parallels between *Fama* and Allecto in the *Aeneid* are especially relevant: Allecto and her allies develop and expand the Paris comparison initiated by *Fama* in book 4.[7]

Section I, "*Aeneas ignotus*," analyzes how Vergil establishes the mechanisms of *fama*, literary tradition and heroic *kleos*, as dynamically constitutive of epic character. Far from bringing Aeneas into focus, however, the multiplicity and ambiguity of *Fama* herself and the prismatic variety of her tales only cast his character and actions into doubt. Heroic repute and lineage will be ambiguously determinative for a son of Venus. Section II, "We'll Always Have Paris," explores the darker side of *fama*, how rumor and slander can create a false Aeneas, a Paris, by the same mechanisms as heroic tradition. The same authorizing appeals to tradition, familiar texts, and even the very Roman habit of thinking in exempla delineate the distinctive outlines of this alternative persona. Though other models for Trojan identity exist in the epic tradition (notably Hector), Aeneas' enemies tendentiously recall Paris as the paradigmatic Trojan. In the *Iliad*, even Paris has his warlike moments, but this version of

---

[4] Toll (1997).
[5] Toohey (1984).
[6] Hardie (2009a) 101.
[7] Hardie (2009a) 102–4.

Paris has been carefully tailored as an effeminate oriental adulterer.[8] Aeneas' enemies generate a negative exemplum from literary and mythological sources, exploiting cultural associations between the East and effeminacy. The multiple referents of this Paris figure authenticate its validity to the Roman audience; while the poem's allusive language evokes the flawed Paris of Homer and Attic tragedy, scornful references to curled hair, luxurious dress, and sexual immoderation equally recall the recent propaganda wars between Octavian and Antony. Aeneas' identification with Trojan Paris creates unease beyond Juno's partial reconciliation in book 12 for the Roman readers who accept him as their founder and Augustus' ancestor.

The intertextual possibilities Vergil absorbed from Apollonius certainly extend to his treatment of character; inasmuch as for Apollonius, character itself embodies a richly textual memory that can mediate and even establish literary genealogy, Vergil's characters also possess this allusive potential. When a Roman reader recognizes that a phrase, a gesture, or a description of a character echoes another text, this echo opens the possibility that these fictional characters convey resonances beyond simply acting out the narrative. Roman self-presentation was studiedly situational and explicitly constructed in terms of reference and imitation; even the harmonious impression of appropriate and admirable self-consistency, *decorum,* was analyzed as a series of successful performances. Fictional character can engage the same model of a referential self through textual allusion, every instance of which depends upon the audience's recognition. Inevitably, the reactions of other characters, especially when augmented by echoes of an authoritative tradition, will also color the audience's perception of a character. Thus in the readings that follow I am less concerned with Aeneas' "personality" than with the mechanisms and significance of constructing an "Aeneas" and his competitors.[9]

---

[8] Suter (1984); de Jongh (1987).

[9] Brief bibliography in Laird (1997), who concentrates on registers of presentation, which informs to an extent my argument on the process of coming into being through the speeches of others; other useful works on Vergilian character are Panoussi (2002); Gill (2004) on the Stoic significance of *furor* in Vergil's characterization; Braund (1998); Conte (1999) a highly psychologizing account, somewhat overly speculative on the "interiority" of Aeneas; J. Griffin (1986), perhaps the most perceptive on the variety and function of sources and models for characters in the epic; Griffith (1985) importantly points out the indistinctness in the early characterization of Aeneas; Moseley (1926); Stahl (1981); Bowra (1990) on Aeneas as a Stoic *proficiens* is perhaps too schematic, though provides some persuasive readings. Feeney (1990a) admirably dissects the registers of Aeneas' speech and silence in his encounter with Dido and in other types of situations. He contrasts Aeneas' language in this instance of personal conflict with his other, more successful public speeches, ultimately concluding that Aeneas' taciturnity reveals a fundamental pessimism about human communication throughout the poem, quite in contrast to the ideals of the Homeric epics.

I. *Aeneas ignotus*

By introducing his relatively obscure protagonist through a series of uncertainties (will he survive the storm? Will he overcome his own anxieties to lead his people successfully to safety?) Vergil emphasizes the fragile contingency of Aeneas' literary existence. In the arrival at Carthage, the swirl of expectations and descriptions surrounding the missing leader call into question who he is meant to be and what role he is meant to perform.[10] The creation of a national epic requires an appropriate founder, a *ktistēs*, to stand at its center. Though attention to Aeneas in Etruria can be attested as early as the sixth century, the Greek and Roman historical tradition posited him as the founder of Lavinium, not Rome. Modern historians suggest that Troy and Trojan origins gained significance through the Republic, both as a tool for diplomacy with the Greek world, and ultimately, as a tool of the Julian clan.[11] That Naevius introduced Aeneas into Roman epic is undeniable; Servius' note *ad Aen.* 1.198 claims, *et totus hic locus de Naevio Belli Punici libro translatus est* ("All of this passage has been adapted from Naevius"). Though Naevius' martial epic may have used the Aeneas legend to provide a suitably mythological etiology for the enmity between Rome and Carthage, it is safe to say that Aeneas was not by any means the protagonist of this epic, or of Ennius' *Annales*, in which he also makes an appearance.[12] The function and character of Aeneas as a hero of Roman epic were yet to be determined when Vergil began his work.

Vergil dramatizes his protagonist's inchoateness at the poem's opening by presenting him as a castaway in a land beyond even Odysseus' travels; his disguised mother's account of the cruelty and treachery of the Phoenicians that led to Carthage's founding compounds the sense of alienation from the known,

---

[10] Barchiesi (1998) 332–3 also asserts that Aeneas "must find himself" at the opening of the poem, and points out the importance of the Homeric *Hymn to Aphrodite* as a model for the encounter between mother and son, and as a symbolic signal of origins.

[11] The pre-Vergilian Aeneas: chapter 1, Galinsky (1969). On manipulation by the Julii, the strongest assertions are found in chapter 1 of Erskine (2001); a corrective to this position in a review by C. B. Rose (2003), though Rose also suggests that the Julii made much of the Trojan legend in the first century in Rose (1998) 409–10. For detailed chronology of the Aeneas legend's development in Italy: Cornell (1975); Cornell (1977); Horsfall (1986). On the usefulness of connections to Troy, Momigliano (1982).

[12] Pease (1935) 21 provides a judicious assessment of the topic in his introduction to book 4 of the *Aeneid*. Though Aeneas undoubtedly appeared in many other works from the Republican era, including Ennius' *Annales*, Fabius Pictor's history, Varro's *Origo Gentis Romanae*, and Cato's *Origines*, no precise characterization of Aeneas may be gleaned from these references. For the development of *pietas* as Aeneas' particular characteristic, probably under Augustus (as evidenced by Vergil), chapter 1, Galinsky (1969); cf. Galinsky (1981) 998–1009 on Aeneas as a synthesis of Hercules and Odysseus that surpasses both.

that is, Homeric, world.[13] Replying to the uncanny huntress' inquiries about himself, Aeneas identifies himself in the conventional terms of heroic genealogy, but his address is also strikingly tentative; Aeneas expresses particular concern for the literary tradition that guarantees his fame: have they heard of Troy, that is, have they done their reading (1.372–85)?

> O dea, si prima repetens ab origine pergam
> et vacet annalis nostrorum audire laborum,
> ante diem clauso componat Vesper Olympo.
> nos Troia antiqua, si vestras forte per auris
> Troiae nomen iit, diversa per aequora vectos
> forte sua Libycis tempestas appulit oris.
> sum pius Aeneas, raptos qui ex hoste penatis
> classe veho mecum, fama super aethera notus;
> Italiam quaero patriam, et genus ab Iove summo.
> bis denis Phrygium conscendi navibus aequor,
> matre dea monstrante viam data fata secutus;
> vix septem convulsae undis Euroque supersunt.
> ipse ignotus, egens, Libyae deserta peragro,
> Europa atque Asia pulsus.

Goddess, if I were to explain, going back from the very beginning, and if you had time to listen to the annals of our sufferings, the evening star would first close Olympus and put the day to rest. We are from venerable Troy, if perhaps the name of Troy has reached your ears; a storm by its caprice drove us scattered in different areas of the sea, to Libyan shores. I am reverent Aeneas, I bear on my fleet the Penates that were rescued from the enemy with me, I am known by my reputation above the heavens; I seek Italy as a homeland, and my ancestry is from Jove the highest. I set sail on Phrygian sea with twenty ships, following the path and destiny indicated by my divine mother; scarcely seven ships battered by the east wind and the waves remain. I wander the Libyan wastes unknown, bereft, driven both from Europe and from Asia.

Aeneas' autobiographical account moves through time, and as in Apollonius, personal memory replicates literary history. Aeneas wearily passes over the earliest part of his tale; however, the conjunction of *dea* and *ab origine* (372)

---

[13] On the negative associations Vergil exploits in his depiction of Carthage in books 1–4, see especially Horsfall (1990a).

prompts an irresistible awareness of Aeneas' own origins, told in the Homeric *Hymn to Aphrodite*, of which this scene is a near rerun. Indeed, the meeting is very much a return to origins, replicating Anchises' own encounter with the disguised goddess and his own cautiously fulsome address, as we shall see further below. Aeneas' evocation of the *Annales* (373) further recalls his own appearance in Ennius, while his Homeric past recurs in the mention of Troy.[14] His Iliadic appearances are suppressed for the moment to emphasize a more important Homeric model, Odysseus' arrival in Ithaca.[15] Aeneas' diffident reference to Troy, "if perhaps the name of Troy has reached your ears" (375), recasts very similar words spoken in a similar situation, namely the disguised Athena's words of homecoming to the incredulous Odysseus, "Stranger, the name of Ithaca has reached the shores of Troy, though they say it is far from Achaean territory" (*Od.* 13.248–9). The literary references ease Aeneas from the past to the present as he turns from textual memory to more prospective allusions. Like Odysseus, Aeneas washes up on an unknown shore, but one that bears some uncanny sense of home as he repeats Odysseus' encounter with a patron goddess helpfully brimming with information.

Through these suggestive similarities, Vergil seems to imply that Carthage could be Aeneas' *nostos*, a possibility immediately contradicted by Aeneas' own self-identification (378–82; *Italiam quaero patriam*, 380), but intriguingly revived during his Carthage sojourn. Initially, Aeneas seems to downplay his descent from Venus, mentioning her only as *matre dea* (382), a misdirection given the outsized role Venus will play at Carthage (a point Vergil stresses early in the episode with an emphatic polyptoton of the goddess' name: *sic Venus et Veneris contra sic filius orsus* 325). Aeneas' assertions of divine lineage foreground Jupiter (380), quite appropriately since he goes on to proclaim his destiny, so recently affirmed in Jupiter's prophecy (1.257–96). Nonetheless, despair at his current situation seems to prevail as Aeneas declares himself "unknown, banished from Europe and Asia" (*ignotus ... uropa atque Asia pulsus*, 384–5). The ritualistic recitations of heroic genealogy hold little comfort outside of the Homeric world. Here Vergil expresses the vast gulf between the Odyssean model and Aeneas' encounter: as her son confesses the deepest fear of the epic hero, Venus inflames them further, interrupting his laments with a dismissive, "Whoever you are ..." (*Quisquis es ...* 1.387). Unlike the comradely Odysseus and Athena, whose reciprocal deceptions affirm their compatibility and Odysseus' successful return to Ithaca, Venus' indifference underscores Aeneas' immediate dilemma, his sudden loss of identity.

---

[14] Also noted by Horsfall (2000) 105.

[15] The harbor at Libya (1.162) combines uncanny familiarity with menace, recalling both the harbor of Phorcys (*Od.* 13.96–112) in Ithaca and that of the Lastrygonians (*Od.* 10.87–94).

The Odysseus model instructs of the dangers inherent in becoming a "nobody" by traveling outside the civilized world.[16] In Vergil's secondary epic, literary texts define the realm of the known, hence the relief Aeneas expresses when he encounters the temple of his implacable enemy, Juno. The images that decorate the temple present an answer to at least one of Aeneas' concerns: Troy and its attendant tales are not unknown in Libya. As Aeneas reassures Achates, *solve metus: feret haec aliquam tibi fama salutem*, "Fear not, this repute will bring you some measure of security" (1.463).[17] This *fama*, their heroic *kleos* and the literary tradition that transmits it, proves that they are still within the familiar, civilized world. As their *fama* comes into focus, painted on the panels of Dido's temple and intricately rendered in the ecphrasis, Aeneas himself strangely fades from view. The ecphrasis' visuality has the paradoxical effect of obscuring Aeneas' physical appearance, an effect anticipated in the narrative when Venus covered the two men in a mist (1.339–40). Ecphrasis is always a counterintuitive poetic feature, translating as it does between verbal and visual media, but in the case of Dido's temple, Vergil evokes the epic tradition as handed down by visual artists as much as poets (1.455–7):

> artificumque manus inter se operumque laborem
> miratur, uidet Iliacas ex ordine pugnas
> bellaque iam fama totum uulgata per orbem,

> He wonders at the hands of the artists and the achievement
> of their collective efforts, he sees Ilium's battles in sequence,
> and the wars publicized by fame throughout the entire world.

Of many remarkable treatments of this passage, Barchiesi's analysis of the temple's metapoetic significance is fundamental here; in his words, "Through the temple of Carthage, the *Aeneid* takes leave of its literary past. It miniaturizes it, distances it, shows a way of re-reading it; in the end, having included it, it marginalizes it from the new tale. [...] the fact that the ecphrasis is a 'miniature' is also a form of control over the weight of tradition."[18] *Fama* here refers to the heroic *kleos* and its poetic transmission so important to Aeneas, but the *bella . . . vulgata*, "publicized wars" of the ecphrasis, also vividly conjure up the visual tradition. The dramatic "sale" of Hector's body (1.483–7), the duel between Achilles and Memnon (1.489), and his encounter with the Amazon

---

[16] Odysseus is "nobody," *outis*, with the Cyclops, who knows nothing of Troy or heroic rituals of courtesy; traditional heroic genealogy proves a disadvantage in the episode, as Odysseus' boastful self-naming leads to the sinking of one ship and Poseidon's ongoing wrath.

[17] See Clay (1988) 197.

[18] Barchiesi (1998) 334–5; Putnam (1998a).

Penthesilea (1.490–3) are some of the most popular images from the epic cycle in vase painting; Vergil evokes the most familiar, even trite iconography available to his audience's visual memory to illustrate his miniaturized version of the epic cycle.[19] This ecphrastic representation of the epic tradition thus seems to respond directly to Aeneas' fears, those left so cruelly unanswered by his mother.

The ecphrasis thus relates very specific literary and visual texts: the Trojan women's vain supplication of Athena in *Iliad* 5 (1.479–82), the abuse and ransom of Hector's body in *Iliad* 22–4 (1.483–4), the well-known iconography of the later epic cycle. But something very strange happens when Aeneas himself appears in the painting, *se quoque principibus permixtum agnovit Achivis*, "He recognized himself mixed in among the Greek leaders" (1.488). Vergil does not tell us how Aeneas recognizes himself, and any possible explanations seem to present more problems. Aeneas might recognize some memorable episode, but which? Unfortunately, the episodes from the *Iliad* in which he features do not show him in the best light; we recall that Aeneas and his mother were both beaten by Diomedes in *Iliad* 5 and saved from certain death at Achilles' hands by Poseidon in book 20.[20] Ancient paintings often had labels identifying even obvious figures, as in Trimalchio's home;[21] is Aeneas literate in Punic, or does the Phoenician Dido's Hellenophilia run to Greek labels on her Trojan murals?[22] Vergil's explicit lack of detail about Aeneas' painted image invites such silly speculation. To *recognize* (*agnovit*, 1.488) oneself suggests a familiar event, one the audience might be expected to know from literature or iconography as in the other episodes Aeneas has recognized. Aeneas' representation recalls no explicit referent. Vergil offers no precise description of either the hero or his portrait. As Aeneas identifies himself in Vergil's miniaturized epic tradition, we confront a void. While acknowledging his protagonist's presence in the epic cycle, Vergil discreetly withholds precise identification with Homer's Aineias. Paradoxically, Aeneas' self-identification illustrates Vergil's willful erasure of his past; he blurs the details of Aeneas' literary past to set the stage for his new identity as the founder of Rome.

"Life" imitates art as Aeneas enters Carthage. Hidden by his mother's mist, Aeneas approaches the assembly unseen: *infert se saeptus nebula (mirabile dictu)*

---

[19] On the popularity of these three episodes in the iconography of the Trojan War cycle, *LIMC*, s.v. "Priamos," "Memnon," "Penthesilea," also Anderson (1997).

[20] *Il.* 5.297–350; *Il.* 20.156–339.

[21] The fresco series of Trimalchio's career is labeled *cum titulis* (Petr. 29.3) despite its entirely mundane and straightforward narrative; even Encolpius has no trouble following the images.

[22] Historically Aeneas' native tongue would have been Luwian, but Vergil follows the Homeric convention by which Trojans speak Greek, Watkins (1986). In Vergil's time, Asia Minor was of course Greek-speaking.

/ *per medios, miscetque viris neque cernitur ulli,* "Encircled by a cloud (wondrous to relate), he entered into their midst, and he mixed with the men and was not perceived by anyone" (1.439–40). Both Aeneas and his companion, Achates, are hidden within the cloud, but Vergil stresses the invisibility of Aeneas, jumbled in but unseen among the crowd, just as he appeared in the temple murals (cf. *permixtum,* 1.488). At the very moment that Aeneas does emerge and one would expect a physical description to flesh out our image of the hero, Vergil obscures, rather than details, Aeneas' appearance in a simile that pointedly returns us to the fashioned world of the ecphrasis (1.588–93):

> restitit Aeneas claraque in luce refulsit
> os umerosque deo similis; namque ipsa decoram
> caesariem nato genetrix lumenque iuuentae
> purpureum et laetos oculis adflarat honores:
> quale manus addunt ebori decus, aut ubi flauo
> argentum Pariusue lapis circumdatur auro.

> Aeneas stepped out and shone forth his godlike face and shoulders; for his mother had adorned her son's hair, imbued him with the ruddy flush of youth and filled his eyes with noble charm: just as when hands add detail to ivory, or when silver or Parian marble is adorned with tawny gold.

Aeneas is divinely beautified in typical epic fashion (the parallel is Odysseus' rejuvenation by Athena before his reunion with Telemachus, *Od.* 16.172–6), but rather than contributing to the specificity of his appearance, he remains as anonymous and generic as an idealized heroic sculpture. These physical and metaphorical works of art seem to represent the static artifacts of the epic tradition that Aeneas must transcend as the protagonist of this new epic. In the opening of the poem, Vergil's Aeneas is still inchoate, contrasted with the immobile figures of the past, but yet to prove himself.[23] He must forge a new persona through the active medium of epic, speech, and provide deeds worthy of commemoration through song. The traditional, historical Aeneas is undistinguished in the temple murals, almost a toy soldier, but he is soon to dominate the poem by taking on the narrator's role in book 2.

The ecphrasis, by dispatching the literary past, serves as a transition to new constructions of Aeneas. From indistinct visual representation, speech and reports become the main modes through which his character will be defined. Throughout the poem, people talk about Aeneas, and he affirms his own identity by narrating his own sufferings to the Carthaginians in book 2. In this

[23] Griffith (1985).

respect, Odysseus' arrival at Scheria provides a template; like Odysseus, who arrives among the Phaeacians as an unknown to be recognized, Aeneas too confronts the expectations of his audience with his own version of events. Whereas Odysseus confirms the heroism of his tales through his physical superiority in the Phaeacians' games, however, the actions Aeneas performs at Carthage suggest a more ambivalent and complex relationship between word and deed. Odysseus' visit demonstrates the otherness of the Phaeacians and their separation from the real cruelties of war and the world outside of Scheria; to them, the sufferings of Troy form a yarn to spin at a banquet; martial skill and dancing are equally valued. Aeneas, in contrast, does not find difference in Carthage, but rather, uncanny similarity. His behavior in Carthage is the opposite of Odysseus': rather than rejecting all that is not home and proving the inappropriateness of his presence, Aeneas envies, embraces, assimilates.[24] Vergil's palimpsestic topography of the Libyan harbor perfectly anticipates Aeneas' problem in Carthage: like Odysseus, he will encounter the perils of the Lastrygonians and misidentify a homeland, simply by treating Carthage as his own adoptive city.

Aeneas' affinity for Phoenician Carthage finds a complement in Phoenician Dido's aspirations to Greco-Roman epic. Their romantic attraction, so intricately developed and, indeed, overdetermined by Vergil, seems in retrospect utterly inevitable;[25] a tremendous feat, considering how unlikely this alliance would have seemed to a Roman contemporary.[26] Like Aeneas, Dido also has a preexistence outside of the *Aeneid*, although the historiographical tradition presented a chronology that prevented Dido and Aeneas from ever meeting, and in fact, elevated Dido as the paradigmatic *univira*, a faithful wife married to a single husband.[27] Naevius seems to have introduced the Dido-Aeneas romance into epic, but Vergil distinctively fashions their mutual attraction around their shared concern for heroic *fama* and the epic tradition. In their

---

[24] Reed (2007) 85–6.

[25] Putnam (1998b) 36–54 analyzes the ecphrasis and its anticipation of major themes in the Carthage episode to trace the poetic connections Vergil establishes for the doomed romance. Vergil places special emphasis on Venus' intervention (1.657ff.), which is utterly redundant considering Zeus' guarantees for Aeneas' future and Mercury's mission to render Dido hospitable (1.296–9).

[26] The peculiarity of Aeneas' response in the eyes of a contemporary Roman audience must be acknowledged. Of all the potential new Troys, Carthage is obviously the most unlikely, as Horsfall (1990a) strongly states in his reading of the sojourn at Carthage. Is it so surprising that a Trojan like Aeneas should feel comfortable in the Phoenician luxury of Carthage?

[27] The Greek historical tradition represented by Timaeus praises Dido as a brave female leader who protected her oath to her dead husband Sychaeus by committing suicide rather than accept the Libyan king Iarbas' proposal—no mention of Aeneas, and Livy follows the historical tradition by omitting Carthage from Aeneas' journey in book 1. Hexter (1992), Lord (1969).

initial encounter, Vergil portrays the Carthaginian queen as a kind of Trojan War follower. Even more distant from the epic tradition than Aeneas, Dido has already revealed her interest in the Trojan War by choosing it as the subject for her new temple's ornament. Though an outsider with little stake in that conflict, she claims familiarity with its texts. In her interactions with Aeneas in book 1, Dido seeks to establish her own place in the tradition through textual references and even reported personal encounters. Like Aeneas, Dido must justify her entry into epic by borrowing the authority of literary tradition. If Aeneas is a bit understated and tentative about his place in the tradition, Dido seems to overcompensate a little.

Thus *Fama* in many guises brings the unlikely pair together, and eventually proves their undoing. In both his encounter with his mother and his relief at Juno's temple, Aeneas demonstrates his commitment to the Homeric concept of *fama* as heroic *kleos*, repute based in genealogy and deeds. The temple ecphrasis further provides a potted literary history that delicately locates Aeneas in the epic tradition with studied ambiguity; *fama* takes on an additional significance as the accumulated texts of the epic tradition. *Fama* as destiny is also poised to separate the pair: if Dido's reputation is as the chaste, loyal, *univira* of her murdered husband, Sychaeus (a tradition alluded to in Venus' pointed retelling of the Timaean tale, 1.335–70), and Aeneas is to become famous as the progenitor of the Romans, his much greater fame to come, as recently prophesied by Jupiter, it is hard to see how this affair will end happily. The *decorum* of their established reputations will not permit their relationship to endure since their individual *famae* offer a script they must follow in divergent directions. The monstrous personification of *Fama* that sets a complicated chain of events into motion, ultimately re-establishing Aeneas' proper course, is the perfect agent to destroy their aberrant idyll: the received epic and historiographical traditions demand that the lovers of the nascent poem follow the plot. Aeneas must continue to Italy, and Dido must die alone.

In a form of simultaneity, at the epic's opening Aeneas appears as yet unformed and indistinct in his new role as nation-builder. Aeneas hungers for the reassurances of the past, and Vergil introduces Dido's eagerness to gratify his nostalgia for familiar heroic courtesies and her welcome acknowledgement of his Homeric status as another element of their mutual attraction. Aeneas and Dido are first introduced to each other through *fama,* complementary reported descriptions: the disguised Venus gives her son an account of the settlement of Carthage, Dido's marriage, and her daring escape from Tyre after her brother's treachery (1.335–70). Likewise Ilioneus offers a glowing, near eulogistic description of the missing Aeneas as he appeals to Dido for mercy and assistance (1.544–9). Confirming Aeneas' relief at the temple, Dido responds that she is well aware of the Trojans and their tradition (1.565–6). Dido's generous offer of aid and welcome to the Trojans seems to validate Aeneas' oddly optimistic interpretation of the temple iconography. Reciprocating her own interest in his identity and repute, Aeneas appropriately asks, "What generations so blessed brought you forth, what glorious parents bore one such as yourself?" (1.605–6), then continues by promising her eternal and far-reaching fame (1.607–10). Aeneas' fulsome eloquence seems to hold tantalizing promise for the *kleos* Dido craves; Aeneas will speak beautifully, perhaps even poetically of her noble qualities and thus inscribe her eternally in epic. *Honos, nomen,* and *laudes* are the prizes he offers (the *praemia digna* he assures will be hers in 1.605), virtually a calque on Homeric *kleos*. That he ends his promise with a reference to his departure anticipates his future betrayal: her affair with Aeneas will destroy her virtuous reputation, and her *nomen* in epic will hardly be glorious. Their Vergilian encounter will cause Dido to depart from her exemplary identity as *univira* in historiography and gain a new, very different *fama* in epic. Dido and Aeneas in their first exchange reveal a shared heroic interest in reputation and its mechanisms, which highlights the *Aeneid*'s powerful intervention in the tradition: after Vergil, neither Dido nor Aeneas will ever be what they were before.

Vergil explicitly indicates Dido's sources of information about the Trojan War and Aeneas himself. The queen addresses him as *nate dea* (a fact not previously mentioned by Ilioneus) and asks if he is really the one from the hymn: "Are you *that* Aeneas (*tune ille Aeneas*) whom nurturing Venus bore to Dardanian Anchises (*Dardanio Anchisae*) by the flow of Phrygian Simois?" (1.618–9).[28] Despite the fact that the Homeric hymn does not give a precise location for Aeneas' birth (in *h.Ven.* 256–58 Aphrodite predicts that the nymphs will raise the infant Aeneas on Mt. Ida), line 618 contains a critical reference to the hymn as the textual source of Dido's knowledge.[29] *Dardanius,* used only twice of Anchises in the *Aeneid,* is applied to Anchises only once in the hymn at a critical moment of revelation. In rousing her slumbering paramour, Aphrodite addresses him with an abrupt, "Wake up, scion of Dardanus (*Dardanide*)" (*h. Ven.* 177). This single occurrence of the genealogical epithet appropriately introduces Aphrodite's speech revealing herself as a goddess and announcing the child she will bear as a result of their encounter. The queen's use of *Dardanius* thus refers to the precise section of the hymn in which Aeneas' birth

---

[28] Servius also notes the emphasis in the demonstrative pronoun, as he says *ad loc., TUNE ILLE AENEAS et hoc admirativum, non interrogativum. "ille" autem honoris est* [. . .].

[29] Though *Il.* 5.311–3 also names Aphrodite and Anchises as Aeneas' parents, the patronymic *Dardanides* does not appear. Surprisingly, this particular deployment of the patronymic has not been noted elsewhere, although on Vergil's uses of the Homeric *Hymn to Venus* and the hymns in Roman literature, see Barchiesi (1999) and Douglas Olson (2012) *ad loc* on this passage.

and upbringing is described, demonstrating her literary sophistication while slyly answering her own question.

Not only the very same Aeneas, but also the very same goddess-mother, as this recurrence of the hymn reminds us: like Apollonius before him, Vergil assembles large-scale echoes of behavior to portray Venus' character. While demonstrating how well versed she is in the Homeric tradition, Dido also confirms the particular text that provides the model for Venus' duplicitous characterization. The earlier encounter between Venus and her son is simultaneously a kind of type scene (hero encounters disguised divinity) and a double imitation of two particular texts: a bitter *oppositio in imitando* of the intimate and playfully reciprocal deception between Odysseus and Athena, and a distressing repetition of Aeneas' parents' encounter.[30] Aeneas reproduces elements of his father's address to Venus in the hymn, and both address her as a goddess, a fact that Aphrodite/Venus denies on both occasions. The goddess consistently perpetuates her deception; while the shameful circumstances of her compulsion may justify her dissembling in the hymn, her persistence with Aeneas verges on the gratuitously capricious, as his outraged response surely indicates (1.407–9). Venus' later suspicions of treacherous *Punica fides* ([. . .] *domum timet ambiguam Tyriosque bilinguis*, 1.661) appear ironically misplaced, since this replay of the Homeric *Hymn to Aphrodite* designates the goddess herself as the untrustworthy figure.[31] As Apollonius' Thetis has shown, mythological lineage can translate into inheritance of character traits: character reveals literary genealogy. Dido's familiarity with the hymn confirms her participation in heroic *kleos* and its texts, but taken with the earlier evocation of a hymnic Venus, these references to the hymn suggest that the son of this duplicitous goddess may also prove untrustworthy.

Dido's sympathies are explained by an earlier encounter with another survivor of the Trojan War: Teucer, the exiled brother of Ajax. Paradoxically, however, the queen's most direct contact with the war only deepens the mystery of who she and Aeneas are and will become in the epic. Dido proves her literary awareness of Homer and the epic cycle, but like Aeneas' appearance in the ecphrasis, this autopsy, which should be definitive in establishing her interstitial place in the tradition, rather generates more telling ambiguities. As Dido recalls the meeting (1.619–26):

---

[30] Distressing potentially to the reader no less than to Aeneas himself for the markedly incestuous implications of this repetition, as Oliensis (2009) 61–3, developing Reckford (1996), disturbingly pursues. Cf. *Od.* 13.187–351, and note that the programmatically solicitous mother Thetis of *Iliad* 1 must also lurk in the background here as another counterexample to Venus' callousness; for further lexical similarities see Gutting (2009).

[31] Venus' appeal to Cupid reprises her destructive role in *Argonautica* 3, another demonstration of her instrumental attitude to human love and suffering.

> atque equidem Teucrum memini Sidona venire
> finibus expulsum patriis, nova regna petentem
> auxilio Beli; genitor tum Belus opimam
> vastabat Cyprum et victor dicione tenebat.
> tempore iam ex illo casus mihi cognitus urbis
> Troianae nomenque tuum regesque Pelasgi.
> ipse hostis Teucros insigni laude ferebat
> seque ortum antiqua Teucrorum a stirpe volebat.

And I even remember that Teucer came to Sidon, after he was expelled from his paternal lands. He was seeking a new kingdom with Belus' help. At that time, my father Belus was laying waste wealthy Cyprus, and once victorious, he held it under his sway. Already from that occasion, the misfortune of the Trojan city was known to me, and your name, and the Greek kings. He himself, though your enemy, spoke of the Teucrians with high praise, and he considered himself born from the ancient stock of the Teucrians.

Teucer himself is not particularly prominent in the epic tradition, though he plays a larger role in tragedy, both Greek and Roman.[32] Dido's account of the encounter attempts to claim a place in the tales of the *nostoi*.[33] As Dido uses the keywords of poetic allusion (*memini, ferebat*), here they underscore her claim's anomaly; she speaks from a position of traditional authority where none exists, and thus Vergil underscores her Zelig-like intrusion into the literary narrative.[34]

---

[32] *Il.* 8.281–4 does not name his mother, only noting that he is a bastard son of Telamon. Sophocles' *Ajax* (1299–1303) and perhaps the lost *Teucer* make his Trojan lineage through the captive, Hesione, more explicit (cf. Xenophon *Kyn.* 1.9, Ovid *Met.* 11.211–7, Apollodorus ApB 2.6.4, ΣAb *Il.* 8.284). There is no mention of Teucer's exile by his father, Telamon, in Proclus' summary of the *Nostoi*, though he does appear on Cyprus in Pindar *Nem.* 4.46–7, and the tale may have been told in Aeschylus' lost *Salaminiai*, the third play in his Ajax trilogy. Pacuvius' fragmentary *Teucer* must have been derived mostly from Sophocles, though other sources may have been part of the background. Gantz (1993) s.v. "Teukros son of Telamon."

[33] The encounter with Dido and Belus' help in the colonization of Cyprus are otherwise unattested outside of Vergil.

[34] Hinds (1988) 17–18 on *Fast.* 3.471–6: "Ovid's, or Ariadne's, *memini* in *Fast.* 3.473 is in effect a refinement of the 'Alexandrian footnote' (D. O. Ross's term for the signaling of allusion by a poet through seemingly general appeals to tradition and report, such as *dicitur* 'it is said,' *ferunt* 'they relate,' or *fama est*, 'the story goes'). And allied too are those ingenious allusions which, rather than being signaled by added comments, are actually so constructed as *through their own wording* to draw attention to their status as allusions." Feeney (1991) 130 also discusses *fertur* (*Aen.* 1.15) as an example of the recurring "language of tradition and authority"; see also his chapter 4, *passim*. Wills (1996) 31 on "external markers of allusion," which for him include *dicitur*,

The problem remains, however: what did Teucer tell her? It seems plausible from what we know of Teucer from later tragedy (notably in Sophocles' *Ajax*) that though he was an ally of the Greeks, resentment against the Atreids and his exile from Salamis might cause him to praise the Trojans as Dido claims he did. The queen's words develop the suggestive etymology of Teucer's name, emphasizing a shared ethnicity: "He himself, though your enemy, spoke of the Teucrians (*Teucros*) with high praise, and he considered himself born from the ancient stock of the Teucrians (*Teucrorum*)" (1.625–6). Vergil employs Teucer's post-Homeric identity as an exile to enhance the parallelism between Aeneas and Dido through allusions to Roman Teucers. In Roman literature, the fragments of Pacuvius' *Teucer* indicate Teucer's return to Salamis as the bearer of unwelcome news from Troy, and recount his banishment by Telamon.[35] Dido's encounter therefore neatly accommodates the Pacuvian Teucer's role as informant and subsequent exile, and further develops the allusions to Pacuvius' storm in the opening of the poem (Servius *ad Aen.* 1.87). Horace's Teucer, the exiled leader nobly encouraging his followers in C. 1.7, has already served as a model for Aeneas' speech to his despondent men earlier in the book (1.197ff.).[36] Teucer's traditional identity in Roman poetry as an exiled *ktistēs* here triangulates the similarity between the future lovers.[37]

Dido's evocation of Teucer triangulates the similarities between the Trojan Aeneas and the Carthaginian queen. His status as a hybrid figure of ambiguous loyalties embodies the uneasy combination of traditionality and the unknown in all three wandering *ktisteis*. Like Aeneas and Dido, this marginal figure from the epic tradition plays a new role in the *Aeneid*. His mixed heritage points to an uncertainty about inherited character traits: Dido should be mercenary, cruel, and deceitful like her treacherous brother, a typical Phoenician/proto-Carthaginian, but unexpectedly shows nobility and generosity.[38] Despite

fertur, perhibent, ut fama est, ut aiunt, ut mihi narratur, certior auctor in the category of reference to another source; he also includes "words of memory," such as *recordor, repeto, refero*, and *memini*, and also opposites, such as *nescio, immemor*, etc.

[35] Pac. *trag.* especially fragments 340–51 on Teucer's tidings and Telamon's violent reaction.

[36] Nisbet and Hubbard (1980) *ad* C. 1.7.30 cautiously suggest a similarity to *Aen.* 1.197ff.: "*peioraque passi* [. . .]. This may be one of the rare places where Horace has influenced Virgil, unless both are indebted to an earlier poet, perhaps Naevius." It seems much more probable that both Horace and Vergil had an image of a wandering Teucer in mind from Pacuvius or even from Sophocles, or that Vergil paid friendly tribute to his friend Horace's successful first book of the *Odes* by adopting his Teucer as model for his own protagonist, than that the similarities between the two passages come from a shared use of the Dido and Aeneas episode in Naevius.

[37] Barchiesi (1999) 337, *pace* Horsfall (1990a) 137, who views Teucer as hostile to the Trojans, warped by his father Telamon's long experience of Trojan deceit and therefore utterly untrustworthy as a positive source on his Trojan enemies.

[38] Horsfall (1990a) 138 characterizes even the ecphrasis as an expression of Carthaginian character: "They illustrate just those qualities which Carthaginians might admire in the victorious Greeks—greed and brutality, for which they themselves had such a fine reputation."

Dido's familiarity with epic tradition, she and the audience have yet to learn what kind of Trojan Aeneas will be; his ambiguous inheritance, like Teucer's, could indicate heroic nobility (from Jupiter), or duplicitous caddishness (from Venus), as the allusions to the Homeric *Hymn to Aphrodite* seem to suggest.

Initially, Aeneas and Dido are both nobodies, vacant signs in the new tradition of Vergil's Roman epic. As the metaliterary medium of the ecphrasis suggests, Aeneas' lack of a distinct physical appearance reflects the poet's attempt to downplay his protagonist's earlier incarnations in the literary tradition; Vergil goes on to fill this void through the reports of other characters. The descriptions provided by other characters and their own words thus fill in the image of Aeneas that Dido and the audience come to expect. The presence of Teucer brings out the similarities between Dido and Aeneas at this point of the narrative: by the time of Horace's poem, this marginal figure has come to represent a philosophical, model *ktistēs*, yet also embodies hybridity, ambiguity, and tragedy. Dido's personal connection to Teucer anticipates the tragic consequences to follow her liaison with Aeneas. The fact that Dido receives her information about Aeneas from such an ambiguous figure further dramatizes how little we know of Aeneas so far. Only hearsay, rumor, and the expectations created by external textual sources provide any hint of what Aeneas might become, both for Dido and for the poem.

II. We'll Always Have Paris

In the beginning of the poem, Vergil dramatizes the novelty of his protagonist by making him a relative "unknown" in a foreign land. His identification with Dido, another interstitial figure plucked from relative obscurity, and their shared awareness of reputation and its mechanisms demonstrate the important generative power of *fama*: we see epic *fama* created as characters recount, trade, and receive versions of themselves. These preexisting versions can even take the form of a literary DNA, as we have seen, in which literary genealogy maps on to mythological lineage with potentially predictive force: Venus' reminiscences of the hymnic Aphrodite suggest that Aeneas may not be the most trustworthy or constant lover to Dido. And despite Jupiter's authoritative prophecy in book 1, the fixity of who Aeneas must become, his *fatum* as the founder of Rome, is challenged throughout by the untrammeled fictionality of epic with its multiplicity of voices, rumors, insinuations.[39] Though the speeches described thus far reflect flatteringly on Aeneas' heroic reputation, not all speakers in the poem are as indulgent, or even polite. Vergil's *Fama* has

[39] Hardie (2002a); Hardie (2002b) 69.

a destructive power, as well as an encomiastic one. Aeneas' lineage, both mythological and literary, recurs throughout the poem to define his character.

After describing the Titan-born *Fama*, the poet presents her as a chthonic double whose tales compete with his own epic (4.188–94):

> tam ficti pravique tenax quam nuntia veri.
> haec tum multiplici populos sermone replebat
> gaudens, et pariter facta atque infecta canebat:
> venisse Aenean Troiano sanguine cretum,
> cui se pulchra viro dignetur iungere Dido;
> nunc hiemem inter se luxu, quam longa, fovere
> regnorum immemores turpique cupidine captos.

> [. . .] she is as dedicated a messenger of vicious falsehood as of the truth. At this time, she was joyfully filling the people with various accounts, and she sang of deeds done and not done equally: that Aeneas, born of Trojan blood had come, to which man lovely Dido saw fit to join herself; now they were warming the winter together in indulgence, as long as it lasted, unmindful of their kingdoms and seized by shameful lust.

Fama's account of the love affair aptly takes the form of reported speech in indirect statement. Though she may be indiscriminate about fact and fiction (4.188, 190), her words have an authority that parallels that of the epic poet (*canebat*, 4.190).[40] *Fama* significantly mentions Aeneas' Trojan blood (*Troiano sanguine cretum*, 191). Does this fact of his birth prompt the elegiac cast of her report? *Fama* tells tales that challenge the epic narrative; Aeneas and Dido are already lovers, but the language she uses to communicate this information implies that the epic is breaking down and becoming an elegy. The contrast between erotic warmth and winter cold (193) and the portrait of lovers self-indulgently neglecting their duties seem to recall Tibullus' programmatic formulation (1.1.45–8):

> quam iuvat immites ventos audire cubantem
>   et dominam tenero continuisse sinu!
> aut gelidas hibernus aquas cum fuderit Auster
>   securum somnos igne iuvante sequi!

---

[40] Hardie (1998) 259, "a demonic double of the epic voice and of the epic tradition itself." Cf. Hardie (1986) 275 n. 118 on the similarities between the Vergilian *Fama* and the "ideal of the poet".

How pleasing to listen to the pitiless gusts and to hold my sleeping mistress in a gentle embrace! Or to sleep peacefully by a comforting fire, when the wintry South wind pours out icy bursts!

Aeneas is a typical elegiac lover in *Fama*'s pseudopoetic account as he ignores his fated responsibilities in favor of personal pleasure.[41] Mercury confirms *Fama*'s elegiac portrait of Aeneas, accusing him of being forgetful of his affairs, *heu regni rerumque oblite tuarum* (4.266) and pursuing *otium* in Libya, *aut qua spe Libycis terris otia teris?* (4.271).[42] Jupiter himself sees both Dido and Aeneas, *oblitos famae melioris amantis* (4.221), where *fama* here signifies both virtuous repute and the epic narrative's progression. *Fama*'s poetic authority mirrors that of the epic poet by mingling truth with fiction (cf. Hesiod *Th.* 27–8), and like the poet, she manipulates genres to create a narrative that her human agents such as Iarbas will pass on as an alternative portrait of the epic hero.

Fama subverts the epic narrative so successfully because of her version's plausibility; like Iarbas, who is primed for credulity by his jealousy, Vergil's readers are primed by the familiarity of elegiac codes. Adducing the familiar, the stereotypical, through the distancing medium of speech enables Vergil to present a sinisterly plausible double for Aeneas: his cousin, Paris. The Paris-figure evoked in hostile speeches about Aeneas is composed of a variety of Greek and Roman traditions, in particular the abuse of Paris in the *Iliad*, which is expanded in Paris' representations in tragedy, combined with Roman rhetorical tropes on effeminacy and oriental excess.[43] By Vergil's time, Paris was already a byword for luxuriousness, effeminacy, and adulterous indiscretion (Cicero on the seducer Memmius, *hic noster Paris, Ad. Att.* 1.18.3). Like a phantom Aeneas fashioned of cloud, this ghostly double misleads and confuses us by its persuasive mimesis.

As Aeneas accumulates symbolic roles such as *pater* in the funeral games of book 5 or Hercules in book 8, he continues to lack the specificity, the distinctive qualities, of other mythological heroes such as Achilles, "tireless, wrathful, ruthless, fierce, / (who) rejects the authority of birth, (who) yields to none in battle" (*impiger, iracundus, inexorabilis, acer, / iura neget sibi nata, nihil non arroget armis*, Horace *AP* 121–2). As a vague and relatively underdefined figure, defined primarily through metaphor and comparison, Aeneas is particularly vulnerable to false characterization. His anodyne epithet, *pius*, is more an

---

[41] Saylor (1986) 75.

[42] On *otium* in an erotic context, see Woodman (1966).

[43] On the invective tradition within the *Iliad*, Suter (1984); Suter (1993). Paris as a stock figure in tragedy, Stinton (1965). The effeminacy of Phrygians in general and Paris as an example of the "Phrygianization" of the Trojans in the fifth century, Hall (1988); Hall (1989). Roman invective tradition: Nisbet (1961), appendix VI; Richlin (1997). Orientalism: Reed (2007).

ethical claim than a personality.[44] The vivid persona of a Paris, with all of his distinctive traits, his glamorously rakish and dangerous qualities, is a much more effective target for abuse—more visible and reassuringly familiar, especially when recast as a eunuch priest of Cybele (a perilously close double) or a lascivious effeminate of Roman invective. The Iliadic second half of the poem introduces no single role for Aeneas to replay, but multiple.[45] Unsurprisingly, Juno and her allies consistently promote *Paris alter* as a negative exemplum (7.321). And not without justification: Aeneas remains persistently Trojan in his relations with goddesses like Venus and Cybele, his origins on Ida, and his inadvisable habit of giving gifts that recall the eastern opulence of his origins.[46] Furthermore, though we might discredit the hostile speeches as partial, their resonances with Aeneas at Carthage continually remind us that the stumbling block for the Trojans is not external (Jupiter has already assured us of that) but internal. Aeneas is haunted by his actions within the poem itself.

III. Looks and Money

By the time Juno lays her charge against Aeneas in Italy as a *Paris alter*, Iarbas has programmatically established this comparison in book 4 in some detail. Inflamed by the slanders of *Fama* (*rumore accensus amaro*, 4.203), Libyan Iarbas prays to his father Jupiter to punish Dido for her ingratitude. He has a surprisingly vivid mental image (4.215–7):

> et nunc ille Paris cum semiviro comitatu,
> Maeonia mentum mitra crinemque madentem
> subnexus, rapto potitur; [...]

> And now that Paris with his effeminate throng, his chin and dripping hair tied up in a Maeonian bonnet, enjoys his seduction.

The phrase *ille Paris* (4.215) resembles Dido's use of the deictic discussed above, though with pejorative force; Iarbas also uses *ille* to refer to an external referent, the notorious Paris. Just as *ille Aeneas* (1.618) points to a tradition outside the poem, so too *ille Paris* indicates a conventional image, a stereotyped figure. Iarbas composes a kaleidoscopic bricolage that mingles realistic

---

[44] Bowra (1990) explores the possibility that Aeneas represents a figure undergoing Stoic testing (*exercitio*) throughout the epic.

[45] Gransden (1984) 122; Aeneas as Achilles, Agamemnon, Menelaus in Anderson (1990) 245.

[46] See Feeney (1990b) 358 on the dangerous symbolism of Troy in Horace and Vergil.

details and facts with unsupported accusations. Dido and Aeneas had indeed embarked on a relationship, but the highly elaborated portrait of Paris reveals a microcosm of destructive *Fama* in action. The *mitra* indicates the iconography of Trojan Paris from fifth-century Athenian stage and vase painting, yet the word itself was considered Greek.[47] In the Roman context, the *mitra* was a feminine article of clothing, but one with particular associations, as described by Servius *ad* 4.216:

> sane quibus effeminatio crimini dabatur, etiam mitra eis adscribebatur; multa enim lectio mitras proprie meretricum esse docet. Ergo ex habitus qualitate mutuatur invidiam; nam eum non iam effeminatum, sed velut meretricem appellat, quod est inimicus non mulierem tantum, sed etiam meretricem vocare.

> Those who were charged with effeminacy also had the *mitra* attributed to them; for much evidence indicates that *mitrae* were actually (the attire) of prostitutes. Therefore, he derives his insult from the type of clothing; for here he does not call him an effeminate, but something like a whore, because it is hostile to call him not only a woman, but also a whore.

If Aeneas resembles a woman, it is a prostitute from the seedy Subura! The phrase *semiviro comitatu* (4.215) introduces a new visual image, the eunuch Galli, Cybele's priests who are always pictured in a noisy throng.[48] Pomaded hair (*crinemque madentem*, 4.216), a sine qua non in a charge of effeminacy, will continue to be an essential element of the depiction throughout the poem. Having received secondhand reports of the lovers at Carthage, Iarbas creates a very specific caricature of Aeneas to despise, drawing on a wide range of iconographic and social cues familiar to Vergil's audience. Incited by *Fama* and acting as her agent, Iarbas similarly contributes his own mix of lies and realistic details to a plausible alternative tradition.

---

[47] Griffith (1985) 315; Reed (2007) 85. *LIMC* s.v. "Paris."

[48] Lucretius on Cybele's worshippers, *Idaeam vocitant matrem Phrygiasque catervas / dant comites* [...] (2.611–2), *comitumque catervas* (2.628), *Phrygias... catervas* (2.630). Martial 3.91.2 also attests to the conventional view of the Galli as a collective, *semiviro Cybeles cum grege*. The Scholia Danielis comments on *Aen.* 4.215, *et bene non solum regi sed et sociis convicium facit. Sane quidam tradunt iure hoc in Phryges dictum; ab ipsis enim ferunt coepisse stupra puerorum*. "Rightly does he lay his charge not only against the king but also against his companions. Quite a few justly relate this tale against the Phrygians; for they say that from them began the practice of violating young boys."

The result of *Fama*'s intervention, Iarbas' prayer reproduces the darker operations of *Fama* herself. A mélange of preexisting referents, both literary and social, Greek and Roman, coalesce to form a super-trope, a version of Paris strongly validated by the audience's familiarity. *Fama* and her human agent, Iarbas, establish the Orientalized portrait of Paris that will continue to haunt Aeneas throughout the poem. This essentialized Paris appears also in Horace, a Paris edited and shaped into a paradigm of effeminate cowardice joined with supernatural attractiveness. C. 1.15, a lyric miniaturization of the *Iliad*, brings together various Homeric elements (C.1.15.13–20):

> nequiquam Veneris praesidio ferox
> pectes caesariem grataque feminis
> imbelli cithara carmina divides,
> >   nequiquam thalamo gravis
>
> hastas et calami spicula Gnosii
> vitabis strepitumque et celerem sequi
> Aiacem; tamen heu serus adulteros
> >   cultus pulvere collines.

In vain, under Venus' protection, will you boldly comb your hair and fit to the timid lyre the songs pleasing to women, in vain will you hide from heavy spears and the barbs of Cretan arrows in your bedroom, and the battle din and the pursuit of swift Ajax; though late, alas, you will smear your adulterer's garb with dust.

Horace assembles this preening, cowardly Paris from various Iliadic *loci*. Before the duel with Menelaus, Hector calls his brother "evil Paris, outstanding of beauty, woman-maddening flirt" (*Il.* 3.39). Paris surely derives his attractiveness (*charma, Il.* 3.51) from Aphrodite, though Hector sourly asserts that this divine favor will not save him, "Nor will your cithara avail you, nor the gifts of Aphrodite, your hair and your beauty, when you are rolling in the dust" (*Il.* 3.54–5). Horace's formulation of Paris draws together the abusive themes found frequently in the *Iliad* and expanded in Attic tragedy, where Paris' musical talent and beautiful clothing are joined with stock themes of Phrygian cowardice.[49] This fifth-century Paris as adulterous dandy makes a further appearance in Horace C. 4.9.13–5, *non sola comptos arsit adulteri / crinis et aurum vestibus illitum / mirata regalisque cultus*, "nor was [Helen] the only one to burn for the

---

[49] Paris' music (barbarian strains on the pipe), *IA* 576–8; clothing, *Tro.* 991–2, *IA* 74, cf. Hall (1989) 137; on Phrygian cowardice, Hall (1989) 124.

coiffed hair of the adulterer, and the gold plastered on his garments, in wonder at his royal appearance." This passage echoes Hecuba's scornful speech describing Helen's infatuation with the exotic foreigner in Eur. *Troades* 987–96:

> My son was utterly gorgeous, and as soon as you saw him, Cypris became your intent. [. . .] Seeing him glittering in his barbarian clothes and gold, you were driven mad with greed. You didn't have much, living in Argos and you hoped that by exchanging Sparta for the Phrygians' city that ran with gold, that it would flood you with extravagances.

Vergil employs Horace's composite Paris in the language of Aeneas' enemies. The strong outlines of the caricature provide a ready-made armature for abuse. Not all of these charges, however, are entirely inaccurate, and the narrative even confirms them to a surprising degree.[50]

The repeated elements coalesce to illustrate a doppelgänger of Aeneas, an alternative version rendered visible through realistic detail. Although he does not mention Paris by name, intratextual echoes and the essentialized motifs in Turnus' vaunt bring him clearly into focus (12.97–100):

> [. . .] da sternere corpus
> loricamque manu valida lacerare revulsam
> semiviri Phrygis et foedare in pulvere crinis
> vibratos calido ferro murraque madentis.
>
> Let me lay his body low and tear the stripped breastplate
> of this unmanly Phrygian to pieces with my powerful
> hand and let me soil his locks, crimped with hot iron and
> dripping with myrrh, in the dust.

Paris' lovely hair (cf. *Il.* 3.54–5; *comptos… crinis*, Hor. *C.* 4.9.13–14) has become the perfumed curls of Ciceronian invective (*in Pison.* 25, *errant illi compti capilli et madentes cincinnorum fimbriae*). Iarbas (4.216), Remulus (*mitrae*, 9.616), and Turnus all show a remarkable consistency in their disapproval of Trojan coiffure, and their manner of expression rings true to stock condemnations of effeminacy in Roman rhetoric.[51] In the Roman context, the Homeric convention of fouled hair as a symbol of ignoble death takes on overtones of sexual

---

[50] Reed (2007) 86 suggests that Aeneas appears perhaps all too comfortable in resplendent Tyrian garb (4.260–64); at *hVen* 279 Aphrodite predicts the outstanding beauty of their son (*theoeikelos*).

[51] See Pease (1935) *ad* 4.216; on the conventionality of physical characteristics as a topic of abuse, Nisbet (1961) 194; Remulus' speech and Roman oratory, Dickie (1985) 172–3.

violence.⁵² This powerful trope has even reconfigured the textual tradition of Horace's Paris in some editions, where *crines* replaces *cultus*: *tamen heu serus adulteros/crines pulvere collines* (C. 1.15.19–20).⁵³ While Horace keeps mainly to the literary high ground in his Homeric and tragic evocations of Paris, Turnus drags this epic figure into the trenches of oratorical warfare.

As Horace's treatment reveals, the Paris figure is inherently and broadly referential and, therefore, attracts multiple sources. Numanus Remulus' abusive speech adds another model to the Paris paradigm, Catullus' self-castrating Attis (9.598–620):

> non pudet obsidione <u>iterum</u> valloque teneri,
> bis capti Phryges, et morti praetendere muros?
> en qui nostra sibi bello conubia poscunt!
> quis deus Italam, quae vos dementia adegit?
> non hic Atridae nec fandi fictor Ulixes:
> [. . .]
> vobis picta croco et fulgenti murice vestis,
> desidiae cordi, iuvat indulgere choreis,
> et tunicae manicas et habent redimicula mitrae.
> O vere Phrygiae, neque enim Phryges, ite per alta
> Dindyma, ubi adsuetis biforem dat tibia cantum.
> tympana vos buxusque vocat Berecyntia Matris
> Idaeae; sinite arma viris et cedite ferro.

> Aren't you ashamed to be trapped again within a walled siege, O Phrygians twice defeated, and to have walls shield you from death? Behold, those who demand our brides with war! What god, what madness drove you to Italy? Here there are no Atridae, nor Ulysses, fashioner of tales. [. . .] You have clothing adorned with yellow and gleaming purple, you cherish lassitude, your pleasure is to abandon yourselves to dances, and your tunics have sleeves, your bonnets bear ribbons. O Phrygian women indeed, not Phrygian men, go to high Dindyma, where the tibia pipes its double note to its devotees. The Berecynthian cymbals and the boxwood pipe of the Idaean mother call you; leave weapons to men and abandon iron.⁵⁴

---

⁵² Reed (2007) 87, "he practically intends a rape." Cf. Troilus depicted on Juno's temple (1.477). Vernant (2001).

⁵³ Nisbet and Hubbard (1980) *ad loc.* prefer *cultus* in both their commentary and in Wickham's OCT.

⁵⁴ Or "yield to the knife," as Horsfall (1990b) 307 n. 54.

Repetition is a defining motif of Remulus' speech. Like Juno's other Italian agents, Remulus shares the goddess' recursive, retrogressive vision (*iterum*, 598, *bis*, 599), in which the Trojans will simply do what they have always done: steal women and suffer the punishment. Remulus' proposed rerun of the Trojan War even contains a coy echo of the *Iliad* proem, "Who of the gods (*tis . . . theôn*), then, set you two (*sphôe . . . xuneêke*) to battle in strife?" (*Il.* 1.8, cf. *quis deus Italiam . . . vos adegit*, 9.600). He repeats Iarbas' accusations of effeminacy with a powerful doubled allusion: his language pointedly echoes Catullus 63, the aetion of the Galli, while simultaneously evoking their contemporary practitioners in Rome.[55] While critique of their luxurious adornment and the feminine *mitra* corresponds to the Paris exemplum, Remulus unmistakably adduces the effeminate priests of Cybele's Roman cult.[56] When Aeneas prays to Cybele in book 7 and again at book 10, he affirms his special relationship with a patron goddess whose rituals and worshippers still caused the Romans some disquiet. Long after her introduction to Rome in 205 BCE, her priests were still imported from Phrygia, it being considered unseemly for Romans to execute her rites.[57] This double imitation of both literature and life generates a vivid sense of recognition.

The verbal echoes underscore the Trojans' foreignness; the most precise verbal repetition occurs in the proper nouns and geographical adjectives denoting Cybele's eastern origins and the Greek names for her musical instruments:[58]

>   agite *ite ad alta, Gallae,* Cybeles nemora simul,
>   simul *ite, Dindymenae* dominae vaga pecora
>   [. . .]
>   *Phrygiam ad* domum Cybebes, *Phrygia ad* nemora deae,
>   *ubi* cymbalum sonat vox, ubi *tympana* reboant,
>   *tibicen* ubi *canit* Phryx curvo grave calamo.
>
>   (Cat. 63.12–13, 20–22)
>
>   O vere *Phrygiae*, neque enim Phryges, *ite per alta*
>   *Dindyma, ubi* adsuetis biforem dat *tibia cantum*.
>   *tympana* vos buxusque vocat Berecyntia Matris.
>
>   (*Aen.* 9.617–20)[59]

---

[55] Horsfall (1990b); Dickie (1985). See also Horsfall in *EV* s.v. "Numano Remulo"; Hardie (1994) *ad loc.*; Thomas (1982) 98–100; Keith (2000); 19–22; Roller (1999) 302–3.

[56] For hostility in Roman sources, see Roller (1997).

[57] Dion. Hal. 2.19.4–5.

[58] Reed (2007) 113 on the exotic sounds of the lines.

[59] Italics in Highet (1972) 257–8.

The gender-bending taunt, "Phrygian women, not Phrygian men," echoes the feminine "Gallae" in Catullus 63 applied to Attis and his fellow eunuchs.[60] With Catullus 63 so forcefully in mind, suggestive correspondences with Aeneas come into view: like Aeneas, Attis is the Phrygian *dux* (15, 32, 34) of a band of exiles in search of a new homeland, *aliena quae petentes velut exules loca* (14).[61] Remulus' speech effectively expands the potential in Iarbas' *ille Paris cum semiviro comitatu* (*Aen.* 4.218): the notoriously effeminate and lascivious Galli further degrade the Paris derived from literary-mythological traditions, a Paris, it should be noted, who is associated with dancing in a most unheroic moment (*Il.* 3.390–4). Like Remulus' Trojans, Homer's Paris gleams in splendid clothing, and though he has just been rescued from a near death experience, looks ready for dancing (cf. *Aen.* 9.614–5). Remulus' Galli palimpsestically merge with the Homeric Paris, and with the taunts of Iarbas and Turnus.

IV. *Hic noster Paris*: Dressed for Adultery

Trojan is as Trojan does: while the Trojans can't help that their costume is considered unusual in Italy, they also seem to conform to an unfortunate Trojan pattern of behavior.[62] Aeneas' special connection to Venus further strengthens the comparison to Paris. No other hero, Trojan or Greek, enjoys the protection of Venus as much as Paris (*Veneris praesidio*, Hor. C. 1.15.13) and her own son. Juno makes this point clear as she accuses Venus of excessive meddling (10.81–93):

> tu potes Aenean manibus subducere Graium
> proque viro nebulam et ventos obtendere inanis,
> et potes in totidem classem convertere nymphas:
> nos aliquid Rutulos contra iuvisse nefandum est?
> "Aeneas ignarus abest": ignarus et absit.
> est Paphus Idaliumque tibi, sunt alta Cythera:

---

[60] As the anonymous press reader pointed out, this evocation of Thersites in *Il.* 2.235 ironically shows Remulus' "deviant allusion": taken literally, Remulus addresses the Trojans as the victorious Greeks of Homer's epic; however, Menelaus does address the Trojans as women in *Il.*7.96, Hardie (1994) *ad* 9.617–20.

[61] Though Aeneas is usually described as *profugus* (most programmatically at 1.2), note Amata's scornful use of the synonym *exul*, 7.359.

[62] Vergil includes numerous incidental details where the Trojans' clothing marks them as unusual to others: Achaemenides' recognition of the Trojans on Polyphemus' island (3.596); Trojans' arrival reported to Latinus (7.166–9, *ignota in veste*); the intricate description of Chloreus' appearance as a priest of Cybele gives more of an impression of barbarism, 11.768–77. On Chloreus' trousers and the significance of clothing more generally, Horsfall (1989).

> quid gravidam bellis urbem et corda aspera temptas?
> nosne tibi fluxas Phrygiae res vertere fundo
> conamur? nos? an miseros qui Troas Achivis
> obiecit? quae causa fuit consurgere in arma
> Europamque Asiamque et foedera solvere furto?
> me duce Dardanius Spartam expugnavit[63] adulter
> aut ego tela dedi fovive Cupidine bella?
>
> You can extract Aeneas from the clutches of the Greeks, and proffer a cloud and empty breezes in place of the man, and you can turn a fleet into an equal number of nymphs: am I forbidden to help the Rutulians against anything? "Aeneas isn't there, he doesn't know": let him remain unknowing and absent. You have Paphos and Idalia, you have high Cythera: why do you provoke a city pregnant with warfare and cruel hearts? Am I trying to uproot your frail Phrygian state from its foundation? Me? Who set the pitiable Trojans against the Greeks? What was the reason for Europe and Asia to clash in war and to break treaties because of seduction? Was I in charge when the Dardanian adulterer sacked Sparta, did I provide the weapons, or foster wars with lust?

Typically, Juno's recursive perspective takes the past war as a model for the present. Like *Fama* and Iarbas, Juno validates her accusations with Homeric referents that trigger audience recognition. Juno conflates (*Aen.* 10.81–2) two episodes from the *Iliad* in which Venus saves her son by whisking him off (*Il.* 5.311–17) and replaces him with a phantasm made of cloud (*Il.* 5.449–53). Juno predictably exaggerates Venus' involvement: Apollo fashions the double in Homer, just as Cybele, not Venus, has transformed Aeneas' fleet in book 9. Nonetheless, Juno's rhetoric pinpoints mist as Venus' favorite tool, as when Venus hides Aeneas and Achates from view in Libya (1.411–2), or removes the mist from Aeneas' eyes to persuade him to flee his doomed homeland (2.604–7).[64] Significantly, Venus also uses mist to save her favorite Paris during his duel with Menelaus in *Iliad* 3 (380–2). By identifying mist as Venus' special form of intervention, Juno artic-

---

[63] I am grateful to an anonymous reader for alerting me to the significance of *expugnavit* (10.92). While the *OLD* (s.v. 1c) cites this line to illustrate the figurative sense of "capturing in battle," it certainly has overtones from the usage more common in erotic contexts (s.v. 5), "To overcome the resistance of, persuade (a person)."

[64] See also A. 12.416–7, where Venus shrouds herself in mist to enhance Iapyx's treatment of Aeneas' wound.

ulates a narrative pattern that further links Aeneas and Paris: Venus' use of mist to aid her beloved, war-inciting Trojan adulterers.

Juno's two-line summary of Venus' culpability for the Trojan War (10.92–3) is carefully articulated to correspond to Aeneas' sojourn in Carthage. Juno's language insistently recalls the earlier narrative: *fovive Cupidine bella* (10.93) echoes the queen's infatuation with the disguised Cupid (*et interdum gremio fovet inscia Dido / insidat quantus miserae deus,* 1.717–9; cf. *Fama*'s tale: *fovere / regnorum immemores turpique cupidine captos,* 4.193–4). Even the verb *expugnavit* (10.92) expresses the same odd valence of erotic siege found in Cupid's *insidat* (1.718). While *Dardanius... adulter* (10.92) is sufficient to denote Paris, an undercurrent of adultery also persists in Aeneas' affair with Dido.[65] In Dido's lap, Cupid actively works to efface Sychaeus' memory (1.720–2); Dido herself considers her liaison with Aeneas as an adulterous betrayal of Sychaeus, as her appearance in the underworld ultimately indicates (6.473–4).[66] In light of how significantly the epithet *Dardanius* identified Aeneas to Dido (1.618), that it denotes Paris here enhances the connection between the two figures and their seductions. The cult locations Juno mentions also return us to this initial meeting; when Venus outlines her plan to substitute Cupid for Ascanius, she proposes to take the sleeping boy to Cythera or Idalia (1.680–1, cf. 10.86) and eventually deposits him in the deep groves of Idalia (1.692–3). Juno's account of Venus' Homeric actions cannily realigns our perspective on Aeneas in Carthage. Juno thus establishes another pattern of Venus' interventions: Venus starts wars by sending her favorites (Paris, Aeneas) to seduce women that do not belong to them. And though she never mentions Dido by name, her pointed language reminds us that Juno's favorite city, Carthage, will also go to war with Venus' descendants, all because of the immortal enmity created by an unhappy love affair. In addition to the external literary and cultural referents for this Paris figure, the narrative itself defines its own Paris-tradition in Aeneas' behavior.

Lavinia's potential marriage to Aeneas is hardly a seduction, but it is repeatedly assimilated to Paris' abduction of Helen, most authoritatively by the Cumaean Sibyl. The Sibyl establishes a theme of repetition, declaring that a wife will *again* bring war on the Trojans: "Again will a foreign wife be the cause of such great devastation, yet again a foreign wedding" (*causa mali tanti coniunx iterum hospita Teucris / externique iterum thalami,* 6.93–4). Amata ventriloquizes Juno's interpretation of events (7.358–64):

[65] For *adulter* as a term used to identify Paris, cf. Prop. 2.34A.7, *hospes in hospitium Menelao venit adulter.* Also Horace C. 4.9.20, discussed below.

[66] Dido herself repeatedly mentions her loyalty to her first husband: initial reservations about her feelings expressed to Anna (4.9–29); the temple to her husband she visits in her grief (4.456–61); her regret about betraying Sychaeus once Aeneas abandons her (4.550–2).

> Multa super natae lacrimans Phrygiisque hymenaeis:
> "exsulibusne datur ducenda Lavinia Teucris,
> o genitor, nec te miseret nataeque tuique?
> nec matris miseret, quam primo aquilone relinquet
> perfidus alta petens abducta virgine praedo?
> an non sic Phrygius penetrat Lacedaemona pastor,
> Ledaeamque Helenam Troianas vexit ad urbes?"

> Weeping much for her daughter and about the Phrygian nuptials (she said), "Must Lavinia be given to Teucrian exiles to lead off, father, do you feel no pity for your child? Nor for her mother—whom he will treacherously leave behind as soon as the North wind blows, heading for deep water, that pirate with his stolen maiden? Didn't the Phrygian herdsman invade Lacedaemon in just this way, and didn't he carry Leda's daughter Helen to Trojan cities?"

Amata displays Juno's allusive and intratextual technique as well as her hostility. Her account of the Phrygian cowherd (7.363) derives from Horace C.1.15, where the first word, *pastor*, identifies the otherwise unnamed Paris.[67] "Phrygian nuptials" all end in tears—never mind Helen, just look at Dido. Amata knows better than to trust Aeneas, a perfidious pirate (*perfidus...praedo*, 7.362)! In book 4 *perfide* is Dido's preferred insult, the only term she uses more than once (4.305, 4.366).[68] This "pirate" has sailed away in haste before, even against the unfavorable North wind, as Dido herself noted incredulously (*quin etiam hiberno moliris sidere classem / et mediis properas Aquilonibus ire per altum, crudelis?* 4.309–11). Amata focalizes Juno's concerns from a mother's perspective, as the matronymic (*Ledaeam*, 7.364) added to Helen's name indicates: Aeneas will treat her daughter like a Helen, tearing her away from her homeland and loving family. Aeneas, like Paris, has a bad relationship history. The Dido episode clings to Aeneas—even those who would have no reason to know what happened in Carthage find themselves talking about it in coded intratextual terms. These reminiscences of Carthage recall Aeneas at his peak of Paris-like indolence and luxury. Dido's fatal disillusionment lends credence to the Paris paradigm. The background of Carthage dogs Aeneas' steps in Italy.

Turnus similarly points out a Trojan pattern of wife-stealing. The Trojans may claim divine destiny for their actions, but to Turnus and Amata, they are

---

[67] See Nisbet and Hubbard's note *ad loc.*, "The noun is sufficient to designate Paris, especially as Ida is mentioned in the context"; and the other literary examples listed.

[68] In *Her.* 7, Ovid employs this adjective as a characteristic of Dido's speech to Aeneas; Ovid's Dido uses the adjective four times in the letter.

all nasty, woman-stealing Phrygians deep down.[69] Turnus compares himself to the wronged Menelaus and suggests that the Trojans are incorrigible womanizers—even the destruction of their city was not enough to stop their predatory urges (9.136–42). In full Atreid-indignation, Turnus portrays Trojans as shifty, sex-mad Orientals and blames the recidivistic Trojans for refusing to learn their lesson. This accusation views the Trojans as trapped in the past, doomed to follow their paradigmatic script and repeat their fatal mistakes.

V. Locating Paris: Topography as Biography

This repeated insistence that Aeneas is "another Paris," indeed, "the same" (*idem*), draws out a surprising amount of evidence to support the comparison, a set of incriminating details that Vergil's narrative does not particularly avoid. Mt. Ida figures as the beginning and the material source of both Aeneas' and Paris' journeys; Aeneas gives "Phrygian Ida" as his departure point from Troy (3.5–6), a location repeated emphatically in book 9, in the metamorphosis of the ships. Vergil notably marks his radical and "indecorous" metamorphic intrusion into the battle narrative with a strong claim to tradition (9.80–7):[70]

> Quis deus, o Musae, tam saeva incendia Teucris
> avertit? tantos ratibus quis depulit ignis?
> dicite: prisca fides facto, sed fama perennis.
> tempore quo primum Phrygia formabat in Ida
> Aeneas classem et pelagi petere alta parabat,
> ipsa deum fertur genetrix Berecyntia magnum
> vocibus his adfata Iovem: "da nate, petenti,
> quod tua cara parens domito te poscit Olympo...."

What god, O Muses, diverted conflagration so fierce from the Trojans? Who deflected flames so vast from their ships? Speak: belief in the deed may be antiquated, but it has eternal renown. At the moment when Aeneas was first building the fleet on Ida and preparing to embark on the depths of the sea, the Berecynthian Mother herself is said to have spoken in these words to the great god, Jove: "My child, grant my request, that which your beloved mother asks of you in return for your dominion of Olympus. [. . . .]"

---

[69] Cf. Amata's very deliberate use of *Phrygiis hymenaeis* (7.358) and *Phrygius...pastor* (7.363); both instances suggest the sexual transgressions of Paris as a national characteristic.

[70] Fantham (1990); Harrison (1995).

The narrator invokes the Muses to affirm Cybele's agency (*quis deus, o Musae*, 80), though even this powerful goddess must defer to her son, Jove, for permission to rescue the ships fashioned from her Idaean trees. As in his account of *Fama* in book 4, Vergil acknowledges his bold fictionalizing with an Alexandrian footnote for his Olympian flashback, *fertur* (85), even as he declares the tale paradoxically "incredible" but nonetheless "famous."[71] But for all the novelty of Vergil's episode, this emphasis on tradition surely reminds us that there is a good precedent for building ships on Ida, namely Paris' expedition to Mycenae. The ambiguous paranomasia with which Cybele describes the recipient of her donation could potentially encompass both occasions, especially since, as Hardie notes, this is the only time Aeneas is (anomalously) called a *iuvenis*: "When he lacked a fleet, I gave them willingly to the Dardanian youth; now an unsettling fear preys on me in my concern" (*has ego Dardanio iuveni, cum classis egeret, / laeta dedi; nunc sollicitam timor anxius angit*, 9.88–9).[72] The epithet *Dardanius* is applied to both Aeneas (1.618) and Paris (10.92), but *iuvenis* much more naturally applies to the callow Paris when he set out for Mycenae than the mature warrior Aeneas[73]—the *nunc* that follows could express a stronger temporal adversative, contrasting that former expedition (already completed to Troy's destruction) with this one-way journey into exile. This time around, Cybele is more worried about her trees, rightly enough: her intervention is required to prevent their immolation in Italy.

These seeming coincidences between the Paris tradition and Aeneas' quest have deep roots in the literary sources. Paris too built his fleet on Ida, and in Proclus' summary of the Cypria, Aeneas even accompanies Paris to Greece at Aphrodite's behest (Proclus *Chr.* 1).[74] Both are infants on Ida: Paris is exposed on Ida (Eur. *Andr.* 295, *IA* 1283–6), while Aphrodite predicts to her consort that their child, Aeneas, will be raised on Ida (*h.Ven.* 256–8, cf. *Il.* 2.820–1). A youthful idyll on Ida seems to be something of a family tradition: Anchises encounters Aphrodite (disguised as a Phrygian maiden) while tending cattle on Ida (*h.Ven.* 54, *Il.* 5.313, Hesiod *Theog.* 1008–10), and Aeneas himself recounts a frightening encounter with Achilles, who rustled the cattle he was

---

[71] Cf. *ut perhibent* (4.179), Hardie (1986) 275 n. 118; Hardie (2002a) 79: "Nor, I think, is it an accident that *Fama* makes her appearance in the course of the story of Aeneas and Dido, the episode in which the Latin epicist is most blatantly caught in the act of manipulating the legends, of fictionalizing." This is especially marked also in Dido's supposed encounter with Teucer; see note 34 above; on Vergil's self-conscious fictionality, Feeney (1991) 186–7.

[72] Hardie (1994) *ad loc.*

[73] Paris is represented as a beardless youth in a set of mid-fourth-century terracotta masks found on Lipari, Webster (1967) 172.

[74] Eur. *Hec.* 631–5 (*Idaian . . . hylan*), Lycophr. *Alex.* 24, Horace C.1.15.1–2 (*navibus/Idaeis*), Ov. *Her.* 16.109–10 (called allusively *Troica . . . pineta Phrygia*), Colluthus 196–9, Pfeiffer's note on Call. Fr. 34.

tending on Ida (*Il.* 20.89–92).[75] Significantly, Paris' most defining moment, the judgment, also occurs while he is tending cattle on the mountain, as Euripides frequently mentions.[76] These associations between Paris and Ida more than sufficiently explain his frequent Euripidean epithet, *Idaios*.[77] Vergil links Aeneas' two patron goddesses, Venus and Cybele, by emphasizing their associations with Ida.[78] They even share epithets in the poem; Venus, most frequently called *alma* or *genetrix* in a nod to Augustan genealogical claims, divides her maternal claim with the Great Mother, whose epithets include *genetrix* (9.82, 117) and, pointedly, *alma parens* (10.252). Thus the topographical network of associations between Aeneas and Paris appears even more detailed than the caricatures of his enemies' taunts.

These overlapping associations figure Ida as the birthplace of all Trojan narratives, up to and including the *Aeneid* itself: Ida "begins" Aeneas and Paris, and its incipiatory force generates the multiple *aetia* of Juno's hatred that open the poem: "the judgment of Paris remained entrenched in her vast memory, the insult to her rejected beauty, that hateful race, and abducted Ganymede's elevation" ([. . .] *manet alta mente repostum / iudicium Paridis spretaeque iniuria formae / et genus invisum et rapti Ganymedis honores*, 1.26–8). Juno's anger encompasses the beginning of the Trojan War and even stretches back to the origins of her ancestral grudge against all the descendants of Tros, Ganymede's father. Beyond their shared ancestry, Ganymede and Aeneas already share a link in the literary tradition as the erotic version of the Ganymede myth first appears in the Homeric *Hymn to Aphrodite* (*h.Ven.* 202–17; cf. *Il.* 5.260–72). Here also Juno's resentment about Zeus' infidelities sets events into motion by inspiring Aphrodite's punishment (*h.Ven.* 38–52) just as it opens the epic. While the hymn does not give a location for the rape, Vergil's ecphrastic account explicitly places it on Ida (5.252, 254). The *Aeneid* locates both causes of Juno's hatred on the mountain that is so fundamental to Aeneas' origins and family history. As seen from the perspective of the Paris paradigm, this most Roman of origin stories, the western movement of the Trojans to Italy, is just another Trojan tale complete with a new princeling to restart the cycle.

---

[75] Allen and Sikes (1904).

[76] *Andr.* 274–91, *IA* 573–85, 1289–1309, *Hel.* 23–30. Cf. Bion 2.10, which states that Paris (*ho bōkolos*) took Helen to Ida. See Nisbet and Hubbard (1980) note *ad* Horace *C.* 1.15.1; Ovid's Oenone describes her marriage to Paris on Ida in *Her.* 5; on Paris and the judgment in Euripides, Stinton (1965) 13–39.

[77] Stinton (1965) 32–3.

[78] Ida and maternal affection or intervention are consistently associated: Venus' medical intervention in book 12 involves the herb dittany plucked from "Cretan Ida," from which the Trojan mountain derived its name (*Hic Venus indigno nati concussa dolore / dictamnum genetrix Cretaea carpit ab Ida*, 12.410–11).

Both the imagery and the occasion of the cloak's donation highlight the problematic significance of Trojan heritage. The Ganymede image appears on a chlamys given to Cloanthus as a prize in a boat race commemorating Anchises' funeral (5.249–57). The Ganymede ecphrasis studiedly avoids the conventional pederastic overtones; rather, the chlamys is a dynastic artifact of the royal Dardanids on which Ganymede symbolizes a familial trajectory from Ida to Olympus.[79] These familial associations, however, can proliferate in problematic directions; the embroidered cloak anomalously depicts the youth as a hunter, a *puer regius* (5.252), a term also used of Ascanius in Carthage (1.677–8) as Venus relates her plan to Cupid.[80] The eroticism of the paradigmatic *puer delicatus* Ganymede appears in a sublimated form in Ascanius' subsequent abduction in Venus' arms (1.692–4); Venus' embrace (*fotum gremio tollit*, 1.691) anticipates Dido's lethal embrace with Cupid (*gremio fovet*, 1.718), while the fragrant *amaracus* of the *locus amoenus* further enhances the erotic mood.[81] Ascanius thus fulfills his requisite youthful stint on an eroticized "Ida," albeit on the suggestively named Cypriot Idalia. Ganymede's unaccustomed virility on the cloak confirms Ascanius' hearty young masculinity, and yet he replays the erotic script of mythical Trojan adolescence—Ida as the locus of Trojan *rites de passage* figured as sexual initiations, from adolescence to manhood, human to divine.

VI. Material Inheritances

The memorial function of the games also provides an important context for the chlamys' significance. Aeneas, newly honored with the epithet *pater* in book 5,

---

[79] On the tradition of Ganymede as a paradigm of pederasty and Vergil's antierotic rehabilitation in the *Aeneid*, Bellandi (1991); Hardie (2002a) 340: "Ganymede passes from hunting boy to apotheosed Trojan in one leap, omitting the rest of the earthly career. The beginning and end of this journey, from Ida to Olympus, coincide with the wider trajectory of the *Aeneid* as a whole, an epic which sees the survivors of the sack of Troy set off in a fleet built from the trees of Mount Ida, and whose ultimate *telos* might be described as a journey to the stars."

[80] Ascanius' hunting at 4.156–9, 7.496–9. Putnam (1998b) 60–6 traces a link between Ganymede and Catullus' Attis initially (*anhelanti similis*, *Aen*. 5.254 ~ *simul anhelans*, Cat. 63.31), that imports an erotic quality to the bond between the beautiful Iulus and Attis' "namesake," Atys: *Atys, genus unde Atii duxere Latini,/parvus Atys pueroque dilectus Iulus* (5.568–9). While Putnam's interpretation importantly points out the subtle homoeroticism in the Ganymede and the Atys descriptions, I am more inclined to agree with Bellandi's and Hardie's emphasis on its unaccustomed suppression for dynastic effect. Atys is after all the ancestor of Augustus' maternal line, the Atii, and as I will argue below in chapter 4, Iulus/Ascanius cannot be too homoeroticized as an ephebe: in Vergil's epic, ephebic allure can be lethal.

[81] Cf. Cat. 61.6–7 and Lucr. 4.1179, Williams (1998) note *ad loc*.; Ascanius "the victim of a temporary rape," Hardie (2002a) 339.

presides over his Aeneadae in the games that represent his transition from son to "father" upon his own father's death. This relic of the Trojan past, the richly dyed purple and gold-bordered eastern cloak, becomes a token in a new act of transmission, a fictional heirloom that symbolizes the connection of the Roman *gens Cluenti* to their Trojan ancestor, Cloanthus (5.122–3). Transmission, but not necessarily transformation—this book, which more than any other illustrates the strong connection between the Trojan past and the Roman present (as in the *lusus Troiae*), can also collapse these categories, perhaps all too soon.[82] How much identification with Trojanness is really desirable? What exactly is being passed on with these heirlooms? Elsewhere in the poem, the Trojans' elegant and well-intentioned gifts often signify the destroyed past and portend destruction for the recipient.[83] Eastern artifacts may be rehabilitated as spoils of war, as Jupiter predicts for Julius/Augustus (*hunc tu olim caelo spoliis Orientis onustum/ accipies secura,* 1.289–90), but the legacy within remains contested. Which Trojan ancestor will their genealogy-obsessed Roman descendants come to resemble?

In the *Aeneid*, the drama of creating character implicates a drama of inheritance. By initially presenting a radically vacant protagonist, Vergil reveals the processes by which an epic character takes form against the multiple narratives of the established tradition. The activities of *Fama* as the transmission of all stories, variously authenticated externally by literary and social referents, and also internally by the narrative itself, create both an Aeneas and his darkling twin, Paris. The barbarous Phrygian, tendentiously formed from a distillation of the literary tradition that also informs Aeneas' identity, is the shadowy double that threatens to detain the gorgeously clad Aeneas at Carthage, recalls Antony at Alexandria, and may still be seen in the eunuch priests of Cybele in Vergil's day.[84] Creating character through schematization, repetition by multiple speakers, reference to the authority of tradition to generate a prescriptively

---

[82] Reed (2007) 74–5.

[83] Gifts from Troy are presented to Dido as part of her fatal seduction by Cupid (1.647–52, in particular, a cloak woven by Helen), and to Latinus before the hostilities begin (7.243–8). Andromache's gift to Ascanius caps the aborted attempt to refound Troy at Buthrotum (3.482–5). A thorough investigation of gift-giving in the poem is Henry (1989) 31–9. Quint (1993) 65 characterizes the Trojans' fatal gifts as a reversal of their previous destruction through the Trojan horse.

[84] Could overidentification with Trojans have had even more pressing urgency in Augustus' day? Nisbet and Rudd (2004) on Horace C.3.3 give a thorough overview of the evidence and conclude that a contemporary debate about establishing an eastern center of power at Troy, or even moving the capital of the empire altogether, may have been the inspiration for the poem. For the hopes of Greek historians in the east that the rise of power at Rome would cyclically lead to a new age of eastern domination once Rome had perished, see Antisthenes of Rhodes (*FGHist*. 257 F. 36), Momigliano (1987).

ideological effect—this certainly resembles the process of establishing an exemplum in Roller's formulation.[85] Creating character may thus be read as a poetic version of exemplary discourse; this means of transmitting character complements the other fictionalized forms of inheritance—genealogy and gift giving—that signal the poem's concern with origins and Romanness. The legendary founder must be exemplary (in all senses of the word) for his descendants, and yet Roman exemplary discourse, like *Fama*, can generate negative as well as positive exempla to hand down with their fictional Trojan genealogies. Paris lives.

---

[85] Roller (2004), and see the discussion of exemplarity in the introduction above.

2

Lucan's Cato and the Poetics of Exemplarity

Unlike the glamorous antihero Caesar, Lucan's protagonist Cato has found few supporters among modern readers; Cato's exemplary rigor challenges plausibility in its absolute perfection, and recent responses have on the whole been unsympathetic.[1] To contemporary critics, Lucan's "hero" requires rehabilitation, seemingly along the same lines as Vergil's "inadequate" Aeneas—our novelistic desire for sentimental identification is hardly fulfilled by the severe and detached figure of Cato Uticensis.[2] This perceived inadequacy, however, may be explained by a process similar to that explored in the previous chapter: the very mechanisms of characterization generate their own trajectories through the poem. In the *Aeneid*, the characterization of Aeneas is initially dramatized as a void to be filled or an enigma to be solved through referential clues, which can (mis)lead to competing alternative identities such as Paris, the effeminate adulterer. For both Aeneas and Cato, these mechanisms similarly present poetic character as composite and referential to models. Furthermore, these principles of composition share a background in Roman rhetorical theory and practice: for the Paris figure a tradition of ethical invective, but in the case of Cato, this process becomes even more

[1] Skepticism about Cato's rectitude in the epic seems to shade into personal dislike or mockery of Lucan's Cato himself, an approach that seems suspiciously subjective: Johnson (1987) 35–66; Bartsch (1997) 101–30; Leigh (1997) 265–82 (arguing for a satirical portrait of Cato, especially in book 9); Sklenár (2003) 59–100.

[2] Significantly, Ahl (1976) 231–79, one of the first Anglophone scholars to exhume Lucan's reputation, conceded some philosophical unorthodoxy in Cato's portrayal, but in the main adhered to the then-conventional wisdom that Cato is presented in a positive light. The most extreme and somewhat unconvincing example of this position is found in Marti (1945), whose schematic analysis of Lucan's three protagonists along a spectrum of Stoic enlightenment has been remarkably enduring. Having established his more nuanced pro-Catonian position in his earliest work on Lucan, Narducci (1979), Narducci (2002) initiated a lengthy, repetitive, and vehement repudiation of Johnson et al.

self-reflexive. Lucan must confront the rhetorical tradition surrounding Cato Uticensis himself. Cato's status as an exemplum seems to exert its own force over other characters in the epic who repeatedly fail to live up to the ultimate Roman model.

By the time of Lucan's composition, Cato Uticensis had achieved martyr-saint status in Roman culture as a Republican hero and Stoic sage, whose exemplary tradition Lucan explicitly incorporates into his characterization.[3] Like other Roman poets, Lucan builds his characters out of models, whose cultural familiarity contributes to the audience's interpretation of the figure. Cato's essentialization as an exemplum in the early empire is, as we shall see, fundamental to his characterization in Lucan's epic. Lucan places Cato in dialogue with himself: his protagonist must engage the intensive tradition of Stoic *memorabilia* that centered on Cato, as well as the cartoonish portrait developed in the rhetorical schools. Cato's persona had already been schematized by the Roman habit of creating exempla to serve a variety of cultural functions.[4] The degree to which Cato fulfills or contradicts the expectations of his mytho-historical persona can illuminate how we read Lucan's enigmatic protagonist in a Neronian context. I examine how Lucan deploys Cato's paradigmatic features in and beyond Cato himself, features that are attenuated and tendentiously shaped by Lucan to suit the poem's doomed politics, and even more pessimistic philosophy. Ultimately, how we understand Cato determines to a great extent how we understand the political and philosophical position of the poem.

For just as the poem's Republicanism is doomed to fail, so too does the ideal of Cato waver, not quite fulfilling expectations. Many scholars have concentrated on the failures of the fictional Cato himself, describing his portrayal as ironized or even parodic; I examine how Cato is constantly at the center of imitation: Cato mimesis throughout the poem effectively signifies his status as cultural hero, a "more reliable exemplar of virtue than Odysseus or Hercules" (Sen. *Const. Sap.* 2.2). Cato's historical exemplarity provides a template against which Lucan's protagonist should be read. That this model looms large in the poem may be seen in its proliferation beyond Cato: I argue that the deaths of Vulteius (book 4), Scaeva (book 5), Domitius Ahenobarbus (book 7), and Pompey (book 8) all reflect a version of Cato's most paradigmatic act: his suicide at Utica. These would-be Catos offer failed versions of the Stoic sage-martyr Cato, and their similarities to type direct the audience to keep the "original" in mind; this process of comparison, the reflexivity inherent in

---

[3] On Cato's development in Roman literature see Pecchiura (1965) and Goar (1987); for a comprehensive overview of all the sources and a thorough biographical examination see Fehrle (1983).

[4] See the introduction on Roller (2004).

the Cato figure, however, continues to operate as we view Cato himself—the danger is that he will disappoint no less than his imitators.

I. Programmatic Paradigms and Failed Doubles

Numerous scholars have provided radically divergent assessments of Cato's first appearance in the poem in book 2, so rather than retread the same contested territory, I will analyze the programmatic nature of this scene, that is, how it establishes the audience's awareness of a Cato paradigm. In this first appearance, Cato establishes his motives for joining Pompey, and Brutus becomes Cato's first passionate imitator. The scene itself is based on a number of models, deriving, for instance, an epic portentousness from Hector's nocturnal visit to Paris in *Iliad* 6.321ff.[5] As a prodigy of the declamation schools Lucan would have had much experience presenting both sides of Cato's dilemma, as the theme was a popular one in both oratorical and philosophical exercises; Miriam Griffin regards Lucan's episode as a particularly successful example in verse.[6]

In this rhetorical set piece cum Homeric type scene the characterization appropriately reflects a self-conscious referentiality. Like Protagoras' Hercules, Lucan's Cato must choose between two paths, or in this case, two personas: Brutus's visit compels Cato to reject a quietist, apolitical version of Stoic ideals in favor of a more active position. Their debate dramatizes a rejection of Seneca's philosophically idealized Cato and the scruples regarding political action this position entails.[7] Lucan's Cato contradistinguishes himself as a Republican activist, a patriotic *sapiens* independent of and even in rebellion against Rome's cosmically ordained doom.[8] As Ahl has suggested, Cato's

---

[5] Fantham (1992a) 122–3.

[6] On the topic of the sage in politics as an educational commonplace see Griffin (1968) 374. Griffin (1968) 374 n. 6 provides further evidence for this philosophical topic in rhetorical exercises: Cic. *Top.* 82; *De Or.* 3.113; Quint. 3.5, 6; cf. *Rhet. Her.* 4.54, "There is no peril so great that the *sapiens* should avoid it if his country is at stake." See also Narducci (2002) 372, Gowing (2005) 78, George (1991) 239–45; Bonner (1966) notes the rhetorical formality of the Brutus and Cato speeches and considers them paired *suasoriae*.

[7] Fantham (1992a) appendix 3, 234–5 asserts the influence of Seneca's already published *Const.* on Lucan's patriotically engaged Cato by contrasting Seneca's and Lucan's "versions" of Cato thus: "Seneca finally preferred to ignore the historical record and preserve the fiction of his hero's integrity, but Lucan, approving the fight against Caesar, was able to respect the record and improve on his hero's motives."

[8] Narducci (2002) 389–95 argues that Lucan's Cato stands as a sage against nature, a Stoic paradox, in order to represent the magnitude of the civil war's evil effects. Thus Lucan magnifies and elevates Cato as the sage who defies the gods and remains the sole guarantor of rectitude in a perverted universe. Johnson (1987) and Sklenár (2003) emphasize Lucan's Stoically impossible evil cosmos, but ultimately condemn Cato's philosophical unorthodoxy and resulting failure as a *sapiens*.

position reverses that of Aeneas in the doomed Troy: unlike the misguided Aeneas, Cato is from the first fully aware of the hopelessness of his actions—his *sapientia* already encompasses Aeneas' vision of the gods destroying the city.[9] Nonetheless, Cato's own patriotism veers perilously close to Aeneas' *furor* at times, just as his inspiration of Brutus uncomfortably resembles an Allecto-like "possession."[10]

Brutus provides the Senecan Stoic orthodoxy in this *agôn* by addressing Cato explicitly as a *sapiens* from the opening of his speech, the *virtutis... sola fides* (2.242–4).[11] Brutus then proceeds to deliver a typical *suasoria* designed to impress this *sapiens* with its unimpeachable Stoic sentiments.[12] His argument for sage-like withdrawal from the growing conflict outlines the ideal response he expects from Cato (2.266–73):

> melius tranquilla sine armis
> otia solus ages, sicut caelestia semper
> inconcussa suo volvuntur sidera lapsu.
> fulminibus proprior terrae succenditur aer
> imaque telluris ventos tractusque coruscos
> flammarum accipiunt: nubes excedit Olympus.
> lege deum minimas rerum discordia turbat,
> pacem magna tenent.

> You will do better to pursue peace in isolation, apart from weapons, just as the heavenly stars, eternally undisturbed, make their own way. The lower air that is closer to the earth is ignited by lightning, and the valleys of the earth suffer the burning winds and the paths of flames: Olympus rises above the clouds. By the law of the gods, conflict stirs up the little things on earth, the great things remain at peace.[13]

Brutus' meteorological metaphors derive from familiar principles of Stoic cosmology and seem especially indebted to Seneca's own fashioning of the ideal

---

[9] Ahl (1976) 241–2.

[10] An observation on *furor* taken too far, perhaps, by Hershkowitz (1998) 81–137; on "possession" as related to "impersonation" in Latin epic, see Hardie (1993) 35–40.

[11] Nussbaum (1994) 359 n. 3 lists sources for the traditional belief in the indestructability of virtue in the sage: *SVF* III.238 apud Simplic. *In Aristot. Categ.* f.102A, 102B; III.240 = Clem. *Strom.* 4.22; III.241 (*Theognetus comicus*), 242; and Alex. Aphr. *De Fato* 199.27.

[12] Lucan takes liberties with the historical record by casting Brutus as the Stoic conservative; evidence indicates that the historical Brutus was more catholic in his philosophical influences: see George (1991) 247 n. 32.

[13] Text of the *BC* is from Housman (1927).

sapiens.¹⁴ Fantham notes the very Senecan use of *inconcussa* in 248 and 268 as a characteristic of the Stoic *sapiens*.¹⁵ Seneca's *De ira* 3.6.1 draws on the same contrast between the peaceful upper and agitated lower regions of the sky to depict *magnitudo animi* as a condition of imperturbable calm in much the same language.¹⁶ Brutus utilizes traditional Stoic imagery in his descriptions of perfect *ataraxia*, reflecting a conventional Stoic position. Lucan's choice of this particular imagery in Brutus' speech perhaps underscores the predictability of the young man's mind; his advice to Cato designates the familiar paradigm of the Stoic sage.

Brutus invites Cato to fulfill his idealized role as the Stoic sage by withdrawing into unsullied philosophical contemplation. Cato's response contradicts this persona in distinctly Stoic terms. In his reply to Brutus, Cato expresses a passionate concern for the welfare of the Roman people and his city. Lucan offers a patriot in place of the serene sage: his Cato declares that individual freedom is not sufficient as long as his beloved city is enslaved. In relating his grief at the city's misfortunes, Cato describes himself as a grieving father performing the final rites for a dead child (2.297–303):

> [...] ceu morte parentem
> natorum orbatum longum producere funus
> ad tumulos iubet ipse dolor, iuvat ignibus atris
> inseruisse manus constructoque aggere busti
> ipsum atras tenuisse faces, non ante revellar,
> exanimem quam te conplectar, Roma, tuumque
> nomen, Libertas, et inanem persequar umbram.

> Just as grief bids a parent bereft of his children to lead the long procession to the gravesite, and it comforts him to thrust his very hand into the black flames and to hold himself the

---

¹⁴ Sklenár (2003) 63–66 offers a thorough assessment of Brutus' speech as Stoic orthodoxy, although he does not emphasize the specifically referential quality of Brutus' language to Senecan philosophical texts. See Fantham (1992a) *ad loc.*, and Sklenár (2003) 66; Chrysippus is the *locus classicus* for the Stoic cosmological layers of earth, water, *aer*, and *aither* (*SVF* 2.527), although it was a common schema in Hellenistic science.

¹⁵ Fantham (1992a) 234 cites *Ben.* 6.28.2, *Epp.* 59.14, 59.16, *Const.* 5.4, 6, and *Q. Nat.* 6.32.

¹⁶ *Pars superior mundi et ordinatior ac propinqua sideribus nec in nubem cogitur nec in tempestatem impellitur nec versatur in turbinem; omni tumultu caret; inferiora fulminant. Eodem modo sublimis animus, quietus semper et in statione tranquilla collocatus.* "The higher and more orderly part of the world that is closest to the stars is never dislodged into the clouds, nor is it driven into storm, nor is it whirled in a tornado; it is free from every disturbance; on the contrary, it is the lower regions that thunder. In the same way as the upper air, the peaceful soul is disposed in a tranquil manner."

gloomy torches to the heaped up mound of the pyre; I will not turn my back before I embrace your dead body, Rome, and before I follow your name and your empty ghost, o Freedom.

This passionate outburst explicitly contradicts the Stoic view of the proper reaction to the death of a child. It seems almost deliberately anti-Stoic that Cato would describe himself as a bereaved father plunging his hands into the funeral pyre, since Seneca in *De ira* and many other Stoic writers dwell upon the loss of a child as the exact moment at which one can display Stoic *virtus* through a proper reaction.[17] The ideal reaction is well documented, especially in the story told of Anaxagoras, who replied to the news of his child's death with the words, "I was already aware that I had begotten a mortal."[18] Cato, the "father of his city" (2.388), starkly contradicts traditional Stoic models of parental mourning.

This "inappropriate" metaphor clearly signals Cato's departure from Stoic orthodoxy. As he had promised to do upon his arrival (*dux Bruto Cato solus erit*, 2.247), Brutus follows Cato's example: in impersonating Cato, Brutus becomes possessed by the same doomed passion that inspires Cato's longing for patriotic self-sacrifice, a *devotio* to end the war (2.306–19). Brutus' conversion is allusively figured as possession: "Thus he spoke and thrust fierce incitements of anger, and roused the young citizen's ardor to excessive love for war" ([. . .] *sic fatur et acres / irarum movit stimulos iuvenisque calorem / excitat in nimios belli civilis amores.* 2.323–5).[19] The language echoes both Allecto's possession of Turnus in *Aeneid* 7 (*saevit amor ferri et scelerata insania belli / ira super*, *Aen.* 7.461) and employs Stoic terminology for the passions (*extollit animos et incitat . . . hinc flamma subdita est et hinc stimulis peragitavit audaces*, Sen. *De ira* 1.7). As he mimics his vehement kinsman, an impassioned Brutus reveals the radical disjunction between this Cato and the conventional *sapiens* he had expected to find. The constant overlap with Senecan language and the theme of imitation draws attention precisely to this conflict with Cato's familiar persona. If Cato is elevated as a kind of divinity in this first appearance, as many have argued, his passions bring him closer to the partisan gods of epic and even their chthonic agents than to

---

[17] Seneca offers examples of paternal self-repression in response to the murders of their children by demented tyrants: the murder of Prexaspes' son by the insane Cambyses (*De ira* 3.13) and the Thyestes-like presentation of Harpagus' children at a banquet (*De ira* 3.15).

[18] Nussbaum (1994) 363 n. 19 cites the story in Cicero *TD* 3.30 found also in Diogenes Laertius 2.13 and Posidonius in Galen *De Placitis Hippocratis et Platonis* 4.7.9–10, 282D.

[19] The unexpected genitive *civilis* modifying *iuvenis* in hyperbaton is placed in juxtaposition with its more common object of modification *bello* in the dative, perhaps to emphasize Brutus' transformation from mild-mannered citizen to bloodthirsty warrior.

the serene divinities of Hellenistic philosophy.[20] Cato's programmatic first appearance in the poem directly confronts the idealized "Cato" of the Stoic hagiographic tradition in a rhetorical set piece and reveals himself counter to expectations. Nonetheless, his status as exemplum is highlighted by Brutus' all too enthusiastic emulation; Brutus' conversion demonstrates Cato's irresistible power as a figure that attracts imitation, a lethal appeal that others in the poem will also evidence.

Catones Manqués

Most scholars accept that Lucan's plan for the poem would have ended with Cato's heroic suicide at Utica; thus the poem's structure would have illustrated Seneca's well-known aphorism that *libertas* and Cato died together.[21] This act more than any other defined Cato as a Republican and Stoic paradigm; like that of the virtuous Lucretia, Cato's suicide provided an irresistible (to the exemplum-hungry Romans) shorthand for their most prized qualities: devotion to *libertas*, both political and philosophical, *fortitudo*, in his unflinching pursuit of his purpose—in short, a distinctly complete and Roman *virtus*. Cato's exemplarity derives almost more crucially from his manner of death than from his conduct in life: as Seneca the Elder designates him, *M. Cato solus maximum vivendi moriendique exemplum*.[22] As firsthand recollections of the historical Cato were carefully crafted into *memorabilia* by his friends and admirers (among them his friends Cicero and Munatius Rufus, and his nephew, Brutus) and Cato was rapidly transformed into an exemplum of the popular imagination through the rhetorical schools, his suicide loomed ever larger as the paradigmatic act of his identity. Indeed, Cato's final soliloquy had become such a topos for declamation that a backlash of sorts seems to have arisen in the early empire: while Seneca himself produces at least three to illustrate Cato's perfect virtue, the satirist Persius and the ever-irreverent Martial profess boredom with the

---

[20] Lucan certainly suggests a numinous semidivinity in Cato throughout the poem, especially through his use of the adjective *sacer*, which is frequently attached to Cato (*sacras... voces*, 2.285; *sacro... pectore*, 9.255, *pectora sacra*, 9.561); cf. Sen. *Suas.* 6.2.5 *pectus sacerrimum*. Marti (1945) and Goar (1987) 43–9 underestimate the Stoic inconsistencies in Cato's portrayal, while Sklenár (2003) 72 goes perhaps too far in arguing for a complete "subversion of Stoic values" in the Cato of book 2.

[21] *Const.* 2.3.1. See Stover (2008) for the most recent reexamination and convincing poetic argument for this hypothetical ending based on Cato's portrayal, which he argues is allusively laden with closural motifs. On the scholarly tradition arguing for Cato's suicide as the end of the poem, see Stover's thorough n. 2.

[22] Sen. *Suas.* 6.2.1.

topic.²³ As Miriam Griffin suggests, the unanimous esteem in which Cato's suicide was regarded "even conferred on suicides undertaken for other reasons some of the glory of the political martyr."²⁴ Cato's exemplarity subsequently inculcated a generation of Stoics in the proper manner of death under Julio-Claudian tyrants. As Griffin states, Cato's example "helped to provide *the etiquette and style* for suicide."²⁵

Cato's suicide created a script for his admirers; its own inherent reflexivity encouraged literary and physical emulation. Cato's hagiographers noted his own emulation of Socrates, signaled by his choice of reading material (Plato's *Phaedo*) after he had resolved on his course of action.²⁶ Geiger's analysis of the similar accounts of Cato's and Thrasea's suicides establishes the script transmitted in Stoic hagiographies:

> The quiet determination, fearless in the face of death, the friends and relatives, anxious over the fate of the hero, some of whom need active discouragement lest they follow his example; the emotions of the friends, who ironically have to be calmed by the serene resolution of the ready-to-die; the preoccupation with the immortality of the soul; the difficulty, almost reluctance, of Death itself to take charge of its suitor; all these point to the death of Socrates and its description in the *Phaedo* as the ultimate example both of the historic deaths and of their literary counterparts.²⁷

Similarly, Griffin also isolates a suicide paradigm: "theatricality," "social character" (i.e., intent to elicit a public reaction, either opprobrium or praise), "calmness of the victim," and "philosophical overtones."²⁸ As we

---

²³ Cato's soliloquies in Seneca: *Epp.* 24.7, 71.8–16, *Prov.* 2.10; Lucilius is imagined as protesting at the triteness of the Cato exemplum, *Ep.* 24.6.1–3. Persius's scornful recollection of his schooldays memorizing the *morituri verba Catonis* (3.45) discussed at length in Tandoi (1965); Martial 1.8.

²⁴ M. T. Griffin (1986b) 197; Griffin (1986a) 68 notes that Ulpian *Dig.* 28.3.6.7 includes *iactatio ut quidam philosophi* among other motives for suicide.

²⁵ M. T. Griffin (1986a) 68. Hill (2004) 186–7 also points to Cato as a template for suicide; Edwards (2007) 154–9 develops the theatrical aspect of Cato's death as a role to play for later Stoics under the Principate.

²⁶ A detail found in Seneca, *Ep.* 24.6; Plut. *Cato minor* 68.2, 70.1 suggests he managed to read it twice. As Geiger (1979) 62 n. 58 notes, reading the *Phaedo* was already in Callimachus' time associated with suicide: *epigr.* 23 Pf. = Page and Gow, *Hell. Epig.* Call. 53.

²⁷ Geiger (1979) 63. Geiger departs from Griffin in emphasizing the literary afterlife and development of the genre of *exitus illustrium virorum*, on which he argues Tacitus' accounts and Plutarch's biographies depend. See also Ker (2009) 53–7 on the genre and Tacitus' reliance on these models as a structuring element in the *Annals*, and for Seneca's suicide in particular.

²⁸ M. T. Griffin (1986a) 65–6; Hill (2004) 184 defines "ostentation, ritualization, political protest, and philosophical allusion."

shall see, these elements reappear in a warped, flawed, and yet still recognizable form in several of the self-consciously exemplary voluntary deaths of Lucan's poem.

Lucan refracts the Cato paradigm throughout the poem in a number of imposters who follow the Catonian script but in a flawed manner. This proliferation of poetic *Catones manqués* thematizes Cato's status as exemplum in the epic; however, as the case of Brutus has already demonstrated, these imitations *in peius* seem to magnify the flaws of the original. In his programmatic appearance in book 2, Cato announces his suicide in a self-conscious reference to his own exemplarity, when he prays for the opportunity to sacrifice himself for the state in an act of *devotio* (2.306–19).[29] Cato's own death is further anticipated several times in the poem, creating what Hill denotes a "suicidal teleology" in the epic, that is, a constant awareness in the reader's mind that Cato's death is imminent.[30] In keeping with his refashioning of Cato, Lucan emphasizes Cato's patriotic motivation for his paradigmatic act in contrast to other receptions of the famous deed. For the rhetoricians of the early empire, the trope of Cato's suicide symbolized a generic *libertas* conveniently divorced from any suspicions of radical Republicanism, while for Stoics under Nero, Cato's self-conscious emulation of Socrates' end provided a template for their own philosophical suicides.[31] How then are we to assess the "flawed" imitations by Vulteius, Scaeva, Domitius Ahenobarbus, and Pompey?[32]

One distinctive element to add when considering Lucan's reproductions of Catonian suicide: Lucan seems especially to reflect a grisly detail found in many sources but particularly prominent in Seneca's description, namely, Cato's double wound (Sen. *Ep.* 24.8):

> Inpressit deinde mortiferum corpori vulnus; quo obligato a medicis cum minus sanguinis haberet, minus virium, animi idem, iam non tantum Caesari sed sibi iratus nudas in vulnus manus egit et generosum illum contemptoremque omnis potentiae spiritum non emisit sed eiecit.

---

[29] On Cato's *devotio* see Fantham (1992a) *ad* 2.306 and Hardie (1993) 31–32; Stover (2008) 573–4.

[30] 6.311 Cato's death is mourned proleptically; 9.208–14 Cato prefers death to complicity with Caesar's tyranny; 9.582–3 Cato at Ammon on the certainty of death; Hill (2004) 225.

[31] Goar (1987) 34 suggests that the Cato of the rhetoricians was more symbolic than politically charged as in Valerius Maximus 2.10.8. Similarly Gowing (2005) 78–9 suggests that Valerius' Cato is politically uncontroversial.

[32] While earlier discussions have acknowledged the self-conscious exemplarity of these spectacular voluntary deaths, none have connected them to a pattern of Cato imitation within the epic itself: Rutz (1960); Leigh (1997); Esposito (2001); Hömke (2010).

Then he inflicted the fatal wound on his body; after being bandaged by the doctors, despite the fact that he had lost blood and was diminished in strength as well as in vigor, at this point, furious not only with Caesar but also himself, he laid hands on his wound and rather expelled than released the noble soul that despised every form of compulsion.

That Cato did indeed resist the doctors and reopen his wound after receiving medical treatment seems to have been a well-known fact, even corroborated by the Caesarian *Bellum Africum* (88.4). Seneca frequently refers to this final evidence of Cato's determination and fortitude (*Ep.* 67.13; *Ep.* 70.19), and yet the gruesomeness of his descriptions can be rather emphatic, as in *Ep.* 70.17, "Cato tore open his wounds more vehemently than he had inflicted them" (cf. Sen. *Ep.* 24.8).[33] Seneca's descriptions of Cato's wound seem uncomfortably close to the graphic violence of his *Thyestes* or his self-maiming Oedipus; the voluntary deaths in Lucan's poem evince a heightened goriness that may well reflect Seneca's account of Cato's death. Catherine Edwards discusses the image of the gladiator in book 2 of Seneca's *De providentia* as the prime metaphor for Cato's suicide as spectacle for the gods—his double wound contains the violent spectacle of the arena performed with the dramatic *fortitudo* of the gladiator.[34]

Both Caesarians and Pompeians provide instances of Catonian suicide, and the narrator's assessments of the acts provide a picture of how they "measure up" to the primary model. In book 4, Vulteius, a Caesarian military tribune, and his crew of Gauls are captured by the Pompeian fleet as they attempt to elude Octavius' blockade at Salonae. Trapped on their rafts like fish in a barrel, yet tantalizingly within sight of their companions on the mainland, Vulteius and his men manage to resist heroically until nightfall; the Pompeians retire to dispatch them at their leisure at daybreak. Vulteius then delivers an exhortation to his men, urging them to regard their hopeless situation as a great opportunity for glory (4.476–520). Vulteius calms his frightened comrades, *tum sic attonitam uenturaque fata pauentem / rexit magnanima Vulteius uoce cohortem* (4.474–5), offering them solace in the face of certain death. The scenario and word choice return us to the nocturnal meeting of Brutus and Cato in book 2: the significant adjective *magnanima* recalls Cato's disciple, Brutus (2.234), while the emphasis on the power of his voice seems to cast him as Cato, *arcano sacras reddit Cato pectore voces* (2.285).[35] The speech itself employs Senecan

[33] See also *Ep.* 13.14.5.
[34] Edwards (2007) 75–7.
[35] Cato's words take on a special power in book 9, where he reassures the wavering troops after Pompey's death and rededicates them to the Republic, 9.292ff.; later, his voice replaces that of the oracle at Ammon (9.564ff.); see also note 20 above.

ideals of suicide as freedom;[36] Vulteius, the noble leader-Caesarian martyr, uses philosophical justifications to call for a dramatic display of *virtus* through self-killing.[37] As in Seneca's injunctions to suicide, Vulteius also appeals to his comrades by stressing the freedom in a voluntary death (4.476–85); and further contrasts their conspicuous visibility on the rafts favorably with a more traditionally heroic but potentially unnoticed death on the battlefield (4.488–502):

> non tamen in caeca bellorum nube cadendum est
> aut cum permixtas acies sua tela tenebris
> inuoluent. conferta iacent cum corpora campo,
> in medium mors omnis abit, perit obruta uirtus:
> nos in conspicua sociis hostique carina
> constituere dei; praebebunt aequora testes,
> praebebunt terrae, summis dabit insula saxis,
> spectabunt geminae diuerso litore partes.
> nescio quod nostris magnum et memorabile fatis
> exemplum, Fortuna, paras. quaecumque per aeuum
> exhibuit monimenta fides seruataque ferro
> militiae pietas, transisset nostra iuuentus.
> namque suis pro te gladiis incumbere, Caesar,
> esse parum scimus; sed non maiora supersunt
> obsessis tanti quae pignora demus amoris.

For we need not fall in an obscuring cloud of battle dust, or when engaged battalions shroud themselves in darkness with their own weapons; when corpses lie heaped together on a field, every death vanishes into the mix, and valor is buried and lost. The gods have put us on a vessel visible to our comrades and the enemy: the waves and the shores provide witnesses, the island will give a view from the highest cliffs, both sides will watch from opposite shores. I know not what great example you are readying, Fortune. Whatever benchmark of loyalty and military duty has ever been transmitted through the ages, our men will outdo it. We know it is a small thing to fall on our swords

---

[36] Hill (2004) 219–221; at his most polemical, Seneca is hyperbolic in his insistence on suicide as freedom, as in *De ira* 3.15.4, where he suggests a variety of "sources of freedom," including the sea, a river, and a well.

[37] On interpretations of multiple and conflicted views of *virtus* within the epic, see the overview in Hömke (2010) 92.

for you, Caesar, but besieged as we are, we have nothing greater, we lack sufficient testaments to our powerful love.

Just as in other political suicides of the Neronian period modeled on Cato, Vulteius explicitly conceives of their act as spectacular (*praebebunt aequora testes*, 4.493) and exemplary (*magnum . . . exemplum*, 4.496–7; *per aevum . . . monimenta*, 497–8): the fatal attraction of Cato's suicide is its imitatability, its instant exemplarity.[38] Like Cato, Vulteius and his men claim ethical nobility: they will exceed all records of *fides* and *militiae pietas* in their dedication to Caesar; thus their voluntary deaths represent a kind of distorted, partisan *devotio* to the Caesarian cause (*tanti . . . pignora . . . amoris*, 502). His speech incites the same passion in his men as Cato's does in Brutus (2.323–5): a dire frenzy for death infects the soldiers as they take on Vulteius' own fervor, *sic cunctas sustulit ardor / mobilium mentes iuuenum* (4.520–1).[39] Vulteius' speech, then, explicitly lays claim to key elements of the Catonian suicide (philosophical motive, exemplarity, political martyrdom), while also relating back to Cato's own programmatic appearance in book 2 (*devotio*, imitation as possession).

The Catonian script also informs the strange manner in which the soldiers very deliberately stop fighting the enemy and turn against each other; Vulteius' men break off the hostilities in a theatrical fashion, while Vulteius himself ceremonially opens the ritual with a formal invitation to annihilation (4.539–44). This marked deliberation looks very much like a version of Cato's quiet resolve, which is quickly followed by an equally Catonian violence: though he asks for but a single blow, Vulteius immediately receives multiple sword thrusts from his devoted followers (4.544–5). A detailed orgy of bloody mutual slaughter ensues that is all the more remarkable for its theatrical setting and awestruck audience; Lucan underscores Vulteius' own promises of spectacularity by introducing the mass violence with similes of the sown men of Thebes and Colchis (4.549–56). Lucan's simile of the Spartoi directs us to Ovid's gruesome account of their frenzied mutual killing in *Metamorphoses* 3, which also "stages" fratricidal violence: the sown men rise from the ground like the side panels of the theater (*Met.* 3.111–2) and immediately perform their fratricidal slaughter under Cadmus' horrified gaze.[40] Cato's deliberate

---

[38] On Vulteius' self-conscious appeal to exemplarity, see Rutz (1960) 466–7. See also Sklenár (2003) 28–31 for a useful discussion of Stoic *virtus* contrasted with conventional epic *virtus* in Vulteius' speech.

[39] Hershkowitz (1998) 237 also links these two passages, but fails to note the Catonian implications of the Vulteius episode.

[40] Note especially the relatively rare compound adjective *terrigenae* (4.553), a particular favorite of Ovid's, occurring six times in his corpus and five of those six in reference to two different sets of sown men (Thebes: *Met.* 3.118; Colchis: *Her.* 6.35, 12.99; *Met.* 7.36, 7.141).

death and messy end become a positive lust for dying in Vulteius' men, as Lucan employs his characteristic love of paradox in his descriptions of bodies thrust onto weapons (4.560–2), and the raft itself grotesquely overflows with the viscera of the slaughtered (4.566–8). In their execution of the script, Vulteius' followers take their cue from their leader's Catonian resolve, but their own mutual killing descends into a bloody, perverse simulacrum of civil war: fathers murdering sons, brother striking brother. As Paolo Esposito has ably discussed, the episode reveals exemplarity perverted: Caesarian *furor* transforms *virtus* into frenzied *amor mortis*, and the spectacle of mass suicide exemplifies *nefas* rather than true martial valor.[41] Imitating Cato is both easier and harder than it seems: although the pattern of action is clear, the spirit is difficult to capture.

The narrator says as much in his evaluation of the deed, bemoaning the false lesson that will be taken from this notorious incident (4.572–9):

> [...] nullam maiore locuta est
> ore ratem totum discurrens Fama per orbem.
> non tamen ignauae post haec exempla uirorum
> percipient gentes quam sit non ardua uirtus
> seruitium fugisse manu, sed regna timentur
> ignorantque datos, ne quisquam seruiat, enses.
> mors, utinam pauidos uitae subducere nolles,
> sed uirtus te sola daret. [...]

> [...] Fame traversing the earth declared no craft more stridently. Yet from the example of these men, benighted peoples will not understand that having escaped subjection by one's own hand does not constitute hardwon courage; rather that tyranny is to be feared, and they will remain ignorant that swords exist that none should serve. Death, would that you would reject those afraid of life, and that only [true] valor could grant you!

Lucan's use of the term *exempla* (4.574) directly targets the inadequacy of Vulteius and his men to provide a model of true *virtus*, of which the truest, of course, is Cato. The narrator asserts that their exempla (4.574) will teach the wrong lesson to an obtuse audience (4.574–5); this contention accords with Matthew Roller's assertion that Roman exempla were defined and accepted by their audiences, and that their message or value was contingent and available for a variety of ideological uses. Lucan dramatizes this process of exemplarity by baldly stating that some people will take the wrong message from their

[41] Esposito (2001).

action: *ignavae gentes* (4.574–5) will mistakenly see their deaths as nobly illustrating the Senecan dictum, "The way to freedom runs through every vein" (*De ira* 3.15.4), that is, as examples of Catonian *virtus*. The traditional valor of suicide is *contemnere mortis*, overcoming the fear of death, but Lucan contradicts this conventional wisdom by explicitly denoting autocracy as more truly terrifying than death itself, *sed regna timentur* (4.576). He thus rejects the proposition that Caesarian martyrdom can partake of *virtus* as long as it ideologically supports monarchy. In this episode, Lucan deploys the Catonian paradigm only to contest its applicability in the case of Vulteius and his men; the striking similarities between their deludedly noble aspirations and the Catonian model paradoxically enhances the gulf between their grotesquely frenzied mutual massacre and the perfect *virtus* of Cato's philosophical and political martyrdom.

Cato as the model that sets the standard, the ultimate exemplum of *virtus* and patriotic sacrifice, similarly shapes the Scaeva episode, whose link to Vulteius has been much discussed.[42] Their common elements establish the Catonian paradigm defined in book 2, much as manuscripts with shared flaws may indicate a common source. As a Caesarian who shares Vulteius' misguided zeal, Scaeva's superhuman heroics also inspire narratorial comment on his perverted *virtus* and problematic exemplarity. The historical Scaeva had already been inscribed as a traditional exemplum for martial valor, canonized in Valerius Maximus and others.[43] And yet, in introducing this famous exemplar Scaeva, Lucan is explicit about the ambiguity of his valor: *Scaeva viro nomen . . . et qui nesciret in armis / quam magnum virtus crimen civilibus esset* (6.144–8).[44] Like Vulteius (and the exemplary Cato), Scaeva's speech declaring his willingness to die for a partisan cause (6.150–65) inspires an emulatory zeal from his men, who become filled with *furor* (6.165), though their passion is to watch, not to fight. Cato's hyperbolic desire for *devotio* expressed in book 2 (*cunctis ego pervius hastis / excipiam medius totius volnera belli*, 2.310–1; *Me solum invadite ferro*, 2.315) is gruesomely fulfilled in Scaeva's single-handed

---

[42] Ahl (1976) 117–20 links the two as examples of perverted *virtus* and partisan *pietas*, as does Sklenár (2003) 13–58; Hershkowitz (1998) 212–18 also regards them as parallel examples of Caesarian *furor*; Hill (2004) 215–37 characterizes Vulteius and Scaeva primarily through their frenzy, or *furor*, which in turn recalls Brutus' programmatic "conversion" (2.323–5). Is Brutus' *calor* (2.323) for battle so far away from the impious boldness that flares up (*incaluit virtus*, 6.240) after Scaeva's deceitful murder of the Pompeian Aulus? See Rutz (1960) 463 for the paradoxical juxtaposition of *incalescere* and *virtus* instead of the more typical *furor*.

[43] Leigh (1997) 158–90 discusses Scaeva as a familiar Roman exemplum and Lucan's distortions of exemplarity in the Scaeva episode, Val. Max. 3.2.23; Suet. *Iu.* 68; App. *B.C.* 2.60; first told in Caesar *Bciv.* 3.53–5.

[44] In a persuasive discussion, Hömke (2010) analyzes the episode as a sabotaged *aristeia* that demonstrates poetically the bankruptcy of heroic values like *virtus* in the epic.

defense of the camp, as he stands alone against the entire Pompeian assault (6.189–92):

> illum tota premit moles, illum omnia tela,
> nulla fuit non certa manus, non lancea felix;
> parque nouum Fortuna uidet concurrere, bellum
> atque uirum. [...]

> The entire force swarmed against him, every weapon directed at him, no hand missed its mark, no spear unlucky; Fortuna sees a new kind of equal combat: man against army.

Scaeva's body eventually becomes so pierced with weapons, the bristling hide of missiles paradoxically defends him from further harm: *tot facta sagittis, / tot iaculis unam non explent volnera mortem* (6.212–3). Shadi Bartsch has intriguingly suggested that at this moment Scaeva seems to represent a perverted sage,

> Lucan's Scaeva now becomes a twisted metaphor for the Stoic sage (even as the narrator condemns him for a *virtus* used only in the service of evil). Pierced by so many weapons that nothing can protect his innards except the spears that have made of him a human hedgehog, Scaeva is now inured to further harm; his ultra-penetrability has become ultra-impenetrability. In metaphorical terms, his willingness to completely relinquish his body to abuse has made him immune to that abuse, just like the good Stoic sage.[45]

In the Catonian paradigm, however, the sage must wound himself as a visible testimonial to his magnificent *virtus*: Scaeva's gesture is no less vehement than Cato's as he rips his own eye out with an arrow and tramples it underfoot (6.214–9). Scaeva's gesture thus translates Cato's dramatic reopening of his wound into a contemptuous, willful act of self-mutilation. Just as Seneca marvels at Cato's perseverance despite his blood loss (*cum minus sanguinis haberet, minus virium*, Ep. 24.8), Lucan observes of Scaeva, *nam sanguine fuso / vires pugna dabat* (6.250–1). His martyrdom ends in failure: unlike Cato, Scaeva fails to make the ultimate sacrifice. Anticlimactically saved by Caesarian reinforcements, he improbably survives.

---

[45] Bartsch (2005) 498; she adduces Seneca *Const.* 3.5: "the wise man is vulnerable to no injury; therefore it does not matter how many spears are hurled at him, since he is penetrable (*penetrabilis*) by none."

Like the exemplary Cato, Scaeva's heroism is conspicuously spectacular—his comrades seem to have stopped fighting entirely—and its self-conscious theatricality is crystallized in the scripted "surrender" Scaeva contrives to deceive an unsuspecting Pompeian into coming close enough for a death blow.[46] Scaeva claims that he will be an exemplum of Caesarian desertion if the enemy presents him alive to Pompey, *sic Scaeva relicti / Caesaris exemplum potius quam mortis honestae* (6.234–5). Scaeva seduces Aulus, his victim, with the cowardly exemplum all the Pompeians desire, but this is nothing more than a deadly ruse, just as his own emulation of the Catonian exemplum is but a vicious distortion of true *virtus*.[47] In the rueful anti-*makarismos* that concludes the episode, the narrator exposes Scaeva's pretensions (6.253–62):

> [...] labentem turba suorum
> excipit atque umeris defectum inponere gaudet;
> ac uelut inclusum perfosso in pectore numen
> et uiuam magnae speciem Virtutis adorant;
> telaque confixis certant euellere membris,
> exornantque deos ac nudum pectore Martem
> armis, Scaeua, tuis: [...]
> infelix, quanta dominum uirtute parasti!

A crowd of his men catch him as he swoons, and raise his exhausted form joyfully on their shoulders; they worship as a god the living facsimile of great Valor enclosed within that punctured breast. They compete to draw the weapons from his transfixed limbs and adorn the deities and Mars' bare chest with your weapons, Scaeva [...] Unfortunate man, how costly the heroism spent only to procure a master.

Unlike the more oblique comment on the Vulteius episode, here the narrator baldly calls Scaeva's efforts a *speciem virtutis* (6.256), a mere imitation. The description of this false *virtus* inside his breast clearly evokes the model of Cato in a moment of intratextual *oppositio in imitando*; later in book 9, Cato will confront the oracle of Jupiter Ammon with his own divine virtue (*ille deo plenus*, 9.564) and the narrator will insist that only Cato is worthy of apotheosis (9.601–4). The comparisons with Cato (both as cultural *exemplum virtutis* and in the intratextual reference to book 9) put Scaeva's "divinity" and

---

[46] On the necessity of an audience to create an exemplum, see Leigh (1997) 182–4, and Roller (2004).

[47] On Scaeva's deception, see Leigh (1997) 178–80, Hömke (2010) 98.

the Caesarians' worship to shame.[48] The elaborately self-conscious claims to exemplarity and their adherence to the Catonian script mark both Vulteius and Scaeva as flawed, debased versions of Cato, who in his function as exemplum exposes just how degenerate they are.[49]

Two significant deaths on the Pompeian side indicate the elevating potential of the Cato paradigm; first Domitius Ahenobarbus, whose magnificent death scene on the battlefield at Pharsalus (7.599–616) is certainly a historical distortion by Lucan.[50] Lounsbury initially observed that Lucan rewrites Caesar's own account of Pharsalus by replacing his heroic centurion, Crastinus, with the Pompeian Domitius, granting him Crastinus' noble death in battle in place of Domitius' ignominious end as a casualty in retreat.[51] Leigh expands this insight, arguing that Lucan's "counter-deformation" of Domitius goes beyond transferring formal aspects, namely Crastinus' role in initiating the battle and his valorous speech, from Caesar's centurion to the Pompeian aristocrat; Leigh's examination of other extant accounts of Crastinus' actions indicates that in the lost versions of Livy and Pollio, Crastinus was probably described as a *devotus*, that is, a "latter-day, Caesarian Decius," and he contends that Lucan's Domitius appropriates this *devotio*.[52]

Lucan's Domitius may be "dressed in the clothes of Crastinus" (Leigh, 142), but his manner of death points yet again to the Cato paradigm. In Conte's terms, Domitius' death scene seems to take Crastinus as a *modello esemplare* (the Caesarian *devotus* of early imperial historiographical tradition), but refers to Cato as the *modello codice*, or master trope, of noble death.[53] As in Scaeva's case, the *devotio* links directly back to the programmatic Cato of book 2, who significantly mentions Decius by name in his own prayer for *devotio* (2.308). Other elements contribute more directly: Lucan underscores the conspicuous virtue of Domitius' death, *mors tamen eminuit clarorum in strage uirorum / pugnacis Domiti* (7.599–600)—in order for a death to bear comparison to Cato's, it must first be seen, the more

---

[48] A similarity observed also by Marti (1966) 254 and Fantham (1995).

[49] Not so different, perhaps, from Priam's metatextual accusation to Neoptolemus in *Aeneid* 2.540–1, *at non ille, satum quo te mentiris, Achilles / talis in hoste fuit Priamo*.

[50] Lounsbury (1975) goes beyond the traditional interpretation that Lucan opportunistically flatters Nero by exonerating his ancestor; Leigh (1997) 140–3.

[51] Lounsbury (1975) 212.

[52] The *Comm. Bern. ad DBC* 7.470 on Crastinus' maddened features; Leigh (1997) 141 posits that Crastinus' frenzy in Plut. *Caes*. 44.6, *Pomp*. 71.2, and App. *B. Civ*. 2.82.347, as they are not derived from Caesar's account, must reflect something in the more Republican accounts of Livy and Pollio.

[53] Hinds (1998) 41 gives the best summary of the *modello esemplare* (constructed through "reproduc[tion of] single *loci*") versus *modello-codice* (embodying an "assimilat[ion of] rules and codifications").

spectacularly the better. Domitius further resembles Cato in his tranquility (he is *securus*, 7.613, practically an epithet of Cato's; cf. Cato *securus sui*, 2.241, with Fantham *ad loc.*; *securi fata*, 9.410), and in his voluntary death he is *liber* (7.612) both philosophically and politically. As Domitius delivers his dying rebuke to the churlishly mocking Caesar, Lucan lays a special emphasis on the voice in his breast, echoing Cato's utterances (*ast illi suffecit pectora pulsans / spiritus in uocem morientiaque ora resoluit*, 7.608–9); like the exemplary Cato, his last words hold special significance. Finally, the requisite Catonian grotesquerie: Domitius demonstrates his willingness to die by rejoicing in his myriad wounds (7.604–5), and his dignified bearing contrasts strongly with the horrific conditions in which Caesar finds him, *in crasso versantem sanguine membra* (7.606). The Cato paradigm serves to whitewash an undignified patrician end; by undergirding the fictionalized account with easily recognizable elements of the Cato exemplum, Lucan manipulates the historical record in an overtly symbolic way. Despite his obvious manipulation of the facts, no one could accuse the poet of falsifying history; rather, he explicitly transforms Domitius into a Republican myth.

The powerfully recognizable elements of the Cato paradigm enable Lucan to ennoble deaths that are not even suicides—merely by presenting the death as voluntary or in some sense welcome, Lucan can import the ethical significance of Cato's suicide to the overtly false account of Domitius' heroic end, and even more paradoxically, to Pompey's murder in Egypt. The poet labors mightily to portray the assassination as tragically undignified while elevating Pompey as a noble victim. The effects, like the models, are mixed. The primary literary model for this scenario is the death of Priam in *Aeneid* 2, which itself references the beheaded *truncus* of the historical Pompey.[54] Over this literary stratum Lucan introduces elements that subtly mold the unphilosophical Pompey into a sage-like figure. Lucan anticipates the murder with premonitions of a Stoic death foretold (8.568–71):

> quod nisi fatorum leges intentaque iussu
> ordinis aeterni miserae uicinia mortis
> damnatum leto traherent ad litora Magnum,
> non ulli comitum sceleris praesagia derant

Unless the rules of the fates and the proximity of his unhappy death, determined by command of the eternal plan, had been drawing Magnus inexorably to his doom, surely someone of his comrades would have had some inklings of betrayal.

---

[54] Definitively established by Narducci (1973).

By overdetermining Pompey's assassination with the language of destiny (*fatorum leges*, 8.568; *iussu / ordinis aeterni*, 8.568–9; *damnatum leto*, 8.570), Lucan activates a Stoic causality for the event. The laws of fate draw (*traherent*, 8.570) Pompey to his wretched end, just as earlier Cato has acquiesced to fate's dictate that he should participate in an unholy civil war: *sed quo fata trahunt, virtus secura sequetur* (2.287).[55] Whereas the enlightened Cato sees and understands the demands of fate (or believes he does), Pompey and his men are actively prevented by divine plan from perceiving the ill-attended welcome party at Pharos as a signal of treachery. By emphasizing the predestined nature of Pompey's end, Lucan prepares Pompey's acquiescence to *fatum*, a Stoic willingness to accept death that Pompey then displays as he sets off in the skiff (8.575–6). Thus Lucan refashions the circumstances to transform this murder into a voluntary death that can be effectively assimilated to Catonian suicide.

Transforming the flawed, fallible Pompey of the previous seven and a half books into a Catonian sage at the moment of his death requires a great deal of groundwork, which Lucan begins to lay with Pompey's defeat at Pharsalus in book 7.[56] The picture is not perfect, and Pompey himself is not the most philosophically promising material, beset as he is with despair and especially anxiety about his beloved Cornelia on Lesbos. Lucan begins his subtle preparations by demonstrating the equanimity with which Pompey bears the disgrace of defeat (7.680–9):

>   non gemitus, non fletus erat, saluaque uerendus
>   maiestate dolor, qualem te, Magne, decebat
>   Romanis praestare malis. non inpare uoltu
>   aspicis Emathiam: nec te uidere superbum
>   prospera bellorum nec fractum aduersa uidebunt;
>   quamque fuit laeto per tres infida triumphos
>   tam misero Fortuna minor. iam pondere fati
>   deposito securus abis; nunc tempora laeta
>   respexisse uacat, spes numquam inplenda recessit;
>   quid fueris nunc scire licet.

>   There was nary a moan nor a tear, and grief to be revered
>   for its nobility intact suited you, Magnus, as one ready to
>   endure Rome's misfortunes. You regard Emathia with visage

---

[55] Cato states a familiar tenet of Stoicism that Fate does not drag (*trahere*) the unwilling, and the true path of virtue is to follow (*sequi*); cf. Seneca *Prov.* 5.4; *Vita Beata* 15.6. Nonetheless, Cato's application of it to the specific circumstances of the civil war is certainly controversial: see Narducci (1985) 1557–8.

[56] For criticism of Pompey, see especially Johnson (1987) 67–100, and Leigh (1997) 110–57.

unmoved: military successes did not see you gloating, nor will setbacks see you in despair; as trivial as fickle Fortuna was to you rejoicing in your three days of triumphs, just so trivial is she in your defeat. You withdraw, now liberated from the burden of doom that has been removed; now you are at leisure to reflect on pleasant times, hope never to be fulfilled has receded; now you are permitted to know what you once were.

Lucan denotes Pompey's impassivity in the face of disaster, shading the hardened general's pragmatism with philosophical overtones, as though his military bearing was in fact an indication of philosophical fortitude (7.680–6). The narrator then addresses a tendentiously Stoic envoi to the hero—who, it must be noted, is fleeing the battlefield—declaring him *securus*, no longer subject to fears of the future (*pondere fati / deposito* 7.686–7), and even well-positioned to begin a course in contemplative self-knowledge. Cunningly, this apostrophe does not assert that Pompey himself is actually philosophically *securus* or planning to spend the remainder of his life in Senecan self-scrutiny, only that he can, now that the worst blows have seemingly been inflicted. In a later repetition of the adjective *securus*, we see how the second-person address imposes an image of a philosophically enlightened Pompey on a highly unsuitable scenario. In this apostrophe the narrator willfully manipulates our impression of his hero's undignified flight (7.709–11):

> aspice securus uoltu non supplice reges
> aspice possessas urbes donataque regna,
> Aegypton Libyamque, et terras elige morti.

> Gaze serenely at kings with no suppliant visage, gaze at the cities held and kingdoms granted by you, Egypt and Libya, and select a territory for your death.

Addressing Pompey (*aspice . . . aspice* 7.709–10), the narrator urges a Stoic course of action that will lead to a *mors voluntaria*, but reveals nothing about the defeated general's actual intentions. This disjunction between the narrator's desires for Pompey and the general's undignified retreat to Cornelia smacks of special pleading. Attempting to transform Pompey into a Stoic figure in the moment of his greatest defeat makes a virtue out of a necessity, much as he finds an ethical bright side to the defeat at Pharsalus, *uincere peius erat* (7.706). These overt manipulations of Pompey's behavior in the aftermath of Pharsalus anticipate Lucan's transformation of Pompey's murder into a Stoic death in the Catonian mode.

Lucan's account of the murder itself places heavy emphasis on Pompey's volition and self-awareness, from the deliberate decision to embark for the shore without protection to the moment of death itself. Following the Cato script, Pompey calmly prohibits Cornelia and his son, Sextus, from accompanying him to shore (8.579–82) despite Cornelia's frenzied protests (8.584–9; 8.639–61). As the lethal blow is prepared, Lucan provides a lengthy internal monologue, the *morituri verba Magni,* as it were, again in line with the rhetorical schema for a Catonian suicide. Pompey delivers the generically philosophical and self-consciously exemplary language required of the model (8.622–35): the ephemerality of success, the invulnerability of the sage to insult, the contempt for death, and especially the heightened awareness of being a spectacle, of setting an example worthy not only of his loved ones, who are witnessing the atrocity, but also for his reputation in the future, *nunc consule famae* (8.624). In his last moments, Pompey polices his own bodily disposition; the rigorous philosophical self-scrutiny advised by Seneca becomes an equally Senecan attempt to compose the final tableau of his death for posterity: immobile and silent (8.613–22). Pompey's perfect physical self-control replicates the exemplary Cato's own indifference to pain in a studiedly self-conscious manner. Martha Malamud has argued that this description represents a pointed impersonation of Cato's death in an attempt to memorialize himself and control his reception; Pompey is caught in a moment of self-exemplification:

> Pompey, belated character that he is, enacts the role of Cato, right down to the costume, when he tries to die as a Stoic sage. The doubleness of Pompey as he plays both actor and spectator at the moment of his death is wittily emphasized by the epigrammatic phrase *seque probat moriens* (8.620): like a Stoic *proficiens,* he proves himself by dying—but *probare* also means to applaud or approve. Like an actor monitoring his own performance, he applauds himself as he dies. Lucan's Pompey creates, in the internal monologue, a text that is terminated by his own death while at the same time attempting to fix the image by which he will be memorialized in future texts.[57]

Like Cato, who courageously opposes the divinities set on Rome's destruction (*uictrix causa deis placuit sed uicta Catoni*, 1.128), Pompey's fixed expression shows his own defiance of the gods who betrayed him, *iratamque deis faciem* (8.666). Pompey's serenely unchanged expression (8.667–8) bears physiognomic testimony to a sage-like consistency and immutability; Seneca praises

---

[57] Malamud (2003) 34. She contends that the phrase *effundere voces* (8.616) links Pompey with Cato at the oracle at Ammon (*effudit dignas adytis e pectore voces*, 9.564) and in his conversation with Brutus (2.285).

Cato in similar terms: *Nemo mutatum Catonem totiens mutata re publica vidit* (*Ep.* 104.30.1; cf. Scaeva 6.224–5). In the very instant of his murder, Pompey seems to achieve the ethical conviction and sanctified beauty of a Cato, despite the gris(t)ly operations conducted on his mortal flesh; Septimius, Achillas' agent, has some trouble sawing through the sinewy tendons and bones of Pompey's neck: *tunc neruos uenasque secat nodosaque frangit / ossa diu* (8.673–4). This detailed description of Pompey's mutilation continues with appropriate horror (his lips and dying eyes still move as the head is impaled on a pike) for another 18 lines until the head is finally embalmed.[58] Cato's gruesome wound is part of the script, but the indignities heaped upon Pompey's mortal flesh prolong the death scene nearly to the point of bathos.

Pompey's unexpectedly rapid and distinctly forceful attack of Catonism as he approaches death inspired a surprisingly influential interpretation of Lucan's Pompey as a Stoic *proficiens* who progresses toward enlightenment through the course of the poem.[59] As there is little evidence of latent Stoic qualities, aspirations, or even awareness in Pompey's characterization until the defeat at Pharsalus, I suggest that Lucan (rather abruptly) employs the highly familiar pattern of Catonian suicide to ennoble and elevate Pompey's murder.[60] This requires a great deal of manipulation and importation of elements quite foreign to Pompey's portrayal thus far, and yet given how productive this paradigm has been in the epic, it is understandable that this enticing model should be imposed at such a critical turning point of the poem. In the epic, Pompey's defeat and ultimately, murder, signify the moment at which the Senatorial forces finally become a Republican army, the last best hope for the Republic's *libertas*.[61] In acquiescing to his own murder, Pompey performs the *devotio* he so conspicuously neglected on the Thessalian battlefield and by his death removes himself as the partisan warlord who compromised the patriotic claims of the Republican side.[62]

By transforming Pompey's assassination into a Catonian *mors voluntaria*, Lucan enables Pompey's death to be seen as a *devotio* that "restores" the

---

[58] On the larger symbolism of Pompey's "undead" head as a meditation on the persistence of his memory at Rome, see Dinter (2010) 189–90.

[59] Marti (1945) 367–73; Johnson (1987) 70 typically regards the strongly Stoic flavor of the characterization at this point as parodic.

[60] Even after Pharsalus, Pompey's desperate flight to Cornelia reveals an enormous amount of inconsistency—he hardly demonstrates the same equanimity toward his wife's fate that he does to his own, or that of the Senate's forces in Thessaly.

[61] Morford (1967) 123 also understands the metempsychosis as a symbolic transference of authority over a newly restored Republican army.

[62] Leigh (1997) 142 posits that Domitius' noble death on the battlefield provides a vigorous contrast with Pompey's behavior at Pharsalus; Leigh does not, however, acknowledge the shared model for both of their deaths that provides them with an effectively fictitious nobility.

Republic, albeit temporarily. Not surprisingly, leadership of this refounded Republic falls to Cato, indicated symbolically by the peculiar metempsychosis that sends Pompey's soul boomeranging back to the paradigm, Cato, and Cato's eventual successor, the future tyrannicide, Brutus (9.1–18). The metempsychosis thus seems to mark out a lineage of the restored Republic's refounders. The exemplum of Cato's suicide operates strongly to signify the *libertas* of the Republic; Lucan attempts to shoehorn Pompey into the role of Republican martyr to underscore the war's ideological transformation: from a civil war to an authentic struggle for liberty. This radical shift in Pompey's portrayal conveys the significance of his elimination as leader of the Senatorial forces; while this sudden transformation may seem awkwardly contrived in light of contemporary expectations of consistency in fictional character, Roman exemplary discourse and the rhetorical tradition that mines it so intensively explain this phenomenon of characterization quite easily. The most economical way a Roman poet trained in oratory could broadcast to his audience that this emotionally fallible man in the last moments of his life struck a great blow for the cause of freedom merely by dying, would be to cast Pompey as Cato at his most paradigmatic moment: his suicide, that *magnum documentum hominibus*.[63]

II. A Catonian Dialogue

As book 9 opens, the poem establishes Cato, the new Republican leader, as the center of attention. Whatever the eschatology signified by Pompey's metempsychosis, the event symbolically and narratively transfers the poem's authority to Cato. Cato's first speech further diminishes Pompey's moment: from sage-like hero and avenging ghost, Pompey is summarily reduced to a dead citizen, *civis obit* (9.190) by Cato's brisk eulogy. Both Cato and the newly legitimate Republican army must define their new roles; the journey across the Syrtes thus promises to be a highly symbolic odyssey that will forge an ideal Republican army, led by the ideal Republican leader. The problem with an odyssey, however, is that Homer's Odysseus lost most of his men. And the problem with crossing the Syrtes is that this desolate wasteland is where another band of epic warriors, the Argonauts, nearly died, and were only saved

---

[63] Val. Max. *Mem.* 3.2.14.1–5. J. Griffin (1986) 191 illustrates the Roman cultural habit of thinking in *exempla* from Cicero: "No wonder he [sc. Cicero] emphasises that the orator must have in his mind 'the whole force of old times and of historical examples,' so that, for instance, he can discredit an opponent by saying something like 'When I looked at Considius, I thought I was seeing the Blossii and the Vibellii of old,' the proud leaders of a Campania hostile to Rome. All this shows how natural Romans found it to 'see through history' and to recognize one event or person in another."

by the accidental intervention of Hercules, the comrade they had earlier carelessly mislaid.[64] These two heroes, so popular as philosophical exempla, are much more problematic as epic models. While Seneca asserts that Cato far exceeds Hercules or Ulysses as an ideal *sapiens*, the poetic associations are not very encouraging.[65] Cato's first authoritative speech addressing the mutinous Cilicians recalls the Iliadic Odysseus in its ruthless efficacy, and yet the elaborate simile of Hyblaean bees returned to their tasks by the clash of cymbals (9.283–93) recalls a different kind of epic, book 4 of the *Georgics* (*G.* 4.51–66) and the mysterious and fantastical epyllion that concludes the book. Book 9 travels far into the supernatural and the mythical, from the Ovidian digression on Medusa's head and the origins of Libya's snakes to the wholly fictitious detour to the oracle of Jupiter at Ammon, not to mention the montage of bizarre deaths by snakebite suffered by Cato's men. Book 9 departs from the limits of historical epic and seems to take its inspiration from more fantastical examples of *epos*: Odysseus' wanderings in books 5–8, Apollonius' *Argonautica*, Aristaeus in the *Georgics*, the *Metamorphoses*. By placing his Cato in an unreal environment that evokes the other primary allegorical exemplars of virtue, Odysseus and Hercules, Lucan provides his own exemplary hero the mythological adventures needed to surpass his competitors.[66]

As Leigh notes, Lucan's account tells us little of the military or strategic objective for crossing Libya: "If the historical Cato marched across the desert with the pragmatic aim of joining Varus and Scipio, from all that Lucan tells us this could be nothing more than an elaborate demonstration of *virtus*."[67] Cato's exemplarity, his ability to inspire and improve those who witness his leadership on this march, should be on display here, as asserted by Fantham (1992b).[68] After witnessing so many flawed, failed versions of Cato-imitation in the poem, Cato's march across the Syrtes, already valorized in Seneca, should be the definitive, authentic representation of successful exemplarity.[69] But rather than providing this ideal, Cato's relationship with his men exhibits yet another problematic dynamic of exemplarity: far from being misguidedly passionate in their imitation of Cato, like Vulteius and Scaeva, Cato's soldiers

---

[64] Leigh (2000) 103–9 discerningly analyzes how the flawed Hercules of Apollonius' epic consistently falls short of the Hellenistic philosophical ideal of the demigod as moral hero, and suggests that Lucan's treatment of Cato in book 9 adapts Apollonius' approach.

[65] Seneca *de Prov.* 2.2.

[66] Fantham (1992b) takes a wholly positive view of Lucan's poetic success in elevating his hero through these supernatural challenges.

[67] Leigh (2000) 108.

[68] Fantham (1992b).

[69] Seneca *Ep.* 104.33.1–5: *Vides posse homines laborem pati: per medias Africae solitudines pedes duxit exercitum. Vides posse tolerari sitim: in collibus arentibus sine ullis inpedimentis victi exercitus reliquias trahens inopiam umoris loricatus tulit et, quotiens aquae fuerat occasio, novissimus bibit.*

have this exemplum forced upon them. Instead of the conventional military service they signed up for, the Roman army will undertake more Herculean tasks, as Cato states his purpose (9.379–81):

> o quibus una salus placuit mea castra secutis
> indomita ceruice mori, conponite mentes
> ad magnum uirtutis opus summosque labores

> O men in my service, whose only idea of redemption is death before slavery, steel your minds for a great task of valor and for arduous toil.

Throughout his speech, Cato assumes that the soldiers share his ethical ambition, to choose death before slavery (9.379), and his *audax virtus* (9.302), which desires to test itself against all the fiercest challenges of this unnatural world.[70] Snakes, thirst, and heat, in Cato's mind, are the delightful challenges to *virtus* and *patientia* (9.402–3). Cato is remarkably explicit in his self-presentation as a model to emulate (9.390–402), promising to serve as their guardian, or witness (*me teste*, 9.391), and to undergo all their hardships first to provide a template for behavior (*primus*, 9.394, 395). If the men see any weakness in Cato, then they too may suffer (9.398–401). Cato describes his relationship to the men in terms of witness and emulation, the mechanisms of exemplarity. His persuasive powers—predictably—stir enthusiasm among the men, who emulate their leader's passion for ethical testing, *incendit uirtute animos et amore laborum* (9.406).[71] After so many debased versions of this scenario, Cato and the Republican army will exhibit true *virtus*. Still, the ominous anticipation of Cato's suicide at Utica in 9.409–10 crystallizes the essential feature of Cato's exemplarity: his willingness to choose death over servitude, the very quality he also attributes to his men (9.379). It appears, then, that Cato's men are eagerly signing up for a one-way mission; their passion to emulate Cato will lead directly to their voluntary deaths. Is this so easily distinguished from the contagious *amor mortis* of the Vulteius or Scaeva episodes? The promiscuousness of the Cato model contaminates the original; in this expedition with little stated military relevance, Cato appears to be leading the Republican army into an irrational suicide mission.

---

[70] Note the direct contradiction of Scaeva's achievement: his *virtus* purchased slavery for himself and for Rome. Cato and his men will despise death because of their hatred of tyranny.

[71] On the troubling conjunction of fire and love in the context of Catonian imitation, see above on 2.323–5.

While Vulteius' men are filled with conviction as they execute their frenzied mutual killing, Cato's men are far more dismayed by the numerous *insolitas . . . mortes* (9.733) they encounter on their journey. Even the most pro-Cato readers cannot ignore the long laments reported in indirect discourse (9.848–80), and the severity of Cato's exemplarity, especially as he witnesses their torments (9.881–9). Cato's *virtus* compels (*cogit*, 9.881) the men to try to live up to his example.[72] In their last agonized moments, the soldiers learn that their sufferings are meaningless from a man who is perfectly intact, *casus alieno in pectore vincit / spectatorque docet magnos nil posse dolores* (9.888–9). Cato's presence thus performs the function prescribed to Lucilius by Seneca, who quotes Epicurus: "You must choose a good man and always keep him before your eyes, such that we live as though he were always watching and we act in all things as though he could see us" (*Ep.* 11.9.1). Like the ideal general, Cato attends every death (9.884), but his outstanding example stifles their cries, *puduitque gementem / illo teste mori* (9.886–7). Even Seneca acknowledges that human nature is vulnerable, and he berates Caligula for denying men sentenced to death their last cries of pain at *De ira* 3.19.3, *cui umquam morituro non est relictum qua gemeret*? The presence of Cato's perfect *virtus* effects this very cruelty.

Lucan continually emphasizes Cato's exemplary status in book 9; Labienus' request to Cato at Ammon contains a sly, self-conscious reference, *quaere quid est virtus et posce exemplum honesti* (9.563).[73] Cato's renowned *severitas* was an essential part of the tradition, as Lucan acknowledges in his stern remarriage to Marcia in book 2 and the subsequent elogium (2.350–91).[74] Even Seneca provides a caveat when suggesting Cato as an imaginary witness for self-improvement: "So choose Cato, but if he seems too strict for you, choose a man of more easygoing quality, a Laelius" (*Elige itaque Catonem; si hic tibi videtur nimis rigidus, elige remissioris animi virum Laelium, Ep.* 11.10.5).[75] Cato's unyielding character and his superhuman endurance

---

[72] Bexley (2010) 144–5 also emphasizes the Senecan quality of Cato's gaze, but is more optimistic about Cato's beneficence to his suffering men. I agree with Bexley that "it is as if Lucan had lifted Cato from the pages of Seneca and made his role as imagined spectator quite literal" (145), but she does not address Lucan's presentation of the men's responses. On Senecan approaches to pain through detached observation, see Edwards (1999).

[73] Ahl (1976) 264 drily comments, "There is humor in Labienus' naivete. Standing before his eyes is the exemplar he would have Cato ask about—Cato himself."

[74] The elogium (2.380–91) clearly draws on Sallust's famous comparison of Cato and Caesar (*Cat.* 54), in which Cato's *severitas* is his most distinguishing feature. As Fantham (1992a) notes *ad* 2.375, *rigidus* was strongly associated with Stoic ethics, and especially Cato himself (*OLD* 5a, b).

[75] Cf. *Const.* 7.1, where Seneca suggests that Cato may be too inaccessible a model for ordinary people.

(he is called *durus* four times in book 9 alone) are on full display in Libya, but Lucan also provides a thorough account of the collateral damage wreaked in Cato's Stoic odyssey.

Cato consistently fails to transform the all too human dross of his troops into Stoic sages. Matthew Leigh convincingly analyzes the deaths by serpent as "flawed Stoic allegory" revealing the "failure of Cato's moral instruction," especially Aulus, whose thirst causes him to open his veins in a parody of Stoic suicide (9.759–60).[76] All of these intensely grotesque deaths demand to be viewed as horrific spectacles, sights that Cato repeatedly denies by hurrying his men away (Aulus, 9.761–2; Nasidius, 9.803–4). Cato cannot allow his men to witness one failure after another. The one victim who survives, Murrus, arguably does so by successfully imitating another Stoic model, Scaevola: Murrus instantly cuts off his own poisoned hand and witnesses the death he escaped, *exemplarque sui spectans miserabile leti / stat tutus pereunte manu* (9.832–3).[77] In the failures and the single "success," Lucan emphasizes viewing as the mechanism of exemplarity. Consciousness of Cato's exemplary status traps the suffering troops in a never-ending ethical surveillance; every event, every death is an occasion for Stoic didacticism, assessment, and, especially, failure. Book 9 actualizes Seneca's advice to Lucilius and places Cato as a living, breathing exemplum before the eyes of his men; unfortunately, the only way in which they can successfully emulate Cato is by dying gruesomely.

In book 9, Cato functions precisely as the ideal *exemplum virtutis* of the Stoic imagination, and this increases the troops' suffering still further, while doing demonstrably little for the Republican war effort. If scholars critique Cato's indifference and inadequacy as a leader in Libya, understanding the character as a personification of the idealized Cato-exemplum may clarify the poetic and ideological mechanisms at work. Lucan the mythographer provides his larger-than-life hero with an appropriately outsized adventure at the edges of civilization; like Hercules or Odysseus, this heroic Cato far exceeds mere mortals on this philosophical quest and easily demonstrates his own perfect *virtus*. And like Hercules or Odysseus, Cato's superiority is also proved at the expense of others' suffering and death. Cato's Stoic perfection is repeatedly contrasted with the woeful philosophical "failures" of his men, and even this exemplary Cato himself cannot successfully effect the ethical transformation a perfect exemplum should promote. In his studiedly conventionalized Cato

---

[76] Leigh (1997) 267–73.
[77] Bexley (2010) 146 on Murrus as sage: "Murrus has managed to save his own life by means of a very literal, highly graphic form of detachment."

and his numerous emulators, Lucan seems to interrogate the effectiveness of exemplarity, revealing instead the superficiality of imitation, and ultimately, the bankruptcy of ideals in a civil war whose ethical boundaries were as uncertain as the boundless deserts of Libya.

Acknowledgment

Much of this chapter is reprinted with some additional text from Seo (2011).

3

Seneca's *Oedipus*, Characterization and *decorum*

This chapter takes a reified figure of Oedipus as a given for Seneca's play: Oedipus is identified with his narrative of self-discovery. Like Cato Uticensis, Oedipus has already achieved the familiar outlines necessary for Roller's definition of exemplary discourse. Seneca's Roman Oedipus is also a uniquely appropriate figure with which to explore Panaetian *decorum* in characterization, given that Sophocles' *Oedipus* takes identity and self-knowledge as its central inquiry. Seneca's play puts a distinctly Roman spin on the tale, portraying an Oedipus in the process of becoming "Oedipus," a protagonist not yet in harmony with his literary persona, but strongly and even improbably aware of his literary and mythological identity outside of the text.

Yet another problem character, Seneca's Oedipus, recently considered unsatisfactory both as a tragic protagonist and as a rewriting of Sophocles' hero, here emerges as a character embodying Senecan philosophical principles and literary responses. Just as in the *Letters* Seneca frequently adduces an "ideal" or normative self that he strives to attain, his Oedipus too gropes toward achieving his normative self throughout the play, that is, his true mythological identity as the paradigmatic tragic figure.[1] In Panaetian persona theory, status and position are nearly as important as essential individual character; with regards to literary character, we see an Ovidian environment dictating what Oedipus must become in Seneca's play. Seneca's Oedipus is warped by his existence in an Ovidian Thebes, and rather than striving to discover the truth about his identity, seems rather to suffer from a surfeit of literary consciousness. Oedipus' quest to harmonize his personae and achieve literary *decorum* in this Ovidian Thebes engages our awareness of literary models and practices of exemplarity. His protagonist's trajectory of self-discovery ultimately reveals a new and very Roman approach to tragedy; our own implication in

[1] On the sage as a "normative self," see Long (2009) 32.

Oedipus' hyper self-consciousness creates a climax all the more shocking for its predictability.

Despite the structural debt Seneca's play owes to the *Oedipus Tyrannus*—the overall plot of discovery and self-destruction is the same in both—Seneca's play emphasizes the Theban environment, and particularly its past: the chorus dwells extensively on themes from Theban mythology (the central odes 2 and 3). Furthermore, the "mystery" of Laius' murder is far less pronounced in Seneca's version thanks to two episodes not found in Sophocles' version: an extispicy (299–402) and a necromancy (530–658), both intended to clarify Delphi's response. These supplementary prognostications reflect the overdetermined nature of the play itself; Seneca's play, in which the murdered Laius denounces his own son from Hades, teems with ghosts, revenants, and specters of the Theban past. Like his protagonist, Seneca performs a reversion to origins by excavating Theban history and exhuming its greatest tragic chronicler: not Sophocles, but Ovid.[2]

My analysis of Oedipus' characterization is itself an Oedipal inquiry into identity and origins. Seneca's Oedipus significantly differs from the Sophoclean protagonist, and I suggest that an explanation of this characterization can only emerge from a reevaluation of Ovid's *Metamorphoses* as a formative source for subsequent Roman paradigms of tragedy and the tragic. Ovid's Theban narrative of *Metamorphoses* 3 and 4 has long been recognized as a virtuosic survey of the tragic tradition; in the *Oedipus*, Seneca's allusions to this Theban narrative impose Ovid's construction of the tragic city on his play and its agents. Ovid's Theban history is their past and their doom.[3] Ovid's massing of Theban events in books 3–4 seems to distill the city's mythographical tradition into a simple tragic paradigm: human error, divine vengeance, repeat. While many scholars have noted the density of Ovidian allusion in the *Oedipus*, none have examined its function in the play: we see the characterization of Oedipus being formed like a sculpture in a mold: Ovid's Thebes is the mold; there is no *Oedipus* without Ovid.[4] Seneca's *Oedipus* seems to position itself intertextually

---

[2] For another study of Senecan tragedy's consistent reference to a Roman text in preference to a Greek model, see Zissos (2009) on the *Troades* as a reworking of *Aeneid* 2.

[3] Seminal here is Hardie (1990a) on Ovid's "tragic Thebes," now augmented by discussion of Ovid's Theban history in the *Oedipus* by Stephen Hinds (2011) in section 2, "Tragic and Ovidian Thebes as Senecan Settings." Hinds economically illustrates the "geopoetical" importance of Ovid's Thebes for Senecan tragedy with brief discussion of Seneca's *Oedipus*. Hinds builds on the crucial arguments of Gildenhard and Zissos (2000), who convincingly develop a laconic suggestion in Hardie (1988) 86 that an Oedipus lies hidden behind Ovid's Narcissus.

[4] Töchterle (1994) is especially valuable for specific textual correspondences. Jakobi (1988) 111–25 also discusses Seneca's *Oedipus* in relation to Ovid. Although Seneca's debt to Ovid has become something of a commonplace since Jakobi's monograph, it is surprising to see how little Ovid appears in Tarrant's survey of Seneca's antecedents, Tarrant (1978).

as the product of the Oedipus-shaped void delineated by the Narcissus tale in *Metamorphoses* 3.[5]

It is surprisingly difficult to claim that there is something odd about Seneca's portrayal of Oedipus, despite the striking differences between Seneca's and Sophocles' portrayals.[6] Although he is known as a figure of tragedy par excellence, Oedipus does not exhibit a consistent set of characteristics in his appearances on the Attic stage; unlike the conventionally "proud" Medea or "grim" Orestes, Oedipus as a character is defined paradigmatically by his actions rather than by personal traits that remain consistent throughout the mythological tradition, or even from play to play.[7] Nonetheless, comparison with Sophocles' protagonist in the *Oedipus Tyrannus* reveals distinct differences from the outset. Whereas the Oedipus of Sophocles moves in an arc from confidence to revelation to despair, Seneca's Oedipus endures the play in a constant state of fear and apprehension.[8] Although many scholars have looked outside the play, and in particular, to Stoic philosophy to explain Oedipus' odd characterization, none (in my opinion) have been able to explain convincingly how Seneca's Oedipus exemplifies the progress of a Stoic *proficiens* or how Seneca's Thebes is anything more than an illustration of an anti-Stoic, malignant universe.[9] In short, while Stoic themes certainly pervade and underpin this as they do Seneca's other tragedies, philosophical motives, be they paraenetic or

---

[5] Following a long chain of scholarly observations, Hinds (2011) 10 appears nimbly on the scene to deliver a Nick Charles-worthy [see *The Thin Man, The Thin Man Returns*, et al.] summation, "Geopoetically (in Alessandro Barchiesi's valuable term) the Thebes inhabited by Oedipus in the Senecan play which bears his name is, inevitably, a post-Ovidian Thebes. That might seem counter-intuitive: when Ovid himself had treated Theban mythology in Books 3 and 4 of the *Metamorphoses*, after all, the story of Oedipus had been a very notable omission. However, recent Ovidian critics have argued that the Theban myths which Ovid does there tell (including Actaeon, Narcissus and Pentheus) can be felt to gesture thematically towards Oedipus as their absent centre and reference-point." Hinds' discussion of the *Oedipus* (from this scholar's perspective) is mercifully short, but sinisterly effective: I obtained a copy of Hinds' paper well after initial drafts of this chapter were in progress and am extremely grateful that (*a*) we agree substantially on our readings of Ovid and Seneca and (*b*) his discussion of the *Metamorphoses* and Ovid's tragic Thebes is only the prelude to an even more interesting discussion of Ovid's exile poetry in Seneca's tragedies.

[6] Garton (1959).

[7] As cited above, Horace *AP* 119–24 on conventional character types.

[8] See the puzzled comment of no less an authority on the mythological Oedipus than Lowell Edmunds (2006) 61: "The largest difference between Seneca and Sophocles lies in the character of the protagonist. In the prologue of the Latin tragedy, Oedipus is anything but the commanding presence he was in this place in Sophocles. [...] For the reception of the Oedipus myth, the striking turn in Seneca's characterization of the hero is his fear."

[9] Stoic interpretations of the *Oedipus* are proposed not very convincingly by Henry and Walker (1983) and Poe (1983). Similar skepticism in Ahl (2008) 15–16; the elegant analysis in Rosenmeyer (1989) of Stoicism in Senecan tragedy does not pursue any individual play as a

cautionary, cannot explain Oedipus' *fear*. Furthermore, Oedipus' fear is consistently associated in a causal way with references to the literary past. Seneca's Oedipus already seems highly self-aware: in a post-Sophoclean *Oedipus*, can the protagonist be anything but terrified? And in a post-Ovidian Thebes, can anything but horrifying tragedy result?[10]

I. Fear

Oedipus' opening monologue establishes his primary emotional register: quaking, nauseating terror with a dash of paranoid persecution. Something is very wrong and highly indecorous in this opening; Seneca signals a strong disjuncture with the Sophoclean version. Oedipus introduces himself by providing a history of his own condition, contrasting an earlier state of confidence with his present panic (12–36):

> Quam bene parentis sceptra Polybi fugeram!
> curis solutus exul, intrepidus uagans
> (caelum deosque testor) in regnum incidi;
> infanda timeo: ne mea genitor manu
> perimatur; hoc me Delphicae laurus monent,
> aliudque nobis maius indicunt scelus.
> est maius aliquod patre mactato nefas?
> pro misera pietas (eloqui fatum pudet),
> thalamos parentis Phoebus et diros toros
> gnato minatur impia incestos face.
> hic me paternis expulit regnis timor,
> hoc ego penates profugus excessi meos:
> parum ipse fidens mihimet in tuto tua,
> natura, posui iura. cum magna horreas,
> quod posse fieri non putes metuas tamen:
> cuncta expauesco meque non credo mihi.
> Iam iam aliquid in nos fata moliri parant.
> nam quid rear quod ista Cadmeae lues
> infesta genti strage tam late edita
> mihi parcit uni? cui reseruamur malo?

whole, but rather outlines strategies of drawing connection between the Stoic principles found in Seneca's prose texts and discrete aspects of the plays; even Rosenmeyer, however, fails to provide a Stoic explanation for Seneca's radical departure from the Sophoclean model. Boyle (2011) *ad* 15 points out the programmatically un-Stoic nature of Oedipus' fear in his opening monologue.

[10] See the quotation of Hinds above, n. 5.

> inter ruinas urbis et semper nouis
> deflenda lacrimis funera ac populi struem
> incolumis asto—scilicet Phoebi reus.
> sperare poteras sceleribus tantis dari
> regnum salubre? fecimus caelum nocens.

> How well I had escaped the inheritance of my father Polybus! As an exile I was relieved of anxieties; while wandering fearlessly (I swear by the sky and the gods), I came into a kingdom; I fear unspeakable things, that my father should die by my hand; the Delphic laurels warned me of this, and they predicted another, greater crime. Is there any sin greater than parricide? Furthermore, as a painful duty (it shames me to speak my destiny), Phoebus warns me against my parents' bedchamber and of their doomed marriage bed violated by a son's sinful torch. This fear drove me from my ancestral realms and exiled by this I left my home: trusting too little in myself, I put your laws, o Nature, into safekeeping. Though you may shudder at it, you may still fear that which you do not think possible. I am terrified of everything and I do not trust myself. Now, even now, the fates are readying some encounter for me. For what can I make of the fact that this plague so widely afflicting the Cadmean people with cursed slaughter spares me alone? For what evil am I being preserved? Amidst the destruction of the city and the deaths constantly mourned with fresh tears and the devastation of the people that I remain unharmed—surely I am Phoebus' accused—could you hope to be given a healthy kingdom despite such intimations of crime? I have polluted the sky!

The sheer density of words for fear and guilt are obviously striking (*infanda timeo*, 15; *timor*, 22, *quod posse fieri non putes metuas tamen*, 26), especially in contrast with Sophocles' Oedipus, whose first appearance features his concern for his people and his vigorous efforts to dispel the plague. In Sophocles, the priest petitions Oedipus as their city's preeminent agent against divine wrath, as evidenced by his success against the Sphinx (*OT* 31–9), whereas Seneca's Oedipus hopelessly dwells on his doom, convinced that his own immunity to the plague indicates some further evil in store for himself (28–36).[11] Oedipus'

---

[11] Fitch and McElduff (2002) 23 also highlight Oedipus' guilt as definitive of his character in both the *Phoenissae* (for obvious mytho-chronological reasons), and more surprisingly, throughout the *Oedipus*. Fitch and McElduff analyze Oedipus' guilt as a "Freudian neurosis"; on the psychological 'readability' of Roman literary characters, see the introduction.

conviction that he is the guilty party seems unmotivated by anything in his own account—as far as he knows at this point, he has escaped Delphi's warnings by fleeing Corinth. Why should his as yet intact health enhance a paranoid conviction that he is being reserved for some special punishment, or that he himself is to blame for the curse on Thebes (*fecimus caelum nocens*, 36)? Seneca's Oedipus claims responsibility much too hastily; the very illogic of his premature "confession" invites further inquiry into this proleptically guilty figure. The audience is of course aware that Oedipus is completely correct, but Oedipus himself is not supposed to know this yet.

The self-contradictory nature of his speech draws attention to the peculiar state of this Oedipus. Oedipus' characterization from the outset therefore expresses a programmatic acknowledgment of the literary tradition's presence within the play; our own awareness of the literary antecedents, and the mythological "plot" easily supplies an obvious explanation for Oedipus' own illogical self-condemnation. This is an especially coy and knowing way for Seneca to reveal a self-consciousness about rewriting a famous play, an endeavor that will surely provide few surprises from plot. Euripides effectively manages the earlier tradition through prologues uttered by wrathful divinities: these introductory figures tend to overexplain their motives and predict the action rather deflatingly, but this seemingly redundant and overexpository feature of Euripides' plays overtly acknowledges—while efficiently quarantining off— earlier versions of Hippolytus or Pentheus. Seneca similarly opens his tragedy with a recognition of the play's venerable antecedents, but he does so through characterization: his irrationally fearful Oedipus appropriates and recasts the audience's literary competence as foreknowledge.

Oedipus' own language encourages this metaliterary awareness: the constant repetition of "something greater" (*aliud ... maius ... scelus*, 17, *maius aliquod*, 18, *aliquid*, 28) certainly presages the familiar events we know are soon to unfold.[12] But this formulation also contains a specifically metaliterary resonance as a description of a text in Propertius' description of the nascent *Aeneid* as "something greater than the *Iliad*" (*nescio quid maius nascitur Iliade*, Prop. 2.34.66). Another significant appearance of the phrase *nescioquid maius* occurs in *Heroides* 12, in a highly self-conscious moment of literary comment by Medea.

---

[12] Barchiesi (2001b) 113 economically outlines the use of *maius* to express tragedy's generic imperative to escalate in Acc. 200R^2 and Sen. *Phoen.* 353–4, as well as its strong metaliterary connotations as a marker of genre escalation. See also Boyle (2011) *ad* 17 on the frequent use of this motif of "enlargement or intensification of evil/crime/sin" in Senecan tragedy and his comparanda. In the *Thyestes*, the phrase parses degrees of ethical fault: Atreus contemplates *nescioquid animo maius* (*Thy.* 267) after deciding to murder his nephews; thus Atreus intensifies "mere murder" by a Stoically deliberate process of culinary contemplation. Thyestes' paternal cannibalism, while providing the generically appropriate denoument, is far less ethically culpable than Atreus' fully conscious act.

As Stephen Hinds has argued, Medea's line, *nescioquid certe mens mea maius agit* (*Her.* 12.212) indicates the letter's status as a prequel to the famous Euripidean (and Ovidian) drama. In Hinds' words, "This epistolary Medea is working herself up to truly tragic stature at the end of *Her.* 12 because ... she is about to 'enter' a tragedy."[13] While the phrase *nescioquid maius* may not be identical to *maius aliquod*, the parallels between Ovid's Medea and Seneca's Oedipus are suggestive: within their respective fictions, each of these infamous figures "senses" a confrontation with the canonical plot just as their authors confront their venerable "originals." Seneca's *Oedipus* must face "something greater," that is, Sophocles' masterpiece—unlike Ovid's epistolary Medea, however, this Oedipus is still at the beginning of his text, so this indication of escalation could also carry a promise to outdo his model.

The emphatic contrast between past and present in lines 12–3 establishes a theme of comparison between past and present versions of Oedipus, a comparison that similarly lends itself to metaliterary interpretation. When Oedipus describes himself as free from fear when he first arrived in Thebes (*curis solutus exul, intrepidus vagans*, 13), this strong contrast between his earlier boldness and his current terror emphasizes the character's literary genealogy: in an earlier incarnation, at the beginning of Sophocles' play, he was a very different man than he is now. As Iocasta chides Oedipus for his timidity (86), her rebuke inspires a further reminiscence as Oedipus describes how boldly he faced the ferocious Sphinx (87–102). Ghosts of Oedipus continually intrude upon the play, enhancing the audience's awareness of Oedipus' past incarnations, both mythological and literary: the references to an earlier, bolder Oedipus evoke Sophocles' vigorous hero. Just as Lucan's Cato performs his own idealized exemplum with dreadful results in book 9, Seneca's Oedipus explicitly signals a contrast with an earlier version of himself. As he bids Creon to reveal Delphi's riddling response to his inquiry about the plague, he claims his previous self: "Speak, even if it is ambiguous: to Oedipus alone is it granted to understand riddles" (215–16). As Boyle notes on these lines, Senecan characters' self-naming projects an "implicit allusion to their own literary and dramatic pedigree."[14] Here Oedipus produces an ironic reference to an idealized Sophoclean self: Oedipus is suddenly invigorated by the challenge of a Sphinx-like conundrum, and yet this very eagerness for interpretation is perhaps the characteristic that most defines him and leads to his downfall in Sophocles' play. This ironic effect, so typical of Senecan drama, underscores Oedipus' own self-consciousness of an expected behavior. Both Oedipus' own mythological biography and our awareness of Sophocles' play demand that he expose the oracle's meaning.

[13] Hinds (1993) 40.
[14] Boyle (2011) *ad* 215–16.

Seneca's Oedipus exhibits fear programmatically in the prologue of the play, quite in contrast to what we might have anticipated. This radically new depiction of Oedipus departs from his received characterization in myth and in Attic tragedy, at least for this plot of his self-discovery. This novelty is further highlighted by backward glances toward the bold, heroic figure we expect, thus creating an impression of self-consciousness in Oedipus himself about who he is "supposed" to be. Seneca relies upon and thus incorporates the audience's sense of familiarity into his new and rather unusual depiction of Oedipus, tyrant of Thebes. Seneca's self-conscious Oedipus, laboring under the burden of literary tradition rendered as destiny, may well have shaped Statius' depiction in the *Thebaid*, an Oedipus whose self-awareness seems so overt as to be nearly parodic. Denis Feeney neatly epitomizes the phenomenon in his comment on and translation of lines 11.614–5:

> In all these cases, the self-sufficiency of the tradition is such that characters and poet appear to have equal access to it. A very remarkable example of the acknowledged weight of the poem's inheritance is seen when Oedipus is made to speak of himself as a canonical character, performing canonical actions:
>
> > o si fodienda redirent
> > lumina et in uultus saevire ex more potestas
>
> Oh If only my eyes could come back so that I could dig them out again, and I had the power to savage my face *according to my normal custom.*[15]

Feeney's reading of Statius seems to support the assertion that Oedipus' actions rather than a personality type define his character. Statius' Oedipus incorporates an extensive mythological and poetic tradition, but this peculiar quality of self-awareness seems to derive from a specific model: Seneca's *Oedipus*.

II. Ovid's Thebes and Divine Wrath

Beyond Oedipus' premature fear, his opening monologue exhibits a paranoid quality that also seems somewhat inexplicable. Oedipus' self-recriminations anticipate special punishments reserved for himself alone: *Cui reservamur malo?* (31) he asks. Even paranoia can have some basis in reality, however; an agent of persecution gradually comes into focus through further intertextual clues.

[15] Feeney (1991) 341.

Oedipus himself proposes a culprit when he addresses the gods at the end of his speech, *o saeva nimium numina, o fatum grave!* (75). This line recalls another famous opening scene with another notable figure crying out to heaven: the beginning of the *Aeneid*. Like the exiled Oedipus, Aeneas also toils under a prophecy *fato profugus* (*Aen.* 1.2), and suffers from a savage goddess's anger (*saevae*, *Aen.* 1.4). Vergil caps his programmatic description of a man persecuted by an unjust divinity with an incredulous apostrophe: *tantaene animis caelestibus irae?* (*Aen.* 1.11). To Vergil's rhetorical question, "Can divine hearts possess such great wrath?" Seneca's *Oedipus* will give an affirmative response.

Although the gods do not appear physically onstage, their malignant influence is ubiquitous throughout the play. Like their ruler, Oedipus, the chorus declare their pessimism in their first ode, a morbid and graphically detailed account of the plague, complete with the grisly deaths of animals and the physical symptoms of illness (*Oed.* 110–200). Far from calling upon the gods to protect them as in Sophocles, the chorus describes the futile attempts of the people to appease their cruel divinities (197–201):

> Prostrata iacet turba per aras
>   oratque mori:
> solum hoc faciles tribuere dei.
> delubra petunt, haut ut uoto
>   numina placent,
> sed iuuat ipsos satiare deos.

> A crowd lies strewn around the altars, praying for death: this alone the gods grant easily. They crowd the shrines, scarcely to appease the gods with their prayers, but in hope of satiating the gods themselves.

The chorus suggests that the hostile gods will devour their very worshippers, and that divine anger is like a hunger that must be satisfied—with death. Of course, the plague is in fact a punishment for Oedipus' unintentional crimes, but the level of horror in Seneca's depiction far outstrips his Sophoclean model. The chorus' terror takes shape through its highly referential descriptions of the illness, which synthesize the greatest hits of earlier literary plagues. The focused references to Lucretius, the *Georgics*, and Ovid's plagues create a palimpsestic impression of familiarity.[16] The Roman texts are much more proximate models,

---

[16] Töchterle's (1994) commentary exhaustively collects all of the individual points of similarity, *ad* Seneca *Oedipus* 37–70 (Oedipus' account) and 110–200 (first choral ode); cf. Thuc. 2.49–52 (plague at Athens); Lucr. 6.1138–91 (plague at Athens); Vergil *Georgics* 3.448–566 (plague at Noricum); Ovid *Met.* 7.523–613 (plague at Aegina). See also Boyle (2011) *ad loc.*

however, as Seneca does not (as he rarely does in his tragedies), directly translate any elements from Sophocles' play, which dwells much less on the actual details of the plague. Although all the Roman accounts use many of the same elements found in Lucretius' close adaptation of Thucydides (origins of the disease, social effects, physical symptoms of the illness), only Ovid's version in *Metamorphoses* 7 and this play take divine anger as their cause. In contrast to Thucydides, Lucretius, and Vergil, who all emphasize contagion from the physical world, in following Sophocles' supernatural causation, Seneca's plague aligns with Ovid's account of the outbreak at Aegina, which also arises from divine wrath (*ira . . . Iunonis iniquae, Met.* 7.523). The allusive language piles up grotesque echoes from earlier texts just as the corpses heap up on one another; the reader picks out scraps of phrases and details of imagery as a Theban citizen might recognize a relative or neighbor in a mass burial. This allusive bricolage accomplishes a house-of-horrors effect, one that aptly illustrates the special quality of the fear gripping Thebes: the citizens witness every kind of death and suffering, but they have seen it all before—there is an uncanny familiarity about this latest affliction sent down from heaven. They are Thebans, after all, and no strangers to divine wrath. Both the chorus and Oedipus have very good mythological and intertextual cause to fear the gods and worry about themselves.

Like Oedipus himself, the Theban citizens seem to express an awareness of their mythological past, an allusive self-consciousness that defines them throughout the play. The choral odes frequently dwell upon the tragic history of their city in highly referential terms. Early in their first appearance, the Thebans seem to draw a connection between their lineage (*Cadmi generosi proles*, 110) and their current affliction as they bewail the constant stream of dead and dying (124–32):[17]

> Stirpis inuictae genus interimus,
> labimur saeuo rapiente fato;
> ducitur semper noua pompa Morti:
> longus ad manes properatur <u>ordo</u>
> agminis maesti, <u>series</u>que tristis

---

[17] *Cadmi . . . proles* is used only by Seneca as a synonym for Theban; cf. *Phoen.* 648. While Ovid never uses this particular phrase, he employs *Cadmeis* for Thebans and descendants of the house of Cadmus: as "Theban" *Met.* 6.217 (Theban territory), *Met.* 9.304 (Theban attendants to Alcmene); as a patronymic *Met.* 3.287 (Semele), *Met.* 4.545 (Ino/Leucothoë), *F.* 6.553 (Ino). All of these stories implicate Juno as a vengeful persecutor of Cadmus and his descendants; Juno stands for Ovid as the Theban enemy par excellence, and Oedipus seems to extend her special vendetta against Thebes to all the gods generally in line 75, *o saeva nimium numina* cf. *Met.* 4.544–5, *utque parum iustae <u>nimium</u>que in paelice <u>saevae</u> / invidiam fecere deae* [Juno].

> haeret et turbae tumulos petenti
> non satis septem patuere portae.
> stat grauis strages premiturque iuncto
> funere funus.

We, a race of unconquered stock are dying, we totter as savage destiny attacks. A new cortege is constantly led for Death, the long column of a mournful troop hurries to the shades, and a grim procession follows. The seven gates are not wide enough for the crowd heading to the graves. The dead burdens come to a halt, and cadaver is crushed by heaped up cadaver.

This vision of the plague's devastation would equally suffice to describe the mythological past of Thebes. Their reference to the seven gates (*septem ... portae*, 130) chillingly links the interminable parade of funerals with their city's most defining architectural symbol in a morbid civic *sphragis*. The chorus thus identifies their city with a continuous procession of corpses, the *ordo* and *series* hastening to the underworld. This grisly self-description suggests a debt to Ovid's own disaster-laden account of Theban history in *Metamorphoses* 3 and 4, which begins with Cadmus' foundation of the city (*Met.* 3.1–130), and is later termed a sequence of evils (*serieque malorum*, *Met.* 4.564). That Ovid's Theban history comes to be seen as a specialized *series* of unfortunate events may be seen in Statius' prologue to the *Thebaid* (1.4–17):

> [...] gentisne canam primordia dirae,
> Sidonios raptus et inexorabile pactum
> legis Agenoreae scrutantemque aequora <u>Cadmum</u>?
> <u>longa retro series</u>, trepidum si Martis operti
> agricolam infandis condentem proelia sulcis
> expediam penitusque sequar, quo carmine muris
> iusserit Amphion Tyriis accedere montes,
> unde graues irae cognata in moenia Baccho,
> quod saeuae Iunonis opus, cui sumpserit arcus
> infelix Athamas, cur non expauerit ingens
> Ionium socio casura Palaemone mater.
> atque adeo iam nunc gemitus et prospera Cadmi
> praeteriisse sinam: limes mihi carminis esto
> Oedipodae confusa domus, [...]

Shall I sing of the origins of the doomed race, the Phoenician rape [Europa: *Met.* 2.833–75] and the unyielding injunction of Agenor's law [*Met.* 3.1–5] and Cadmus who scoured the waters [*Met.* 3.6–10]? It would be a long succession backwards, if I were to follow the anxious sower of hidden Mars, as he founded warfare in his cursed furrows [*Met.* 3.99–130], the song by which Amphion bid the mountains to assemble into Tyrian fortifications, whence came Bacchus' baleful wrath directed against his kindred walls [Pentheus: *Met.* 3.511–732; Minyeides: 4.1–415], what were the works of savage Juno [Semele: *Met.* 3.253–315], against whom unhappy Athamas turned his bow, why the mother in her leap with her companion Palaemon did not tremble at the vast Ionian [(Juno, Ino, Athamas: *Met.* 4.416–542]. And for now at this point allow me to pass over the sorrows and successes of Cadmus: let the muddled house of Oedipus form the boundary of my song.

This extraordinarily long praeteritio, in which Statius passes over all of the Theban subjects he will omit from his epic on the Seven against Thebes, provides a distillation of Ovid's Theban sequence in the *Metamorphoses*.[18] This list omits some other famous Theban fatalities from the *Metamorphoses*, especially Actaeon and Narcissus, but it is surprisingly comprehensive and rigorously Ovidian in its order. It is perhaps no surprise that Statius, in the work most influenced by Seneca's tragedies in both style and register, here reveals how canonical Ovid's version of Theban history has become.[19] After Ovid's comprehensive treatment, Roman literature treats Thebes as a lengthy list of devastation, and synonymous with tragedy.

In books 3 and 4 of the *Metamorphoses*, Ovid equates Thebes with the tradition of Attic tragedy; although the tragedians hardly limited themselves to Theban topics, Ovid's rearrangement and explicit rewriting of Theban tragedies into a continuous narrative promotes a view of the city as the paradigmatic *locus tragicus*.[20] In this observation, Ovid shares his intuition with Froma

---

[18] An observation made in passing also by Hardie (1990a) 226 n. 13.

[19] Keith (2002) 389 ably discusses Statius' appropriation of an Ovidian Thebes in the prologue, and her approach to Statius' Ovidian formulations of character is very acute throughout, though she underestimates Seneca's influence on the *Thebaid*.

[20] Hardie (1990a) 226 n. 14 suggests that Ovid "signposts entry into a stagey, tragic world" through his simile of the Spartoi rising from the earth like figures painted on the *aulaea* on the Roman stage (*Met.* 3.111–2); my arguments owe a great deal to this critical observation so casually made. Braund (2006) 264–8 on the contemporary significance of Thebes in Statius' epic provides a useful survey of Thebes in classical literature but says surprisingly little about Ovid's influence on the subsequent tradition except to note that Ovid's "interest" was further "developed" by post-Augustan authors. It is especially interesting that Braund (263 n. 9) considers Apollodorus 3.5.7–3.7.1 the "fullest continuous ancient account of Theban legends," which while factually accurate, rather misses the point of Ovid's significant impact on the canonical order and reception of Theban tales in later literature.

Zeitlin, who has brilliantly analyzed Thebes' central significance in Attic tragedy.[21] As Philip Hardie has formulated,

> The subunit formed by the episodes in book three constitutes a set of variations on the (appropriately tragic) themes of sight, blindness, and recognition. But the recurrent narrative structure that links all the Theban stories (with the exception of the inset songs of the Minyeides) is that of the intervention of a vengeful god to punish a mortal who errs, wittingly or unwittingly [...].[22]

Ovid's selection of Theban tales that share themes and narrative structure provides a template for tragedy that becomes canonical for his successors. Presenting lists of Theban misfortunes cannot help but evoke Ovid's repetitiously tragic Thebes and the malignancy of the gods. The chorus consistently evokes the Ovidian tragic history of Thebes, even in supposedly pious contexts like the second choral ode (403–508). This ode to Bacchus, the city's patron god, takes appropriately hymnic form, but as the god of tragedy par excellence, it is not surprising that, as they expound his feats, some regrettable incidents emerge.[23] They recall Pentheus' dismemberment in particularly grisly terms (432–4), and the miraculous transformation of Ino and Melicertes into the sea gods Leucothoë and Palaemon (445–8), while conveniently omitting how Juno drove Ino's husband Athamas mad through the chthonic intervention of Tisiphone, as we recall from *Metamorphoses* 4.[24] The last moderately positive feat they can mention is how Bacchus transformed the Tyrrhenian pirates into dolphins (449–67). As in the *Thebaid* prologue, the collection and order of these Bacchus-centered episodes recalls their arrangement in

---

[21] Zeitlin (1986).

[22] Hardie (1990a) 231. Hardie's analysis has recently been augmented by Gildenhard and Zissos, who explain the Narcissus episode as a retelling of the Oedipus myth. Rather than disrupting the unity of his tragic Cadmeid genealogy with the intrusion of the flashy Labdacids, Ovid substitutes a covert version of the Oedipus story under cover of Narcissus, another individual doomed by self-knowledge. As they explain (141): "Thus, Oedipus and Narcissus are related through inverse mimetic correlation, as Narcissus reenacts an Oedipal destiny and experiences the thematic concerns and plot structures of his tragic alter ego within the codes of eroto-elegiac discourse and a pastoral environment." Thus even the supposed "light relief" of book 3 conforms to the tragic rule of Thebes.

[23] See Boyle (2011) 207–8 on the metapoetic qualities of the hymn: "Since Bacchus is also the god of poetic frenzy, and the Greek god of tragedy and is featured here in a literary form (the dithyramb) regarded by commentators such as Aristotle as the originating precursor of tragedy itself, the ode has a metapoetic and metatragic function, indexing the transformative powers of tragic drama."

[24] Here I would go further than Mastronarde (1970) 306, who merely suggests that "crime and gloom" "lurk beneath the surface" of this ode.

the *Metamorphoses*, where all of these events were caused by vengeful gods. In conclusion, the chorus returns gratuitously to Pentheus again, this time obliquely (*Sacer Cithaeron sanguine undavit / Ophioniaque caede*, 484–5). The marriage of Ariadne and Bacchus on Naxos is the last extended vignette they offer, but their account of Ariadne's elevation to heaven neglects to mention Ariadne herself (*telum deposuit Iuppiter igneum / conditque Baccho veniente fulmen*, 501–2).[25] The chorus' panegyric fails to convince with their ambiguous exempla; even the patron god of their city is recalled in his most vindictively destructive guises.

Creon's report of the necromancy, a Senecan addition to the plot, continues the play's emphasis on Thebes' tragic history. It is no longer fashionable to abuse Seneca for being a poor dramaturge, but in this scene, Seneca egregiously spoils the plot with gratuitous glances backward into the past, and a premature revelation from Laius' ghost that Oedipus is his murderer. The process of discovery that occupies most of the *Oedipus Tyrannus* is here short-circuited by Laius' postmortem testimony. In many of Seneca's plays, obvious violations of classic Aristotelian principles (which surely were well known to himself and his audience) often occur; usually these transgressions reveal Seneca opportunistically sacrificing dramatic unity or action for some localized literary effect. By Seneca's time, katabasis was already a staple of epic,[26] as he seems to signal in the weary recapitulation of Vergil's underworld personifications (*Furor, Horror, Luctus, Morbus, Senectus, Metus*) that precedes the spectral visions to come, but we will have occasion to return to a Theban novelty among them (*avidumque populi Pestis Ogygii malum*, 589).[27] Creon reluctantly describes how Tiresias and his daughter Manto performed the ritual and then recounts the ghosts who appeared. Creon sees, yet again, a list of violent Theban personages from the Spartoi (586–8) to Zethus and Amphion, the builders of the city walls, Niobe, Agave (her third appearance in the play), and Pentheus, yet again (609–18):

> [...] primus emergit solo,
> dextra ferocem cornibus taurum premens,

---

[25] Ariadne is mentioned as a new bride ascending to heaven, *ducitur magno nova nupta caelo* (497), but by the end of the section (502–3) has utterly disappeared. Ovid's accounts of Ariadne, strongly shaped by the bleak Catullus 64, are famously pessimistic and ambiguous about the nature of her katasterism (cf. *Her.* 10 and *F.* 3.459–516) and may well be interpreted as a negative display of divine power.

[26] Feeney (1991) 341–2: "No subject was more vulnerable to the charge of being hackneyed; not only did such scenes go back to the origins of the epic tradition, in the *Odyssey*, but they enjoyed a particular vogue in Statius' immediate predecessors and contemporaries."

[27] *Oed.* 589–95, cf. *Aen.* 6.273–81; I accept Leo's transposition of 589 between 594 and 595 as printed in Zwierlein's text.

> Zethus, manuque sustinet laeua chelyn
> qui saxa dulci traxit Amphion sono,
> interque natos Tantalis tandem suos
> tuto superba fert caput fastu graue
> et numerat umbras. peior hac genetrix adest
> furibunda Agaue, tota quam sequitur manus
> partita regem: sequitur et Bacchas lacer
> Pentheus tenetque saeuus etiamnunc minas.

> Zethus first rose from the earth, clutching the struggling bull by the horns with his right hand, and in his left hand Amphion held the lyre that drew boulders with its sound, and finally the daughter of Tantalus among her children, safely bearing her solemn head high in lofty arrogance as she counts her shades. Here is a worse mother than her, maddened Agave, her entire troop follows her after apportioning their king: and mutilated Pentheus follows the bacchants and still violently makes his threats.

Each of the ghosts appears in tableau, frozen in their most defining mythological actions. This highly literary form, the necromantic katabasis, is a very appropriate vehicle through which to replay literary history, especially the tragic history of Thebes. These four figures are all depicted as they appeared in Greek tragedies: Zethus and Amphion in Euripides' lost *Antiope*, Niobe in lost plays by Aeschylus and Sophocles, and Agave and Pentheus in Euripides *Bacchae*.[28] This very Greek series might seem to challenge the assertion that any list of Theban topics should be considered implicitly Ovidian, since Zethus and Amphion do not appear in the *Metamorphoses* in their tragic guises. Furthermore, Niobe, while certainly a descendent of Cadmus, only receives her punishment in book 6 (6.146–312). Ovid's tale of Niobe, however, follows the tragic Theban template established in books 3–4: Tiresias and Manto make a cameo appearance in Lydia at the opening of the Niobe tale to warn the queen of misfortunes to come (*Met.* 6.157–62). Their unexpected presence in Asia signals a reversion to the Theban pattern; just as Ovid has shoehorned Tiresias into the Narcissus story to encode it with an Oedipal structure, thus Tiresias and Manto intrude into the Niobe myth to signal its typically Theban tragic qualities.[29] Departing from the standard version of the myth, Ovid alone relates that Amphion stabbed himself

---

[28] For fragments of the *Antiope* see Nauck² fr. 179–227.

[29] My interpretation applies to Niobe the reading of Gildenhard and Zissos (2000) 133: "In short, the figure of Tiresias and the specter of the Delphic Oracle locate Ovid's tale of Narcissus within Sophocles' Oedipal imagination, delimiting from the outset the textual boundaries of the static epyllion through a dynamic, intertextual 'frame.'"

after his children were slaughtered (*Met.* 6.271–2); thus Amphion performs the denouement expected of this tragic template. By restoring Niobe, suggestively denoted by the Ovidian patronymic *Tantalis*, to her rightful place among her Cadmeian relatives, Seneca recognizes her affinity with the Theban tales of books 3–4 by "correcting" her displacement in the *Metamorphoses*.[30] That this occurs in a necromancy led by Tiresias and Manto, who is never named on the Greek stage but unaccountably present in Ovid's Niobe story (her only appearance in the epic), further confirms Seneca's Ovidian reference.[31] The necromancy conjures up literary revenants to produce a commentary on Theban literary history; does spoiling the mystery of Oedipus' identity really matter, in a work this crowded with textual ghosts?

The central choral ode lays out Seneca's Ovidian associations most explicitly. As far as the chorus is concerned, Ovid's Theban history is their past, and their doom. It is Ovid's catalogue of divine punishment and human suffering that renders Thebes synonymous with tragedy as a genre. The play rather surprisingly continues after Laius' revelation (one would think this would tie things up expeditiously) and Oedipus evades conviction a little longer by accusing Creon of colluding with Tiresias to usurp the throne. Oedipus seems to be heading off track and possibly avoiding further investigation of his own guilt. The chorus, however, through their account of Thebes' tragic history reminds us that no one gets away unscathed (709–63):

> Non tu tantis causa periclis,
> non haec Labdacidas petunt
> fata, sed ueteres deum
> irae secuntur: Castalium nemus
> umbram Sidonio praebuit hospiti
> lauitque Dirce Tyrios colonos,
> ut primum magni natus Agenoris,
> fessus per orbem furta sequi Iouis,[32]
> sub nostra pauidus constitit arbore
> praedonem uenerans suum,
> monituque Phoebi

---

[30] Used by Ovid of Niobe only in *Met.* 6.211.

[31] Manto appears but is unnamed in Euripides *Phoenissae*; in Seneca and Statius' *Thebaid* (much indebted to Senecan tragedy) Manto is a more prominent figure. Keith (2002) 400–401 similarly notes Ovid's innovation in adding Manto to the Niobe narrative in her discussion of Tiresias and Manto's necromancy in Statius *Thebaid* 4.406–645. Her discussion, however, largely neglects the significant role that Seneca's necromancy in the *Oedipus* must have had in consolidating and concentrating the Ovidian resonances for Statius.

[32] Cf. *Met.* 3.6–7: [...] *quis enim deprendere possit / furta Iovis?*

<u>iussus erranti comes ire uaccae,</u>
<u>quam non flexerat</u>
<u>uomer aut tardi iuga curua plaustri,</u>
<u>deseruit fugas nomenque genti</u>
<u>inauspicata de boue tradidit.</u>[33]
Tempore ex illo <u>noua</u> monstra <u>semper</u>
protulit tellus:
aut anguis imis uallibus editus
annosa circa robora <u>sibilat</u>
superatque pinus,
<u>supra Chaonias celsior arbores</u>
<u>erexit caeruleum caput,</u>
<u>cum maiore sui parte recumberet;</u>[34]
aut feta tellus impio partu
effudit arma:
sonuit reflexo classicum cornu
lituusque adunco stridulos cantus
elisit aere

*

non ante linguas agiles et ora
uocis ignotae clamore primum
hostico experti.
Agmina campos cognata tenent,
dignaque iacto semine proles
uno aetatem permensa die
post Luciferi nata meatus
ante Hesperios occidit ortus.
horret tantis aduena monstris
populique timet bella recentis,
<u>donec cecidit saeua iuuentus</u>
<u>genetrixque suo reddi gremio</u>
<u>modo productos uidit alumnos</u>—[35]

---

[33] Cf. *Met.* 3.10–14:

> "Bos tibi" Phoebus ait "solis occurret in arvis,
> nullum passa iugum curvique inmunis aratri.
> hac duce carpe vias et, qua requieverit herba,
> moenia fac condas <u>Boeotiaque</u> illa vocato."

[34] Cf. *Met.* 3.38–45: [...] *longo caput extulit antro* / <u>caeruleus</u> *serpens horrendaque* <u>sibila</u> *misit.* [...] *ac* <u>media plus parte leves erectus in auras</u> / <u>despicit omne nemus</u> [...].

[35] Cf. *Met.* 3.124–5: *iamque brevis vitae spatium sortita* <u>iuventus</u> / <u>sanguineam tepido plangebant</u> <u>pectore matrem</u> [...].

> hac transierit ciuile nefas!
> illa Herculeae norint Thebae
> proelia fratrum.
> Quid? Cadmei fata nepotis,[36]
> cum uiuacis cornua cerui
> frontem ramis texere nouis[37]
> dominumque canes egere suum?
> praeceps siluas montesque fugit
> citus Actaeon agilique magis
> pede per saltus ac saxa uagus
> metuit motas zephyris plumas
> et quae posuit retia uitat—
> donec placidi fontis in unda
> cornua uidit uultusque feros,[38]
> ubi uirgineos fouerat artus[39]
> nimium saeui diua pudoris.

You are not the cause of our great peril, nor do the fates intend harm for the Labdacids, but the ancient grudges of the gods assail us. The Castalian grove offered shade to the Sidonian immigrant and Dirce watered the Tyrian colonists, from the time when the son of noble Agenor, wearied from pursuing Jove's adulteries over the globe, rested anxiously under our tree and worshipped the ravisher he sought. Instructed by Apollo's counsel, he followed a wandering heifer whom neither the plow nor the curved yoke with its dragging cart had ever broken; he abandoned his pursuit and took a name for his people from that ill-omened cow.

From that time the earth has always produced new monstrosities: either a serpent born in the hollow valleys hisses around the venerable oaks and towers over the pines, it lifted its cerulean head higher than the Chaonian trees though most of its body remained at rest; or the earth poured forth war born of wicked birth: the trumpet blasts from its bent horn and the pipe shrilled its piercing melodies in curved bronze.

*

---

[36] Cf. *Met.* 3.138–40: *prima nepos inter tot res tibi, Cadme, secundas / causa fuit luctus, alienaque cornua fronti / addita vosque, canes satiatae sanguine erili* [...]. Also *nepos Cadmi* (*Met.* 3.174).

[37] Cf. *Met.* 3.194: *dat sparso capiti vivacis cornua cervi* [...].

[38] Cf. *Met.* 3.200: *ut vero vultus et cornua vidit in unda* [...].

[39] Cf. *Met.* 3.163–4: *Hic dea silvarum venatu fessa solebat / virgineos artus liquido perfundere rore.*

Though their tongues were unpracticed and mouths had untested voice, they were immediately proficient in a battle cry. The kindred armies face off on the fields, offspring worthy of the seed that was sown, and with a life span of a single day, these children born after the morning star's passing died before Hesperus' rising. The newcomer was aghast at such prodigies and watched the bloodshed of his new people in terror, until the savage youths finally fell, and he saw their mother receive into her embrace the children she had just borne. Thus may the sin of civil war pass us by, so that Herculaean Thebes may know only those fraternal battles.

Why should we go on to tell the fate of Cadmus' grandson, when the horns of a sprightly stag covered his forehead with strange branches and his dogs hunted their own master? Actaeon fled headlong through the forests and mountains, swifter on fleet foot. Wandering through the glades and cliffs he shied at feathers ruffled by a breeze and he avoided the traps he had himself placed—until he saw his horns and bestial visage on the surface of a quiet spring, where a goddess of excessive modesty had once refreshed her maidenly limbs.

In the first lines of the ode, the chorus directly contradicts the mythological tradition, Sophocles' plot, and even the direct accusation of Laius just reported moments before. "It's not you," they tell Oedipus, "it's us" (709–12).[40] The chorus goes on to illustrate their theory that the gods just have it in for Thebes; all the evidence is unmistakably framed as Ovid's Theban narrative, from Cadmus' foundation through Actaeon's death.[41] Seneca carefully follows Ovid's language here as well as the narrative order of events, and almost exclusively refers to Ovidian episodes he has not yet employed, except the Spartoi, whom, we shall see, he had a very good reason to include. Like Statius' Ovidian introduction to the *Thebaid*, the ode follows very precisely Ovid's order of events. From the very beginning, the gods have always hated Thebes and have always afflicted their city with supernatural threats and dread. Even the founding of

---

[40] Hinds (2011) 11–13, following Jakobi (1988) 121–5, also elucidates the Ovidian echoes in this choral ode to argue for a Senecan linkage of Actaeon and Narcissus, 13 n. 15: "i.e. in Seneca the moment of self-recognition in the pool, rather than preceding the pursuit of Actaeon by his dogs, becomes the climax of the chase." This assimilation of Actaeon to Narcissus in "aquatic self-recognition," according to Hinds, "allows *both* Actaeon *and* Narcissus to prefigure the plot, most forcefully realized in Oedipus, of delayed self-knowledge."

[41] As Boyle (2011) 276 notes, Seneca draws parallels between Cadmus, "the exile who becomes king of Thebes and eventually an exile again," and Oedipus, and points out the essential similarities between Theban "transgenerational" destruction and Oedipus' own impending doom.

the city was cursed, and the gods had deceived them: first Jupiter's licentiousness (*furta*, 716) brings Cadmus to Thebes; then Phoebus' prophecy convinces Cadmus to settle there. Seneca's chorus, while summarizing Ovid's own etymologizing aetiology (*moenia fac condas Boeotiaque illa vocato, Met.* 3.14), adds the editorializing adjective *inauspicata* (724) to Cadmus' heifer. The chorus continues to follow Ovid's foundation story closely, but they emphatically claim that Thebes has always produced unnatural monstrosities (*nova monstra semper*, 724). This may recall the *semper nova pompa* of line 126—there is always some new item to add to Thebes' lethal laundry list.

Next in both Ovid and the choral ode comes the giant serpent that slaughters Cadmus' fellow Tyrians: Seneca again closely imitates Ovid's language, incorporating the hissing and the vast size, of which the towering head and body are only partially visible (*Oed.* 730: *cum maiore sui parte recumberet*; cf. *Met.* 3.44–5: *media plus parte leves erectus in auras*). In both narratives, after Cadmus successfully kills the beast, he then sows the teeth to create the Spartoi, whose murderous and short life span Seneca repeats here, despite having mentioned them earlier in the necromancy (598). As Oedipus will soon learn the truth about his incestuous relationship, Seneca colors his description of the Spartoi with suggestive language, [. . .] *feta tellus impio partu / effudit arma* (731–2): as Boyle (2011) notes *ad loc.*, the parallel with Jocasta's own "impious birth" is "patent." For obvious reasons, Seneca fixes on Ovid's image of the dead soldiers "striking their bloodied mother with still warm breast" as they collapse on the earth (*Met.* 3.124–5), but apparently found the language too subtle. Seneca rewrites, "The mother saw the children she had just borne return to her embrace [lit. "lap"]" (*genetrixque suo reddi gremio / modo productos uidit alumnos*, 746–7).[42] This incestuous overtone must have been irresistible to Seneca: in a tragedy about Oedipus, reference to a maternal "lap" can hardly be without sexual connotation.

The culmination of the ode presents Actaeon, the paradigmatic unwary Ovidian victim of *error*, hitherto unmentioned in the play but required by the Ovidian sequence. Ovid himself introduces Actaeon as the *first* of Cadmus' doomed descendants with a coy joke: when Ovid says that his grandson was the first *inter tot res, Cadme, secundas* (*Met.* 3.138) the positive adjective *secundas* is delayed just enough by the apostrophe to Cadmus to create a sense of surprise. Cadmus' line is hardly known for its run of good fortune, so the brief

---

[42] Noted also by Boyle (2011) *ad loc.* as a reference to "Oedipus' 'return' to his mother's bosom." For *gremium* with an explicitly sexual meaning as "female sexual parts" see *OLD* 3 s.v. *gremium*. Unsurprisingly, one of the texts cited is Statius *Theb.* 1.234 of Oedipus and Iocasta, *immeritae gremium incestare parentis*; cf. Cat. 67.29–30, a facetious (if tasteless) mention of incest: *Egregium narras mira pietate parentem, / qui ipse sui nati minxerit in gremium*. For a discussion of the terminology, Adams (1982) 92.

hiatus generated by the apostrophe allows the reader to fill in an adjective that complements the *res* of Cadmus: when *secundas* follows, it catches us off guard. Through this subtle aural device Ovid plays on our own knowledge that the line of Cadmus will produce a series of unfortunate events. Seneca's chorus echoes this familiarity as they ask, "Why should I even mention the fate of Cadmus' grandson" (751), adopting Ovid's periphrasis, *Cadmei nepos* (*Met.* 3.138). The chorus hardly needs to mention him by name; we all know what is coming next in the Ovidian sequence immediately after the foundation of Thebes: Actaeon.[43] In this section Seneca imports entire phrases wholesale from Ovid's account (*vivacis cornua cervi; in unda / cornua vidit vultusque; virgineos ... artus*), rendering his debt unmistakable.

Ovid's version of Actaeon certainly supports the chorus' contention that the gods are especially cruel to Thebans, as they characterize Diana *nimium saevi diva pudoris* (763).[44] Actaeon's story is the first of three Theban tales in Ovid that includes a judgment on divine behavior, a progression that begins with an equivocal assessment for Diana (*Met.* 3.253–5):

> Rumor in ambiguo est: aliis violentior aequo
> visa dea est, alii laudant dignamque severa
> virginitate vocant; pars invenit utraque causas.

> Opinion was divided: to some the goddess seemed unfairly savage, while others praised her and adduced her appropriately harsh chastity; both sides found justification.[45]

In book 4, Ino's devoted attendants, horrified by their mistress' apparent suicide, abuse Juno for her cruelty to Semele, since Ino was persecuted for the mere fact of being Semele's sister. Juno's words effecting the attendants' metamorphoses into rocks and birds appropriately names her preeminent characteristic, *saevitia* (*Met.* 4.545–50):

> nec dubium de morte ratae Cadmeida palmis
> deplanxere domum scissae cum veste capillos
> utque parum iustae nimiumque in paelice saevae

---

[43] Ovid anticipates the quick deterioration of Cadmus' good fortune hard upon the foundation of the city in *Met.* 3.130–1, *Iam stabant Thebae, poteras iam, Cadme, videri / exilio felix.*

[44] The negative judgment of Diana in Ovid's narrative also noted by Boyle *ad loc.*

[45] Actaeon's denouement in Seneca repeats Ovid's emphasis on Diana's moral culpability; Hinds (2011) uncharacteristically neglects an Ovidian allusion in *Oed.* 763: the unusual formulation *nimium saevi ... pudoris* with the intensive clearly evokes Ovid's *violentior aequo ... severa virginitate*, reminding us that Actaeon's punishment is the first occasion in the *Metamorphoses* where any comment has been raised explicitly about the gods' morality.

> invidiam fecere deae. convicia Iuno
> non tulit et "faciam vos ipsas maxima dixit
> saevitiae monimenta meae." res dicta secuta est.

> Certain that she was dead, they mourned the house of Cadmus and tore their hair and clothing, intending to bring opprobrium on the goddess so unjust and excessively cruel to her rival. Juno did not tolerate their accusations, declaring "I will make you the greatest testaments to my cruelty." And her word was done.

Far from refuting their accusations, Juno rather confirms her insatiable vindictiveness by punishing even the servants of Semele's sister; Ovid consistently depicts the gods as excessive toward Thebans.[46] The attendants' transformation into rocks connects this episode to the displaced Theban tale, that of Niobe, who also turns into a figure of stone. After her sons have been murdered, Niobe condemns Latona and asks her to spare her daughters (*Met.* 6.280–1):

> pascere, crudelis, nostro Latona, dolore,
> pascere' ait 'satiaque meo tua pectora luctu!

> Cruel Latona, feed on my grief—feed, sate your heart with my mourning!

Like Juno with Ino's servants, Latona will not be satisfied until all of Niobe's children are slain. Ovid's gods are consistently immoderate where the Theban house of Cadmus is concerned. Seneca's Theban citizens seem to understand the situation perfectly when they try to satiate, rather than propitiate, the gods at their altars (*satiare, Oed.* 201). Similarly, Seneca's addition to the standard Vergilian underworld personifications (*avidumque populi Pestis Ogygii malum*, 589) appropriately embodies Ovid's view of Thebes: supernatural forces are all too greedy for Theban suffering. In this ode, the chorus attempts to exculpate Oedipus by making the point that it's not his fault alone: the gods hate Thebes. This conclusion, however, only damns Oedipus more securely by presenting an explicitly Ovidian view of Theban history as a never-ending sequence of divine persecution.

Oedipus sensibly replies to the chorus, "My mind swirls with anxieties and my fear returns" (764). Seneca's constant return to the Ovidian narrative of Thebes provides an explanation for Oedipus' fear and the citizens' pessimism

---

[46] Juno is also judged *gravius . . . iusto* in her punishment of Tiresias, *Met.* 3.333; on human standards of ethical judgment problematically applied to the gods in Ovid, see Feeney (1991) 201–2.

that is generated by the audience's own literary knowledge. This emphatic use of Ovid's Theban narrative demonstrates how intertextuality can shape characterization. But if Ovid's Theban history will also dictate Oedipus' future, how can Seneca, while emphasizing our foreknowledge of events, still represent his account as something new? The anagnorisis scenes are, as one might expect, rather perfunctory after Laius' revelation. Once Oedipus has discovered his true identity, however, he unexpectedly becomes the fearless figure we expected at the beginning of the play. A long messenger speech reports his response, introducing it with the statement, *secum ipse saeuus grande nescioquid parat / suisque fatis simile. "quid poenas moror?"* "He was violently readying some dreadful thing for himself, and something befitting his destiny. 'Why should I delay my punishment?'" (925–6). The phrase *grande nescioquid* again signals a metatextual level: we are now aware that a predetermined event is about to happen, one we expect from earlier texts. But can it be *maius*? What could be worse than Oedipus' blinding and Iocasta's suicide?

III. Transgressing *decorum*

Oedipus' rejection of delay also reminds us that the entire play has delayed the inevitable and expected conclusion. But now that he has achieved *decorum*, reached his true identity as the cursed, incestuous parricide, he is no longer afraid but hastens toward the punishment he seems to have dreaded all along. First he calls up Thebes' ghosts, the beasts of Cithaeron, Actaeon's raving dogs, even Agave to punish him (931–3), then he plans to stab himself, but decides that this is too quick a death for his crimes. As he dwells on his unnatural sins, he declares (943–7):

> Natura in uno uertit Oedipoda, nouos
> commenta partus, supplicis eadem meis
> nouetur. iterum uiuere atque iterum mori
> liceat, renasci semper ut totiens noua
> supplicia pendas—utere ingenio, miser [...].

Nature collapses Oedipus into one, she has produced new births, let her be transformed for my punishment. May you live and die again and again, and be constantly reborn so that you may constantly be punished afresh—use your cleverness, wretch [...].

Oedipus simultaneously claims his identity as the hero who outwitted the Sphinx, and his inheritance as but the latest of Thebes' never-ending monstrosities.[47] Nature, like the earth, has devised her latest monster to afflict Thebes, and Oedipus seems to appreciate the need for appropriateness—his punishment too will constantly be renewed, in a familiar Theban pattern: *semper nova*... To do so, however, he will need to exercise his famous cleverness, a quality that has not yet been seen in this play.

Seneca's characters seem to become especially self-conscious of their literary pasts as they conclude their tragedies, most famously Medea, who finally "claims" her identity once she is resolved to murder her children, *Medea nunc sum* (*Med.* 910), and to Jason, after murdering their children before his eyes, *coniugem agnoscis tuam?* (1021).[48] Similarly, once Oedipus acknowledges and accepts his true identity, he plays the part enthusiastically. The messenger goes on to relate Oedipus' blinding in gory detail (960–70):

> violentus audax vultus, iratus ferox
> iamiam eruentis; gemuit et dirum fremens
> manus in ora torsit. at contra truces
> oculi steterunt et suam intenti manum
> ultro insecuntur, vulneri occurrunt suo.
> scrutatur auidus manibus uncis lumina,

---

[47] The irony of Oedipus' *ingenium* also noted by Boyle *ad loc.*

[48] As Rosenmeyer (1989) 52 observes, Thomann (1961) vol. 1, 43 had already noted Senecan protagonists' tendency toward "self-revelation." The often-cited Fitch and McElduff (2002) provides some valuable observations on the linguistic means of self-construction in Senecan drama (self-naming; recourse to precedent; social/familial roles). Littlewood (2004) 103–71 assumes literary self-consciousness in Senecan characters but attempts to go beyond self-reflection by demonstrating how "framing" myths, especially of Phaethon or of the Golden Age, are also presented as models for the protagonists. Bartsch (2006) 265 draws a provocative connection between these metatheatrical moments and the Stoic principle of ethical *decorum* (see above, introduction): "In the *Medea*, as in other plays, the question of what befits her often takes a metatheatrical character in that Medea may seem to look to prior versions of her own story to discover what exactly *decet* her *persona* or is *dignum* of it; she comments of her role as a mother that 'greater crimes befit me now, after childbirth' (*maiora iam me scelera post partus decent* [*Med.* 50]) in the same way that Oedipus, after putting out his eyes, remarks that 'This face befits (an) Oedipus' (*vultus Oedipodam hic decet* [*Oed.* 1003]) or in the same way that Atreus comments on his plan for child-cookery, 'This is a plan that befits Thyestes—and befits Atreus' (Dignum est Thyeste facinus et dignum Atreo [*Thy.* 271])." Most recently, Hinds (2011) 22–28, "Ovid's *Medea* in Intertextual Repertory," returns to the figure of Medea and carries on her afterlife in Seneca's *Medea* as an example not only of literary self-consciousness, but also of an Ovidian "Medea code," a kind of "super-*topos*" in Senecan tragedy, fashioned from references to *all* of Ovid's Medeas (27): "In the *Metamorphoses*, in *Heroides* 12 and back in the lost tragedy, it is arguable that the cumulative effect of Ovid's interventions in the already-crowded Medea tradition is to program all subsequent Medeas in Latin, and perhaps the majority of subsequent tragic (and quasi-tragic) protagonists in Latin, as post- and propter-Ovidian." See below, chapter 4, "Parthenopaeus and *mors immatura* in Statius' *Thebaid*" for an exploration of another Ovidian "super-*topos*," the Doomed Ephebe.

> radice ab ima funditus uulsos simul
> euoluit orbes; haeret in uacuo manus
> et fixa penitus unguibus lacerat cauos
> alte recessus luminum et inanes sinus
> saeuitque frustra plusque quam satis est furit.

> His face—savage, reckless, furious, bestial as he starts excavating; moaning and raving horribly he flings his hands on his face. And the eyeballs are bulging in challenge, they even aim directly at his hand, they seek their own wounds. He digs greedily at his eyes with clawed hands; extracting them by their innermost root he twists at them as he tears them out; his hand burrows in the empty socket, and jammed deep inside, he scrapes at the hollows with his nails, and as he mauls the deep recesses of his eyes and their empty cavities he excessively vents his futile rage.[49]

Seneca embellishes Sophocles' description of the blinding with enhanced violence.[50] Oedipus becomes a man at war with himself; as parts of his body enact a physical civil war, Oedipus becomes a physical embodiment of the self-destructive Theban tradition. The incredibly graphic imagery here gives an impression of excess—Oedipus does have to dig out his own eyeballs. But does he have to be so vehement, so disgusting, about it? Even the messenger is appalled, *plusque quam satis est furit*. This excess seems even more striking if we recall the relatively modest punishment Oedipus himself had declared for Laius' murderer earlier in the play. At that time (257–63) he declared that the killer should suffer exile, commit incest, and kill his father, in short, as he states presumptuously, "whatever I myself escaped." He did not mention, however, anything about clawing at his empty eye sockets with his fingernails. But in a stark perversion of Stoic conceptions of cognition, the very organs that transmit knowledge to the mind suffer utter oblivion at the moment that Oedipus recognizes his true identity. Oedipus' quintessential gesture of recognition appropriates a Senecan image of willful ignorance found in the

---

[49] Both *eruo* and *scrutor* bear some important connotations; a surprising number of citations in the *OLD* implicate *eruo* in physical acts of blinding or mutilation. Most significantly for Oedipus, *eruo* and *scrutor* also can be used of research or investigation, which makes them doubly significant for Oedipus' blinding, the result of his all too diligent pursuit of the truth. As Henderson (1998) 253–4 and Keith (2002) 384 have noted, Statius too associates these verbs, especially *scrutor*, almost exclusively with Oedipus. While both mention Seneca's depiction of the blinding, Henderson concludes that Seneca must be Statius' immediate model, while Keith pursues further Ovidian connections.

[50] For further discussion of Oedipus' blinding, see Seo (forthcoming) on Senecan tragedy.

letters: critiquing other schools of philosophical thought, Seneca singles out the Skeptics for special condemnation: "The former do not furnish illumination by which one's vision may focus on the truth, but the latter [the Skeptics] gouge out my eyes" (*oculos mihi effodiunt*) (*Ep.* 88.45). Oedipus' recognition of his own monstrous existence aptly takes the form of knowledge perverted.

Once he has completed his punishment, Oedipus then asks the gods to cease and desist, a respite we know from Ovid's Theban history will not be forthcoming (974–7):

> […] uictor deos
> conclamat omnis: "parcite en patriae, precor:
> iam <u>iusta</u> feci, <u>debitas</u> poenas tuli;
> inuenta thalamis <u>digna</u> nox tandem meis."

> Conqueror of the gods, he shouts to everyone, "Now spare my country, I beg you. Now I have enacted justice, and I have borne the requisite punishment. Finally a night has been found that befits my marriage."

Oedipus has already surpassed the limits of Sophocles' version by scraping at his bloody eye sockets. This, he thinks, should be enough to satisfy the vengeful gods, hence his Pyrrhic "victory." This is what must be required, this is *iusta*, this is *digna*. Justice, *iustitia*, however, is hardly a limiting criterion in the gods' dealings with Thebes, and in light of Thebes' history, Oedipus' language of justice and closure contains an ironic expectation of transgression. As he declares shortly thereafter, *Bene habet, peractum est: iusta persolui patri.* / […] *nil, parricida, dexterae <u>debes</u> tuae: / lux te refugit. uultus Oedipodam hic decet.* "Good, it's done. I have justly atoned for my father. […] You owe nothing more for the deed of your hand, o parricide. The light itself flees you. This is the face that suits Oedipus" (998–1003).[51] Now that we have reached what surely must be the end, Oedipus' language is filled with terms for repayment, justice, satisfaction, suitability, in short, the language of *decorum*. He has fulfilled his destiny to be the blinded, incestuous parricide, and there seems to be almost a sense of relief in the closure. The chorus too in its final ode philosophizes, "All things progress along a fixed path (*certo tramite*), and the first day gives rise to the last" (987–8). It seems that we have all gotten what we came for: Oedipus

---

[51] Cf. Schiesaro (1992) 59, on *Thyestes* 105, *actum est abunde* (cf. *Aen* 7.552, *terrorum et fraudis abunde est*), and Bartsch (2006) n. 48 above; Boyle (2011) *ad* 1003 also underscores the "metatheatrical effect" of *vultus Oedipodam hic decet*. Schiesaro also regards these statements as signals of the inevitable repetition of poetry, almost a Freudian compulsion to return to the painful origins.

has finally taken his place among the doomed victims of Thebes; he has fulfilled his literary and mythological destiny, and the play can safely conclude.

Hardly. All of this reassuring closural language, its satisfying indications that our expectations have been finally satisfied, the presumed fulfillment of the character's *decorum*, these are all a fraud. There is still more to come, for unlike in Sophocles' play, Iocasta emerges onstage in the last act, and in her final speech of self-recrimination demands that Oedipus kill her: *Agedum, commoda matri manum, / si parricida es: restat hoc operi ultimum* (1032–3): "Go on, lend your mother a hand, if you are a parricide. This last deed remains!"[52] Without waiting for a response she stabs herself. Iocasta here turns the logic of his identity against Oedipus: now that he has finally become the incestuous parent-slayer we knew he was all along, he should finish the job. Oedipus in response castigates Apollo (1042–5):

> Fatidice te, te praesidem ueri deum
> compello: solum debui fatis patrem;
> bis parricida plusque quam timui nocens
> matrem peremi: scelere confecta est meo.
> o Phoebe mendax, fata superaui impia.

> You, "prophet," I accuse you, the gods' bulwark of truth: I owed only my father to fate, but as a double parricide I am guiltier than I feared—I have killed my mother: she died by my crime. O lying Phoebus, I have exceeded my cursed fate.

Oedipus claims the guilt for his mother's extraordinary onstage death, but objects that as a double parricide he has surpassed his anticipated "quota" of parent-murder. Again, the language of excess reminds us of our own limiting expectations: we wait for Iocasta to die, but did we foresee this startlingly indecorous form of suicide? Apollo's prophecies to Oedipus are like the mythological tradition to us: Oedipus thinks there can be a limit, a "sure path," as the chorus put it earlier, to what he must do to be Oedipus, but Seneca cultivates these limiting expectations only to reveal that there is always more (*plus*), something greater (*maius*), something beyond (*ultro*). For Oedipus, Delphi's prophecies seem to promise some kind of finality, some closure or ending. Similarly, our own notion of who Oedipus should be is conditioned and, to a certain extent, limited by our experience of the literary tradition Seneca so explicitly defines throughout the play. Seneca reflects our own understanding of Ovid's tragic

---

[52] Another perspicuous observation from an anonymous reader has sharpened the translation of "*commoda*" (1032): the colloquial ring of "lend a hand" (OLD s.v. 2b: ~ *manum*) expresses Iocasta's eagerness to die.

Thebes through Oedipus' fear. Oedipus' characterization therefore operates in a dialogue with Ovid's Theban history. Seneca employs the Ovidian material to solve the puzzle posed by his unexpectedly terrified protagonist. To accomplish this he must rely on our competence as readers to understand the template of Ovid's tragic Thebes: human error, divine vengeance, repeat. And yet, at the end of the play, Seneca reveals that despite our jaded surfeit of literary knowledge, we can still be horrified when the blinded Oedipus mutters to himself, [...] *siste, ne in matrem incidas*: "Wait, don't trip on your mother" (1051). The punning on *incido* is certainly significant: one chance encounter (*incido* OLD s.v. 4) with his mother has proven quite enough for Oedipus.

Seneca's *Oedipus* establishes the model, the literary background shared by the audience, through his distinct evocations of Ovid's Thebes. In doing so, he cultivates a sense of familiarity and expectation that may initially seem counterproductive to tragedy in an Aristotelian sense. Seneca telegraphs Oedipus' doom in a far more obvious and overdetermined manner than the subtle wordplay of Sophocles' drama. Seneca, however, cultivates a heightened environment of dread, an oppressive air of pessimism and doom that runs counter to the reversal required in Aristotelian tragedy. Rather than moving from fortune to disaster, Seneca's Oedipus is already wretched at the play's opening. The only trajectory is down, and the only question is how low we can go. By emphasizing the literary past (Sophocles, Ovid), Seneca creates a floor that continually drops to reveal even further depths (Jocasta's onstage suicide, the gruesomely enthusiastic self-blinding, the bizarrely comic pragmatism of the blinded Oedipus). Seneca's excesses as a tragedian work in tandem with his methodical evocations of literary limits, limits that derive from the audience's shared awareness of his literary models. In the *Thebaid* Statius similarly elicits the audience's complicity through literary consciousness, exploiting a Senecan sense of doom in his depiction of Parthenopaeus, and creating audience surprise at his depiction of Amphiaraus. The following chapters trace the communication between poet and audience in the *Thebaid* and the precise effects of the literary and cultural cues deployed in Statius' portrayal of these well-known figures. Which models emerge and what they signify reveal where the audience should think they are going. Statius exploits the larger scope of the epic to develop his characters' allusive potential: they incorporate more models from a greater diversity of sources, and their trajectories develop over longer duration, but this increased referentiality only enhances the audience's sense of predetermination. Epic raises the stakes for poets and readers, and the relation between them further defines their shared sense of place in the literary tradition and their cultural environment.

4

Parthenopaeus and *mors immatura* in Statius' *Thebaid*

> By now it is clear how the [Bond 007] novels of [Ian] Fleming have attained such a wide success: they build up a network of elementary associations to achieve something original and profound. Fleming also pleases the sophisticated readers who here distinguish, with a feeling of aesthetic pleasure, the purity of the primitive epic impudently and maliciously translated into the current terms and who applaud in Fleming the cultured man, whom they recognize as one of themselves, naturally, the most clever and broadminded.
>
> Such praise Fleming might merit if he did not develop a second facet much more cunning: the game of stylistic oppositions, by virtue of which the sophisticated reader, detecting the fairy-tale mechanism, feels himself a malicious accomplice of the author, only to become a victim, for he is led on to detect stylistic inventions where there is, on the contrary—as will be shown—a clever montage of *déjà vu*.[1]

These next case studies from the *Thebaid* examine the details of Statius' characterization and especially the effects in the reading audience. But how, as Eco's devastating assessment of Fleming implies, can a work be pleasurable to an audience through its sense of reassuring familiarity, and yet not be cynically mediocre? Statius, like Fleming, develops characters as synthetic generalities, stock figures rendered familiar by their similarity to multiple antecedents that constitute a comfortingly broad field of reference.[2] Statius guides the reader's sensibility by recalling literary models, and the sense of familiarity thus engendered in turn authorizes his idiosyncratic reinterpretation of Theban narrative's actors. Statius emphatically draws attention to the conventionality of his characters, only to reverse the assumed predictability he himself has fostered.

---

[1] Eco (1979) 163.

[2] Smolenaars (1994) xxvi–xxxv on "combinatorial imitation" as a typical Statian trait, also Van Dam (2006); see Hinds (2011) 27 on the Ovidian "super-*topos*."

Though this process can be successful only when the conventions of epic are relatively established, this heightened awareness of conventionality allows the poet to illuminate epic conventions as a device to generate audience surprise when he derails or subverts our carefully engineered expectations.

In his Theban epic, Statius draws his characters by consolidating literary models into composites, very much like Vergil's Paris. Statius employs a variety of models to make his characters Parthenopaeus and Amphiaraus into "super-tropes," the Doomed Ephebe and the Predestined Prophet respectively.[3] Like exempla, these reified figures require the assent of the audience to function successfully; Statius' long chain of careful literary and cultural allusions activates and even co-opts the audience's assent by fulfilling expectations.[4] Once we place a textual *locus* in a framed pattern of associations, as in Vergil's Paris, we have become what Eco calls the "malicious accomplice of the author." A smug overconfidence in our literary sophistication may even lead us to predict what will happen in the narrative. We do know how it all ends, mythologically speaking, but as in Seneca's *Oedipus,* we may still be surprised, even ultimately misled, by our authorial accomplice. These next two sections highlight the familiarity and predictability of Statius' epic characterizations to track their effects on both the narrative and the audience.

Amphiaraus and Parthenopaeus may seem relatively minor figures, but as in art connoisseurship, the less prominent details often reflect the author's style accurately. Tragic representations of the fratricidal conflict at Thebes focused on the intestine conflict. As Froma Zeitlin has authoritatively argued, Thebes and the problematic family connections literally embodied by the Labdacid ruling family provided useful material for conceptualizing the problem of

---

[3] Hardie (1990b) examines multiple correspondences between Vergil and Flavian epicists in a similar vein, but he argues only for Flavian readings of Vergil, whereas I am concerned with even larger fields of reference. As he states (3), "I take individual passages from the Flavian epics in which *two* (or more) passages of the *Aeneid* are laid under contribution; analysis of such passages reveals that the later poets were reading Virgil with an eye to structural correspondences or contrasts, and to image-structures reaching from the small scale of the 'multiple-correspondence simile' to the large scale of patterns that arch over the whole text, features that have been at the centre of much modern Virgilian criticism." I will argue that Ovid and Seneca are far more influential in shaping Statius' epic sensibilities.

[4] Cf. Levene (2010) 178 on the influence of rhetoric in generating stereotypical character: "But rhetoric has an entirely separate dimension also, because as well as providing a framework for evaluating characters as evidence for one's case, it also offers techniques for presenting a character—whether the speaker, the client, or (less often) a third party—such that the audience is emotionally engaged with their experiences. This is not precisely identical to the sort of emotional engagement that one might find in narrative or dramatic literature—it is typically far more overt and the sympathy it seeks to evoke is narrowly focused on the requirements of the case—but there is an obvious overlap." Statius seems closer to this version than Vergil.

distinction and separation of the individual from his community at Athens.[5] John Henderson and Susanna Braund have argued for a similar reading of Statius' *Thebaid* as large-scale metaphor for civil conflict in Rome.[6] While the fratricidal theme remains central, Statius' version of the Theban cycle goes far beyond the dramatic conflict within the family. Employing many well-known modes of epic digression, such as etiology and historical exegesis, the poet also fills his poem with conventional set pieces such as sacrificial rites, funeral games, lament, or *aristeia*. In each of these episodes, minor characters such as Hypsipyle, Lycurgus, and Atalanta take on larger roles in the narrative than the Theban cycle requires of them.[7] The extended development of relatively minor characters allows Statius to augment the mythological narrative with themes outside of the traditional fratricidal conflict. Statius' minor characters crowd the stage with their own narratives and literary histories, perhaps all the more because they are less central to the "action" of the epic. We might see this as a Stoppard-like phenomenon: the conceit of *Rosencrantz and Guildenstern are Dead* reminds us that we all know that Hamlet kills his uncle and everyone else ends up dead, but we as audience members are also perfectly aware that no one is more conscious of this familiar narrative than Stoppard himself.

Both Amphiaraus and Parthenopaeus feature in lengthy battle scenes that culminate in their deaths; their detailed death scenes in turn cap their highly detailed representations. Both appear in Attic tragedy, though Amphiaraus plays a larger role in the tradition of the Theban cycle because of Eriphyle's betrayal.[8] In Statius' epic, these relatively marginal figures become magnified representatives of tragedy and loss, as their significant appearances at the beginning and the end of the poem indicate. Amphiaraus, were it not for Tydeus' familiar aggression, would have been the first hero named by the poet (*quem prius heroum, Clio, dabis? Immodicum irae / Tydea? Laurigeri subitos an vatis hiatus?* 1.41–2), while the end of the poem contains a lament for Parthenopaeus (killed two books earlier) in a peculiar three-line epitaph that ends the narrative: *Arcada quo planctu genetrix Erymanthia clamet, / Arcada, consumpto servantem sanguine vultus, / Arcada, quem geminae pariter flevere cohortes* (12.805–7). As will be seen below, this pathetic anaphora contains its own closural sense, which links the death of Parthenopaeus with larger themes of grief and mourning in the poem as a whole.[9] Statius encourages us to pay attention to the margins as part of the poem's thematic architecture.

---

[5] Zeitlin (1986).

[6] Braund (2006) analyzes the historical context, whereas Henderson (1998) takes the Domitianic context as a starting point for a larger discussion of the psychological and literary-historical strands exemplified by the poem.

[7] On *mora*, see Brown (1994).

[8] Gantz (1993) 506–19, 525–8; *LIMC* s.v. "Amphiaraos, Eriphyle."

[9] Fantham (1999).

The analysis of Parthenopaeus explores the audience's cued and manipulated sense of the ephebe's overdetermined doom. We know that Parthenopaeus will die because he is one of the seven Argive leaders attacking Thebes, but Statius also elicits this consciousness through frequent references to Parthenopaeus' appearance. We will trace the literary lineage of this "Doomed Ephebe" figure through Greek genres and Roman texts and examine its effect within the epic and beyond: Statius incorporates Flavian sexual aesthetics as well.

From the evidence of Statius' oeuvre, the *puer* in Roman poetry should inspire a shudder of dread. Especially the cute, curly-haired, rosy-cheeked ones. The very beauty of the boy, particularly when it generates erotic attraction, leads one to think hard about ... death. Parthenopaeus, the tender young *deliciae* of the *Silvae*'s *epikēdia*, and the juvenile Achilles of the *Achilleid*, are the primary exhibits in the Statian corpus. In the *Thebaid*, the reader finds these associations between eroticism and death as inescapable as Parthenopaeus' sorry and predictable end. By making Parthenopaeus a repository of Roman conventions of eroticized ephebic beauty, the poet defines our horizon of expectations for the character. In his allusive characterization of Parthenopaeus, Statius goes further than mere reference; he defines an image of the doomed, beautiful ephebe, not only for his poem, but for the entire epic tradition. Through Statius' morbid lens, even the venerable Homer and Vergil exhibit this tendency to eroticize untimely death (no surprise that the virtuosic Ovid and his assiduous emulator, Seneca, are fundamental to Statius' sensibility). Silius Italicus too will not remain indifferent to the wiles of the Doomed Ephebe.[10]

I. Models Greek and Ovidian

First a brief account of the imagery and the language that enable this counterintuitive linkage between youthful male beauty and death. Greek pederastic lyric, funerary epigram, and the *Iliad* establish the poetic motifs, albeit with different emphases.[11] Lyric eroticizes the transience of male beauty, while funerary epigram and epic tend to concentrate on nonerotic representations of "beautiful death," in Vernant's phrase, namely, death at a physical peak.[12] All three genres emphasize a paradoxical goal: the commemoration of an ephemeral physical perfection. All of these literary evocations of youthful male beauty tend to freeze an instant to reflect on the inexorable passing of time and

---

[10] Podetus in *Pun.* 14 is explicitly derived from Statius' Parthenopaeus, as Lorenzo Sanna has shown, Sanna (2004); for Hylas as a model in the *Punica*, see Vinchesi (2004).

[11] Griessmair (1966).

[12] Vernant (2001).

its potential destructive power. Time threatens the attractions of the youthful *erōmenos*, while funerary epigram and epic commemorate the potentiality and glory of the young warrior in a poetic monument to loss. Poetry celebrates its power to capture ephemerality, to extend *kairos*, the perfect moment: Kyrnos will always be young, beautiful, and eternally reanimated by the singers of Theognis' poetry, while funerary epigram mourns and commemorates beauty forever intact. Epic and funerary epigram associate beauty with death as a way to amplify untimely loss, though also to celebrate the glory of a fallen youth.[13] Lyric and pederastic epigram as seen in the *Anthologia Palatina* are more interested in beauty's erotic appeal and its fading; the emphasis is on persuasion, and mortality appears as a protreptic motif; that is, "Physical attractiveness is of a short duration, by the way, so is life, so let's sleep together and then you'll be young and beautiful in my poetry forever." Stopping time through poetic commemoration therefore paradoxically emphasizes its passage as inscribed in the body of a young man, either in untimely death or a first growth of beard.[14]

While these Greek evocations of male beauty, loss, and desire inhabit their own contiguous genres, each with their own functions, an Ovidian intervention realigns their relation to one another. Just as for Senecan drama, Ovid's distillation and revision of these Greek models reveals their shared elements even as they come together to create a new narrative, or script. Ovid's song of Orpheus in *Metamorphoses* 10 represents a decisive intervention that makes Statius' Parthenopaeus possible. Orpheus' repetitious commemorations of young men loved to death by the gods establish a fatal linkage between pederastic poetics and death. The Orpheus narrative dramatizes a new pederastic genre coming into being, established by the ur-poet of mythology; like the operations of *Fama* in the *Aeneid*, this author-surrogate exemplifies the process of Ovidian poetics in miniature, creating a new genre from earlier models.[15] Statius' Parthenopaeus implements the codes of this novel Ovidian genre, much as Seneca's Oedipus inhabits an Ovidian Thebes.

In *Metamorphoses* 10, after losing his beloved Eurydice, Orpheus retreats to the wilds of Thrace and becomes a missionary of pederasty. Ovid's introduction to the Orpheus narrative anticipates the themes to come, aptly employing the metaphorical language of spring and first blossoms typical of Greek pederastic verse as a euphemism for pederasty (*aetatis breve ver et primos carpere*

---

[13] Peek (1955); Cleobis and Biton in Herodotus exemplify an extreme form of this glorification, as their physical perfection seems to create the glory surrounding their death (Hdt. 1.31).

[14] Tarán (1985) offers an excellent discussion of the theme of unwelcome hair growth as a protreptic in Greek epigram. Richlin (1983) 39–44 details imitation of Greek pederastic lyric in Statius' contemporary Martial.

[15] Janan (1988). For general comments on overlapping narratives in the *Metamorphoses*, Barchiesi (2002).

flores, Met. 10.83–5).¹⁶ A digression that precedes Orpheus' song further establishes a paradigm for the tales to follow: Cyparissus, the *puer dilectus* of Apollo, abandons himself to mourning after accidentally killing a pet stag and transforms into a cypress tree. Apollo's words to the new tree set the morbid tone for the pederastic narratives to follow: "The saddened god groaned, and said, 'I will mourn you, you will mourn others, and you will be a presence to those who grieve'" (*Met.* 10.141–2). Orpheus' own accounts of divine-mortal pederasty will cement the lethal outcomes of these relationships.

The formulaic prooemion to Orpheus' song explicitly engages a discourse on genre (*Met.* 10.148–55):

> Ab Iove, Musa parens—cedunt Iovis omnia regno—
> carmina nostra move! Iovis est mihi saepe potestas
> dicta prius: cecini plectro graviore Gigantas
> sparsaque Phlegraeis victricia fulmina campis.
> nunc opus est leviore lyra: puerosque canamus
> dilectos superis, inconcessisque puellas
> ignibus attonitas meruisse libidine poenam.

> Mother Muse, begin my tales from Jove, for all things yield to Jove's rule. Jove is the power I have often recounted before: with a more substantial plectrum I have sung of Giants, and the victorious lightning strikes on the Phlegraean plain. Now I need a more delicate instrument: I will sing of boys loved by gods, and girls maddened by forbidden flames who deserved the penalty for their lust.

Orpheus overloads on incipiatory signals: he combines the conventional trope of *ab Iove principium*, asserting the grand scope of his work, with a peculiarly intimate invocation of the muse, his mother Calliope.¹⁷ After this grandiose opening, Orpheus makes a programmatic statement contrasting genres. It seems to follow the model of typical Roman *recusatio*, but with a supremely authoritative twist: Augustan poets usually claim that their powers are too feeble to permit them to sing of Gigantomachy, a favorite paradigm for epic,

---

¹⁶ See examples in Tarán (1985); Richlin (1983) 35–7 discusses the rosebud as a common metaphor for a boy's anus in the *AP*.

¹⁷ As Bömer (1969–86) notes *ad loc.*, the *ek Dios archometha* incipit has a long history in many different poetic genres. Note especially Alcman fr. 29 Page; Cleanthes fr. 1 Powell; Aratus *Ph.* 1 = Theocritus 17.1, supposedly Orphic in origin; Cicero *Arat.* fr. 1 with Soubiran (2002) notes *ad loc.* In particular see Strato *AP* 12.1, a pederastic poem in which he begins with Zeus and then claims his young lovers rather than the muses as his inspiration. More immediately relevant to Ovid see Vergil *Ecl.* 3.60 and Ovid *F.* 5.111; on the motif, see also Fantuzzi (1980).

but Orpheus dismisses the topic nonchalantly (*cecini . . . Gigantas*, 10.150).[18] Having rejected these larger subjects, Orpheus turns to his own, idiosyncratic genre: divine-human pederasty and the revilement of women. Amusingly, Orpheus "invents" the conventional terms, for instance, *plectro graviore* to describe epic, and *leviore lyra* to describe his new type of erotic song.[19] Orpheus clearly defines his subject matter: "I will sing of boys loved by the gods, and girls driven mad by illicit passions who earned punishment by their lust" (*Met.* 10.151–2); as Barchiesi has argued, he will sing as the homoerotic Orpheus of the Hellenistic poet Phanocles.[20] As the very first poet, the self-described son of Apollo and a Muse, Orpheus sings before generic categories: his themes and genre should be idiosyncratic. Paradoxically, the mythological *auctor* of poetry affirms his authority through typically Ovidian referentiality.

In addition to defining the subject matter of his new song, Orpheus also prescribes the literary topoi and elements that constitute this genre. As promised, he begins with Jupiter, whose passion for Ganymede provides the highest authority for pederastic relations (10.155–61, quite in contrast to Vergil's virile Ganymede). Apollo follows, but his tale is less fortunate: his grief at Hyacinthus' accidental death produces a double etiology from a single metamorphosis, namely, the origins of the eponymous flower and the invention of the dirge. This tale programmatically illustrates the poetic self-consciousness of the proem as the young boy's body undergoes multiple transformations, both metaphorical and physical.[21] Orpheus begins by anticipating the physical metamorphosis and Hyacinthus' attendant immortality (*Met.* 10.164–6):

> qua licet, aeternus tamen es, quotiensque repellit
> ver hiemem Piscique Aries succedit aquoso,
> tu totiens oreris viridique in caespite flores.
> te meus ante omnes genitor dilexit [. . . .]

> Inasmuch as is allowed, you are eternal, and as many times
> as the spring dispels the winter and the Ram yields to watery
> Pisces, so many times do you rise and flourish on a grassy knoll.

Hyacinthus is simultaneously addressed as a human and as a flower: *tu*, line 166, in initial position refers to the flower, while initial *te* in the following line

---

[18] Detailed account of Gigantomachy in Roman *recusationes* in Hardie (1986) 85–7: Prop. 2.1.19f., 39f.; Hor. *C.* 2.12.16ff.; Ov. *Am.* 2.1.1ff., *Tr.* 2.69ff., 3312f.; Man. 3.5f.; *Culex* 27f.; *Ciris* 29ff. For Gigantomachy as a paradigmatically grand theme in contrast to slighter topics, Innes (1979).

[19] On the significance of *gravior* to mean weightier genre see McKeown (1989) on Ovid *Am.* 1.1.1.

[20] Barchiesi (2001b) 56–7.

[21] Hardie (2002b) 229–30.

addresses the erstwhile human. Orpheus rehearses the poetic commonplaces of pederastic eros in the transformed body of Hyacinthus: the brief spring and the first flowers of youthful male beauty evoked in line 10.85 take a literal form in the transformed *puer* (*ver . . . flores,* 85, echoed by *ver . . . flores,* 165–6). The flower's annual reappearance in the spring botanically represents the poetic immortality promised to countless generations of young *erōmenoi* like Kyrnos. Orpheus thus opens with the punch line: physical metamorphosis leads to poetic immortality in pederastic song.

As the narrative continues, Orpheus turns to a hyperpoetic figure, simile, to depict Hyacinthus' death. The flower simile appropriately anticipates Hyacinthus' physical transformation in a kind of poetic "proto-metamorphosis."[22] With typically Ovidian irony, the first poet uses one of the most imitated similes in ancient literature to illustrate this programmatic erotic death (*Met.* 10.190–5):

> ut, si quis violas riguoque papaver in horto
> liliaque infringat fulvis horrentia linguis,
> marcida demittant subito caput illa gravatum
> nec se sustineant spectentque cacumine terram,
> sic vultus moriens iacet, et defecta vigore
> ipsa sibi est oneri cervix umeroque recumbit.

> Just as when someone bruises violets, a poppy, or a lilies bristling with golden pistils in a well-watered garden, weakened, they immediately bow their withered heads, unable to support themselves and they gaze at the earth with their tops, just so his dying head droops; his enfeebled neck cannot bear its own weight and lolls on his shoulder.

The subject, image, and language are primarily a synthesis of two ephebic deaths in Vergil, Euryalus and Pallas (*Aen.* 9.435–7, 11.68–70). In Don Fowler's influential reading of "Vergil killing virgins," the deaths of Euryalus and Pallas contain an erotic charge imparted by the densely layered allusions; he traces its origins from the death of Gorgythion in *Iliad* 8 through the epithalamia of Sappho and Catullus. Fowler emphasizes how the interchangeability between defloration and death amplifies the pathetic youthfulness of the victims.[23] The Ovidian version transparently recalls the entire poetic genealogy of this image, even literalizing Sappho's hyacinth in Hyacinthus. Whereas each of the models employs virginal beauty and loss in their own generic contexts ("beautiful death" in Homer; sexual

---

[22] Barkan (1986) 20.
[23] Fowler (1987): *Iliad* 8.306–8; Sappho 105; Catullus 62.39–47; Catullus 11.21–4; *Aen.* 11.68–71.

initiation in Sappho and Catullus; tragically untimely death in Vergil), Orpheus' simile synthesizes all the target texts into an image of homoerotic ephebic death.[24] Hyacinthus' first transformation is literary, as well as metaphorical.

This allusive proto-metamorphosis is followed by a physical transformation into a floral text. The ephebe's corpse becomes physical material for written poetry: "He [Apollo] inscribed his own laments on the petals, and the flower displays the text 'alas!' and (each) funereal character was traced out" (*ipse suos gemitus foliis inscribit et AI AI / flos habet inscriptum funestaque littera ducta est*, 10.215–6). The painfully overemphatic, and even crudely physical, description of the text carved into each petal emphasizes Hyacinthus' physical embodiment of this new genre, pederastic lament.[25] Untimely ephebic death, even unheroic ends met in sporting accidents (Apollo's stray discus, 10.182–5), is judged worthy of poetic and botanical commemoration. The venerable Spartan festival, the Hyacinthia, is tacked on as an afterthought (10.217–9), seemingly quite secondary to the poetic aetiology that has taken place.

The Hyacinthus tale dramatizes the origins of a new genre. Ovid endows Orpheus with the most authoritative genealogy possible as the son of a Muse (*Musa parens*, 10.148) and Apollo himself (*meus ... genitor* 10.167).[26] His poetic authority is further demonstrated by his exceptional mastery of poetic formulae, traditions, and texts. Orpheus' homoerotic poetic agenda defines his new genre, essentializing distinct models to feature their common components: beautiful boys, eroticism, death. Hyacinthus' "double" metamorphosis and hypertextualization make him an emblem of this new genre of pederastic lament. Ovid's Orpheus reads backward into the tradition, revealing strands of morbid pederastic eroticism in even the most venerable epic models, Homer and Vergil. This overheated, eroticized pathos associates ephebic beauty with untimely death, a lethal linkage that guides audience expectations for Statius' Parthenopaeus.[27]

II. Deadly Coiffures

From his initial description of the ephebic hero, Statius focuses on his exceptional beauty. His attractiveness is programmatically associated with his impending doom (*Th.* 4.251–3):

---

[24] Dyson (1999) argues for Lavinia's blush as the primary referent of Orpheus' obsession with red and white.

[25] Surely the repeated cry *aiai* and the aetiological bent here are forcing a parallel to the ancient folk etymology that derived *elegos* from cries of lamentation *"e e legein"* (*Suda*).

[26] Ovid chooses Apollo's paternity over that of the mortal Oiagros.

[27] Ephebic beauty becomes the cause of untimely death in Seneca's *Phaedra*; see appendix below.

> pulchrior haud ulli triste ad discrimen ituro
> vultus et egregiae tanta indulgentia formae;
> nec desunt animi, veniat modo fortior aetas.

> Hardly anyone about to set out for the grim conflict had a more lovely countenance, and so great an endowment of outstanding beauty. He did not lack for courage, if only his hardier years had come.

Statius explicitly links physical beauty to youthful vulnerability; his rueful tone (*veniat modo*) editorializes for the reader, already anticipating the painful loss. Parthenopaeus' beauty is his distinguishing characteristic (*pulchrior ... vultus et egregia tanta indulgentia formae*), whereas his martial spirit is but an afterthought (*non desunt animi*, 4.251). The war, here significantly called a *discrimen*, will ultimately separate this boy from the men. A Vergilian echo embedded in this description enhances the sense of foreboding: Euryalus' first depiction emphasizes youthful beauty (*forma insignis viridique iuventa*, Aen. 5.295), while his bond with Nisus contains a suggestion of eroticism barely hidden below the surface.[28] In contrast with Statius' Parthenopaeus, however, Vergil's many beautiful young warriors go beyond the merely pathetic, amplifying themes of paternal loss, gender transgression, or even dynastic success in the case of Ascanius.[29] Euryalus, Lausus, Pallas, and Camilla, as Hardie has conclusively shown, all serve as epic models for virginal death; as he concludes, "Statius concentrates the Vergilian sequence of dying virginal warriors into the one figure of Parthenopaeus."[30] Statius adopts a bandwidth of representation already narrowed by Ovid: the catalogue of doomed youths in *Metamorphoses* 10 reduces the equation to "attractiveness = death," in which young men transformed into plants literalize Vergil's metaphor of "green/thriving youth" (*viridique iuventa*).

---

[28] Oliensis (1997). Discussion in Hardie (1994) 31–4 of Achilles and Patroclus as homosexual models for Nisus and Euryalus. La Penna (1996) also discusses Statius' amplification of Nisus and Euryalus as models for multiple pairs of young homosexual lovers. His article treats many of the same Statian passages discussed here but his point is rather more limited: La Penna concludes merely that homosexual *eros* is much more prominent in Statius' poetry than in his predecessors.

[29] *Aen.* 10.433–6 on the mirroring of Pallas and Lausus, both of an age and *egregii forma, sed quis Fortuna negaret in patriam reditus*. See Conte (1986) 185–95; Ascanius' epithet, *pulcher*, is less pederastic than genealogical; cf. Ennius *Annales* 1.15, where Venus is described as *pulcra* as she fills Anchises with divine inspiration for Aeneas' journey, Hardie (1990b) 11, n. 35. But Ascanius may still be a dead end after all—which son will found the city of Rome (cf. Livy 1.1)? Cf. Hardie (1994) 14–18 on *rites de passage* in *Aeneid* 9.

[30] Hardie (1990b) 9; "combinatorial allusion" in Statius, Smolenaars (1994) xxvi–xxxv.

Statius strongly limits Parthenopaeus' characteristics to youth and beauty, unmistakable signifiers for untimely death in epic. As epic constantly affirms through counterexamples like Camilla or Parthenopaeus, war belongs to men; androgynous youths are as at risk as transgressive huntresses.[31] Two repeated motifs define the poetics of this lethal beauty: a pink-and-white complexion and blonde coiffure. The first programmatic description of Parthenopaeus in Statius' Argive catalogue clearly defines ruddy cheeks as a sign of youth, "blushing sweetly and marked by his cheeks flushed with burgeoning youth" (*dulce rubens viridique genas spectabilis aevo*, 4.275). This brief phrase exemplifies Statius' presentation: Statius adapts the Vergilian phrase to evoke Euryalus' programmatic first appearance in the footrace (*viridi ... aevo; viridique iuventa*, Aen. 5.295); the modifiers *dulce* and *spectabilis* underscore the intensely voyeuristic visuality of his blushing cheeks. These sentimentalized descriptors of youthful beauty recur in book 9, where Parthenopaeus rides out to the battlefield (*Th*. 9.701–3):

> [...] tunc dulce comae radiisque trementes
> dulce nitent visus et, quas dolet ipse morari,
> nondum mutatae rosea lanugine malae.

Then his tresses gleamed sweetly, his gaze sparkled sweetly
with rays of light, and his cheeks whose lateness he resented,
had not yet been transformed by rose-tinged down.

The repeated adjective *dulce* again dictates an emotional response to the youth's physical appearance; his hair's appearance cannot be objectively "sweet," but rather entrancing only to an implied viewer. The youth's appearance on the battlefield invites erotic attention rather than inspiring intimidation. Parthenopaeus' countenance is again called rosy (a variant on *rubens* above), the sign of a beardless, unwanted juvenility.[32] Parthenopaeus' pink cheeks are presented erotically as an androgynous beauty; his beardless cheeks, also infused with pederastic allure, indicate his excessive haste to become a man by going to war. The narrator's editorializing focuses the reader on Parthenopaeus' youthful attractiveness. The visual cues emphasize Parthenopaeus' youth by employing the homoerotic descriptors of fleeting male beauty; the narrator's

---

[31] Hinds (1997), Keith (2000) 65–100.

[32] His own overprotective mother, Atalanta, has already made the same point (*Th*. 4.335–7):

> expecta dum maior honos, dum firmius aevum,
> dum roseis venit umbra genis vultusque recedunt
> ore mei [...].

Thetis also uses similar appeals on her son with similar ineffectiveness, *Ach*. 1.164–5.

voyeuristic comments thus signal the prematureness of the handsome young hero's martial enthusiasm.

Ovid's metamorphosis of Hyacinthus establishes the cosmetic tropes of homoerotic death. At the climactic moment of transformation, the hyacinth flower takes on the color of the dead youth's blood (*Met.* 10.210–3):

> ecce cruor, qui fusus humo signaverat herbas,
> desinit esse cruor, Tyrioque nitentior ostro
> flos oritur formamque capit, quam lilia, si non
> purpureus color his, argenteus esset in illis

> Behold, the blood, as it soaked into the earth and stained the plants, ceased to be blood, and a flower brighter than Tyrian purple emerges and takes shape like a lily though these flowers are purple, whereas lilies are white.

Ovid's Orpheus takes a commonplace of ephebic beauty and makes it literal: in lines 211–3, the contrast of red and white flowers pathetically echoes the glowing pink-and-white complexion traditional to attractive boys. Ovid's Hyacinthus is used as a paradigm of the *puer delicatus* in *Silvae* 2.1, where he compares unfavorably to Glaucias, the dead foster child of Atedius Melior (*S.* 2.1.112), whose complexion was so vividly beautiful: "Where is that alabaster, tinged with ruddy flush?" (*O ubi purpureo suffusus sanguine candor, S.* 2.1.41).[33] Statius reuses the same sentimentalized juxtaposition of red and white in his programmatic first description of Achilles, the figure of untimely death par excellence, "His visage was still tender: a crimson flame flickered in his snowy pale skin, and his hair shone more alluringly than gold" (*dulcis adhuc visu: niveo natat ignis in ore / purpureus fulvoque nitet coma gratior auro, Ach.* 1.161-2).[34] As in Parthenopaeus' first description, the affective adverbs frame the red, white, and blonde color scheme to maximum voyeuristic and deadly effect.

After the complexion, the hair. Hair also features in Parthenopaeus' iconography in Aeschylus' *Seven against Thebes* (*Septem* 532–7):

> [...] Such the loud vaunt
> of this creature sprung of a mountain mother, handsome,
> something between man and boy.
> The beard is newly sprouting on his cheeks,
> the thick, upspringing hair of youth in its bloom.

---

[33] Cf. Van Dam (1984) *ad loc.*

[34] Griessmair (1966) 87–89 on Achilles as the paradigmatic *pais aōros* in funerary inscriptions.

> His spirit unlike his maiden name is savage,
> and with a grim regard he now advances.[35]

Parthenopaeus' name, the "virgin-faced one," is obviously suggestive, and Aeschylus indulges in some etymological play, glossing the name as *andropais anēr* (*Septem* 533). As Philip Hardie observes, "His name itself entraps him in a perpetual epicene adolescence," and his ephebic appearance suits the etymology: the down has just come into his cheeks and his hair is appropriately thick, though in a menacing way (*Septem* 534–5).[36] Nonetheless, in the messenger's report to Eteocles, Parthenopaeus appears menacing and fearsome, one to challenge the gods. Froma Zeitlin locates his union of opposites (man/boy, male/female) as the source of his uncanny power: "Parthenopaios, like all hybrids, owes his malignant strength to the union of contraries which defines him."[37]

Parthenopaeus' youthful appearance in the post-Ovidian *Thebaid* strikes quite a different kind of dread; rather than serving as signifier of transgressive power, in the *Thebaid*, Parthenopaeus' first beard and flowing locks demonstrate his vulnerability and inadequacy for war.[38] Since Homer depicted Hector's hair flowing in the dust as he is dragged around the walls of Troy, the defilement of hair has strongly pathetic and lethal associations.[39] As the troops gather for the expedition, Parthenopaeus also feels war lust (*Th.* 4.260–3):[40]

> prosilit audaci Martis percussus amore,
> arma, tubas audire calens et pulvere belli
> flaventem sordere comam captoque referri
> hostis equo [....]

> Impelled by foolhardy love of war, he leapt to arms, burning
> to hear the trumpets and to sully blonde hair with the dust
> of battle, and to ride back on the seized horse of an enemy.

---

[35] Grene (1953).

[36] Hardie (1990b) 11.

[37] Zeitlin (1982) 100. Capaneus in the *Thebaid* seems to have taken on some of the impiety of Aeschylus' Parthenopaeus: *Septem* 529–532; cf. *Thebaid* 10.899–939, Fantham (2006).

[38] Sanna (2008) explores the symbolism of dust and sweat for Statius' vulnerable young warriors. I am grateful to him for sharing his unpublished dissertation chapter on Parthenopaeus; though I received it after this chapter was completed, it is reassuring that we followed many of the same textual traces.

[39] See chapter 1 above. Fowler (1987) 197; Vernant (2001) *passim*. Troilus as depicted on Dido's temple is the closer model for Parthenopaeus, *infelix puer atque impar congressus Achilli,* / [...] *huic cervixque comaeque trahuntur/per terram, et versa pulvis inscribitur hasta* (*Aen.* 1.475–8).

[40] All *Thebaid* text taken from Shackleton Bailey (2003a) and Shackleton Bailey (2003b), except text from *Thebaid* 9, taken from Dewar (1991).

Parthenopaeus naively imagines himself "sullying blonde hair with the dust of battle," an appropriate image for martial epic, as long as it is not one's own. The negative connotations of the verb *sordere* imply that he resents his own androgynous beauty and wishes to appear rugged and battle-stained like a real warrior.[41] The combination of battle dust and hair can never really have a nonlethal connotation in the epic tradition; "fouling hair" (*foedare in pulvere crinis, Aen.* 12.99) practically becomes a synonym for dishonorable death. In the *Thebaid*, ephebic hair exerts its own narrative pressure. Parthenopaeus comes to learn how dangerous it will be to let his hair down in war, an action whose consequences the doomed youth does not quite fully understand.

While hair in epic has its own trajectories, Statius also exploits the special ephebic associations of hair. The erotic, androgynous beauty of youth is affirmed by luxurious hair but also lost with the arrival of a first beard. In ritual vows, the cutting and dedication of a lock signifies the passage into adulthood.[42] The hairstyle, the first growth of beard, and the votive lock are all symbols of ephemerality and transition that Statius uses to create a heightened sense of fatality around the alluring young hero. Statius, like Ovid before him, has a special affinity for hair. Statius imports the social into the mythological, by translating the gendered, symbolic language of the body into heroic terms.[43] An overcultivated coiffure, a suspicious indicator of effeminacy, becomes in epic a sign of fatal ephebic androgyny.[44] Just as the wrong kind of hair can indicate a failure of adult masculinity in imperial Rome, in epic, having androgynous, feminine hair clearly signals martial inadequacy. Already in the *Aeneid*, descriptions of hair can contribute to a picture of pathetic death, as in the death of Lausus, [...] *et terra sublevat ipsum / sanguine turpantem comptos de more capillos*, "He [Aeneas] lifted him from the earth where he was fouling his hair with blood, his beautifully arranged hair" (10.831–2).[45] But hair is not as prominent a feature in the Vergilian descriptions of youthful heroes. In Statius quite the opposite is true: hair is overcultivated not by the heroes but by the poet himself. It would quickly become tiresome to cite all of the occasions on which Statius describes attractive hair; it is sufficient to note that in descriptions of youthful beauty, golden locks are a sine qua non for Parthenopaeus (*Th.* 9.701), Glaucias (*S.* 2.1.34–45), and especially Achilles (*Ach.* 1.162).

---

[41] I am grateful to Gianpiero Rosati for raising the connection between Statius' Parthenopaeus and descriptions of Hippolytus' manly attractiveness in Ov. *Her.* 4. In *Her.* 4.78 dust is observed on the face, *et levis egregio pulvis in ore decet*, but not on the hair. The case of Hippolytus is significant and will be discussed in the appendix below.

[42] Also an important marker of the transition from life to death; cf. Dido and Iris in *Aen.* 4.

[43] Connolly (1998).

[44] Gunderson (2000) 59–86, also Edwards (1993) *passim*, and Gleason (1995).

[45] See also Turnus' threats against Aeneas' Paris-like hair, *Aen.* 12.97–100 and the discussion in chapter 1.

Hair seems to have had a special importance in the imperial court of the balding Domitian. Llewellyn Morgan has noted Domitian's preoccupation with hair (or the lack thereof), and the emperor's own use of Achilles as an exemplum in the dedication of his work, the *de cura capillorum*. Domitian exploits Achilles' traditional association with long hair and untimely death in his humorously consoling dedication to a bald friend.[46] Elsewhere in the *Silvae* and in Martial's epigrams, beautiful hair is a characteristic of youths both in poems of consolation and especially in poems about Domitian's favorite eunuch, Earinus, an example we shall consider in more detail below. In *Silvae* 2.6, a *consolatio* to Flavius Ursus on the death of his young favorite, Philetas, Statius praises the youth's masculine beauty with an rather paradoxical comparison to a martial Parthenopaeus (S.2.6.38–47):[47]

> non tibi femineum vultu decus oraque supra
> mollis honos, qualis dubiae quos crimina formae
> de sexu transire iubent; torva <at>que virilis
> gratia nec petulans acies blandique severo
> igne oculi qualis bellus iam casside visu
> Parthenopaeus erat, simplexque horrore decoro
> crinis et obsessae nondum primoque micantes
> flore genae; talem Ledaeo gurgite pubem
> educat Eurotas, teneri sic integer aevi
> Elin adit primosque Iovi puer adprobat annos.

There was no womanish affectation in your features, nor effeminate beauty in your face, as in those whom the reproach of androgynous beauty forces to transgress their sex: your charm was bold and masculine, and your gaze was not flirtatious; your eyes were gentle, but with a noble cast, like Parthenopaeus, now handsome in his helmet. Your hair was elegant in its shaggy adornment, and your glinting cheeks were not yet bound by a first growth; just like a boy whom Eurotas might raise near his Ledan stream, unsullied in his tender age he approaches Olympia and commends his earliest years to Jove.

Statius is at pains to portray youthful, masculine beauty, but the (over)emphasis on masculinity with its repeated denials (*non . . . femineum*, 38; *nec petulans acies*, 41) and striking oxymorons (*torva <at>que virilis / gratia*, 40–1; *blandique severo / igne oculi*, 41–2) appears to be special pleading. The comparison

---

[46] Morgan (1997).
[47] Text of the *Silvae* from Shackleton Bailey (2003c).

to Parthenopaeus on the battlefield and to a Spartan youth should guarantee Philetos' uprightness. Despite the poet's praise of the healthy young masculinity in Philetos' appearance, the comparison with Parthenopaeus seems less than convincing, especially in light of Statius' own portrayal of the young hero in the *Thebaid*.[48] Again, the beardless cheeks import a sense of erotic desirability, though the funereal context also suggests the pathos of untimely death. Still, the adjective *simplex* applied to hair, especially with the ablative of description, *horrore decore* (*S.* 2.6.43), irresistibly draws us back to the infamous courtesan Pyrrha of Horace *Odes* 1.5.4–5: *cui flavam religas comam/ simplex munditiis*. Just as Pyrrha's hairstyle makes an art of elegantly austere luxury, Philetos' hair seems to possess a similarly paradoxical studied neglect. Pyrrha's seductive knowingness in the matters of hair casts a hint of feminizing doubt on Philetos' innocence.

This *Silvae* passage thematizes a number of important aspects of ephebic hair in a funeral context. The point is not that the ephebe is explicitly effeminate, but that the preciousness of his beauty lies in transient androgyny. The ephebe moves into manhood via two types of haircutting: dedication of locks and the first growth of beard. Hence the pointed reference to Spartan education and the importance of the Eurotas in *Silvae* 2.6.46: the practice of dedicating a lock of hair to a river god represents a young man's transition to adulthood. In epic, however, this convention is more often seen subverted than successfully executed. Homer presents the locus classicus for the connection between haircuts and untimely death in Achilles' great vow and dedication of his lock at Patroclus' pyre (*Il.* 23.140–51). Achilles dedicates his lock to Patroclus' shade as a gesture of mourning, but also in explicit anticipation of his own death. The lock that should symbolize a successful transition to manhood, here accelerates into premature death. In Homer, just as Patroclus substitutes for Achilles in battle, cutting the lock before fulfilling the vow attached to it symbolizes Achilles' imminent death.

In the *Aeneid*, Ascanius' vow to Euryalus before his fatal night mission suggests some tantalizing parallels. At 9.300, Ascanius promises to take care of Euryalus' mother in suggestive terms: "I swear by this head, by which my father was accustomed to swear before." After Euryalus' death, Ascanius fulfills his oath, thus proving his own trustworthiness to be as great as his father's

---

[48] Critical opinion is split on Statius' portrayal of Philetos: Shackleton Bailey (2003c) reads Statius "literally" as rejecting any hint of effeminacy in his appearance, as does Newlands (2011) *ad loc*. Van Dam (1984) accepts the identification in the transmitted *titulus* of Philetos as a *puer delicatus*, and thus admits the possibility of exaggeration on Statius' part. As so often, Statius seems to have his cake and eat it too: while it is appropriate to praise the healthy virtues of the deceased, surely the bereaved would miss certain erotic charms as well? My reading of 2.6 has affinities with Asso (2010) on *Silvae* 2.1, another epicedion for a young slave.

confidence in his survival. Both Peleus and Aeneas use their sons' heads as symbols of their greatest hopes for the future. Vergil, however, does not emphasize Ascanius' hair, perhaps because of the lethal Homeric associations; rather, the pathetic death that ensues from this vow is displaced onto Euryalus. The essential pathos of both of these vows, Peleus' unfulfilled promise and Ascanius' unhappy duty, lies in the destruction of the future, hence the importance of swearing oaths on this most transient part of the body. In his lament for the young Glaucias, Statius recalls Atedius Melior often swore oaths on the boy's future beard (*S.* 2.1.52–4):

> O ubi venturae spes non longinqua iuventae
> atque genis optatus honos iurataque multum
> barba tibi? [...]

> Where is that hope of adolescence, not far off in coming, and the glory anticipated for the cheeks and your beard, so much used as a token of oaths?

The sense of imminence in the phrase *venturae spes non longinqua iuventae*, the adjective *optatus*, and the implicit view to the future in *iurata* all exploit the poignant juxtaposition of ephebic potential and its loss. In Parthenopaeus, we find all of these associations maximized.

Statius focalizes Parthenopaeus' childish imaginings of war as a glamorous transition to adulthood: his lovely hair will take on the martial dust appropriate to the warrior. The erotic prominence of hair in descriptions of the young warrior's beauty takes on a more lethal connotation as the Achillean similarities emerge. In book 6, Statius also uses the funeral games for the baby Opheltes to anticipate events from the climactic battle to come.[49] Before the footrace, Statius establishes the symbolism of Parthenopaeus' lock as a synecdoche for the youth's life (*Th.* 6.607–10):[50]

> flavus ab intonso pendebat vertice crinis
> Arcados; hoc primis Triviae pascebat ab annis
> munus et, Ogygio victor cum Marte redisset,
> nequiquam patriis audax promiserat aris.

> The Arcadian youth's blond hair was hanging down from his unshorn head; he had been cultivating it from his

---

[49] Lovatt (2005) 31.
[50] Cf. the repeated use of this epithet of Diana at 9.863, when Parthenopaeus prays in vain to *Trivia* as he begins to fade in battle.

earliest years as a dedication to Diana, and in vain, he had boldly promised it to his native altars when he returned victorious from Theban war.

Statius evokes the personified sense of cultivation found in Homer's *trephein* (*Il.* 23.142) in the verb *pascebat*. Like Achilles' lock, Parthenopaeus' hair is also intended for a special divinity and will be delivered on the hero's return from war. The mortality that shadows Achilles also hangs over Parthenopaeus; Diana proves unable to help her favorite despite his promised dedication, and his return, like Achilles', will be lost. Even the contrafactual adverb, *nequiquam*, corresponds to Achilles' self-conscious *allōs* (*Il.* 23.144), though Parthenopaeus knows much less than Achilles about his own fate.

Immediately following this vignette of Achillean, untimely death, Parthenopaeus loses a footrace to Idas, his juvenile twin (*Th.* 6.583–6). Idas gains the lead by foul play; he seizes Parthenopaeus' conveniently long hair and passes him at the finish. This parallel to Euryalus' victory through Nisus' self-sacrifice in the footrace of *Aeneid* 5 has the same predictive force. Just as the lovers' actions in the funeral games for Anchises represent a rehearsal for their deaths in book 9, Parthenopaeus' failure games anticipates his own end in battle.[51] The importance of hair in the footrace is profoundly overdetermined; before the start of the rematch, Parthenopaeus prays to Diana directly, demanding her help because his pious cultivation of her lock caused his earlier downfall: "O powerful goddess of the woods (this is yours, this is the lock owed to you for your glory, and this insult comes from your dedication)" (*diva potens nemorum (tibi enim hic, tibi crinis honori / debitus, eque tuo venit haec iniuria voto), Th.* 6.633–4). His petulance pinpoints a truth that will be revealed in the moment of his death: this is but a preliminary insult that Diana's failure will inflict upon him. Like Achilles' lock in *Iliad* 23, this votive lock with its implicit promise of the future paradoxically indicates Parthenopaeus' doom. The lock's prominence in this replay of Euryalus' race only enhances the sense of dread.

After his *aristeia* in book 9, aided substantially by Diana's arrows, Parthenopaeus finally returns to himself. As his strength fails with the goddess' departure, he sees himself with clarity. His weapons get heavier and heavier, "and he seems a child, even to himself" (*puerque videtur / et sibi, Th.* 9.855–6). Like Vergil's Troilus, he is a *puer*, unequal to the demands of battle (*infelix puer atque impar congressus Achilli, Aen.* 1.475). At this moment of self-

---

[51] On the funeral games of Anchises as a *prolusus* for the deaths of Nisus and Euryalus, cf. Hardie (1994) 28–9.

recognition he receives the fatal wound from Dryas, and as he is carried off the battlefield, his vision of himself as a child is confirmed by his trivial concerns (*Th.* 9.877–9):

> at puer infusus sociis in devia campi
> tollitur (heu simplex aetas!) moriensque iacentem
> flebat equum. [...]

> But as the stricken boy is carried to the edge of the battlefield by his companions (alas, the ingenuousness of his youth!) in his last moments he wept for his fallen horse.[52]

Like Euryalus, Parthenopaeus entrusts a young companion, Dorceus, with his last words to his mother in which he returns to the lock that embodies his *mors immatura* (*Th.* 9.900–907):

> "hunc tamen, orba parens, crinem," dextraque secandum
> praebuit, "hunc toto capies pro corpore crinem,
> comere quem frustra me dedignante solebas.
> huic dabis exequias, atque inter iusta memento
> ne quis inexpertis hebetet mea tela lacertis
> dilectosque canes ullis agat amplius antris.
> haec autem primis arma infelicia castris
> ure, vel ingratae crimen[53] suspende Dianae."

> "My bereaved mother, you will take this," and he offered it for cutting in his right hand. "Take it in place of my body, the lock that you used to brush while I protested in vain. You will give it a funeral, and remember amid the rites, let no one dull my hunting weapons with untrained hands, and let no one guide my beloved hounds anymore through rocky glens. These weapons, however, that were so unsuccessful in their first campaign, burn them, or dedicate them as a reproach to the remorseless Diana."

Here Statius elaborates on Homer's scenario in book 23: the lock is cut at the very moment of death, and the implicit identification with the lock in Achilles' speech is made explicit (*hunc toto capies pro corpore crinem*, 9.901).

---

[52] Echoes of Persephone's rape, in which she naively laments her lost flowers, *Met.* 3.398–401.

[53] Dewar 1991 *ad* 907: *crimen Imhof*: munus crimen B^3: crinem P: munus ω.

Parthenopaeus' climactic death scene with its emphasis on the lock studiedly completes the parallels to Achilles' funereal offering in book 6.

III. Flavian Ephebes

Statius draws liberally on literary representations of untimely death from Homer, Greek pederastic and funeral epigram, and Ovid's Orpheus. Contemporary visual culture may also provide a context for the theme of eroticized *mors immatura*. Elizabeth Bartman has suggested that the image of a "sexy boy" (her term) became popular in Roman sculpture in the late first and early second centuries CE.[54] She argues that far from being copies of singular Greek models, these Roman sculptures incorporate the more *soigné* elements of Praxitelean and fourth-century Greek models into a more generic portrait of alluring, androgynous beauty. For Bartman, these "sexy boys" are indicative of a particular aesthetic that Roman sculptors and audiences themselves desired and created, not slavishly copied out of some unthinking philhellenism. From Bartman's evidence, it seems that this eroticized ephebic figure, also used on sarcophagi, was a familiar element of a distinctively Roman aesthetic.[55] John Pollini's study of late first-century CE sculpture finds more evidence for a strongly homoerotic aesthetic.[56] He argues that many representations of boys have been misidentified in the past as female figures because their hairstyles reflect female fashions of the Neronian, Flavian, and Trajanic periods. Pollini identifies boys with female hairstyles, in particular, long hair with bangs, as slave boys. Their effeminized appearance to Pollini signifies their sexual function as *pueri delicati*.[57] Pollini compares these sculptures in the round to the memorials recorded in Statius' *Silvae*; these sculptures are the plastic equivalent of the *consolationes* offered by Statius for his grieving patrons.

The preeminent "sexy boy" of the Flavian period was Domitian's favorite, Earinus, who has a strong presence in literature of this period.[58] In Statius' *Silvae* and in Martial, Earinus very much resembles the alluring Parthenopaeus except in one significant difference: the emperor's favorite, like Ascanius in

[54] Bartman (2002).

[55] Bartman herself uses contemporary literature as evidence of this very point, though none of the Statian passages adduced here.

[56] Pollini (2003).

[57] Pollini's provocative connection between the religious and sexual function of these slaves (some of them appear as religious ministrants in relief sculptures) and his analogy to contemporary scandal within the Catholic church may be excessive, (2003) 159.

[58] Pollini discusses Earinus in the poetry of Martial and Statius, *passim*. Bartman does not mention Earinus specifically, which is understandable since the works she discusses are only vaguely dateable in most cases.

Vergil, must not be associated with untimely death. Both Statius and Martial composed poetry on the dedication of the eunuch's locks in the temple of Asclepius in Pergamum; Martial also adds several poems in praise of his beauty (S. 3.4; Martial 9.11; 12; 16; 17; 36). The fact that Earinus is a eunuch, presumably to preserve his androgynous good looks, poses a sticky problem, as Domitian had issued an edict outlawing castration, probably in CE 85, several years before the dedication commemorated in these poems from CE 95.[59] These poems about Earinus must dodge a Skylla and a Charybdis: on the one hand, the castration itself is embarrassingly illegal, and on the other hand, the poets must praise his ephebic beauty and even the cutting of a votive lock, without introducing unwanted morbid associations.

The uncomfortable issue of castration is deftly turned to the poets' advantage. The castration is the remedy to the *mors immatura* theme: inoculated by the procedure, Earinus, flowery little Mr. Springtime, according to Martial's etymologizing epigram 9.11, will never grow a beard and thus lose his beauty. His symbolic immortality is such that he can be compared to the disadvantage of a petulant Ganymede (S. 3.4.12–24; Martial 9.36), and both poets make a point of emphasizing his "eternal" youth through the image of his beardlessness. Statius even uses the dedication of the tresses to remark upon the absence of the expected beard clippings (S. 3.4.78–82):

> tu quoque, nunc iuvenis, genitus si tardius esses,
> umbratusque genas et adultos fortior artus
> non unum gaudens Phoebea ad limina munus
> misisses: patrias nunc solus crinis ad oras
> naviget. [...]

> And you would by now be a young man [a *iuvenis*, not a *puer*] had you been born later, and your cheeks would have been shadowed and your mature limbs stronger. You would have proudly sent more than one gift to Phoebus' door: but now, only a single lock makes the journey to its native shores.

The castration seems to have been a blessing that Earinus might have missed had he been born after the edict in 85. These lines demonstrate the eunuch's anomalousness: the lock travels alone, *solus*, to Pergamum, Earinus' native city; if he were capable of growing a beard, he would have more offerings to send to Asclepius' shrine. Statius follows these lines with the mythological locks that Earinus' hair will surpass in beauty: the fatal purple lock of Nisus, and

---

[59] See Garthwaite (1984). Vessey (1986) 28 calls the effect of these verses "emetic" on the modern reader.

the lock that Achilles had promised to the river Sperchios (*S.* 3.4.84–5). Those pieces of hair portend doom, while Earinus is guaranteed a kind of immortality: he plays Ganymede to Domitian's Jupiter.[60] Earinus' solitary gift makes him superior to these famous mythological figures because his lonely piece of hair, missing the beard clippings that would ordinarily accompany the offering of an intact youth, demonstrates his freedom from the expectations of *mors immatura* that accompanies ephebic beauty in the literary tradition. Earinus embodies a permanent erotic juvenility in his poetic depictions, one that is defined in terms opposed to conventions and examples that Statius himself has established elsewhere.

The success of Earinus' near immortality depends upon the reversal of a now familiar trope. His beauty carries no lethal overtones because his beardless youth is surgically guaranteed by the god Asclepius' intervention. In Earinus, we see the inversion of Parthenopaeus, Euryalus, Pallas, Glaucias, and Philetos. The conventions that bind these figures together rely heavily upon poetic allusion, gathering critical mass to become their own minor poetics of ephebic death. Though built upon earlier Greek traditions, Ovid's importance to the development of this poetics cannot be underestimated. Ovid's Orpheus demonstrates the tendentious way in which the subject of song can be circumscribed. In the *Metamorphoses,* Orpheus self-consciously reshapes the Greek traditions of pederastic lyric and funerary epigram to create his own personal micro-genre. Orpheus' formulation leads us to read backward in pre-Ovidian epic and to find the essential poetic traces that validate his claims. By translating Orpheus' pederastic laments into epic and *epikedia,* Statius finds a *langue* that from the first signals to the reader the pathos and inappropriateness of Parthenopaeus' martial action. Nonetheless, Parthenopaeus and his 'unepic' qualities also trace backward to cast doubt on the fundamental purity of all epics, including the most canonical poems, such as the *Iliad* and the *Aeneid*.

The Doomed Ephebe super-trope betrays its precise Ovidian origins in a final allusive moment, Parthenopaeus' wound (*Th.* 9.880–3):

> aegraque per trepidos expirat gratia visus,
> et prensis concussa comis ter colla quaterque
> stare negant, ipsique nefas lacrimabile Thebis,
> ibat purpureus niveo de pectore sanguis.

> A weakened charm breathed out through his wavering countenance, and three and four times they seized his hair and shook his neck, but they could not prop it up,

---

[60] Martial 9.11.7; an overgrown and unattractive Ganymede expresses jealousy: Martial 9.16, 9.36.

>   and then, a pitiable calamity even to the very Thebans,
>   the crimson blood started spreading on his snowy chest.

As the fatality of his wound becomes obvious, Parthenopaeus' head slumps down, despite the efforts of his companions to revive him. The weakened neck, *colla*, certainly holds a hint of something we have seen before, while the rough handling of his hair contrasts pathetically with the radiance and otherworldly beauty it has represented up to this point. Line 883 brings in a familiar color scheme: his crimson blood stands out on the snowy chest in an elaborate chiastic arrangement, and suggests a kind of botanical metamorphosis by allusion. In the moment of his death, Parthenopaeus adopts the familiar posture of a young hero like Gorgythion, but his erotic charms seem amplified by the intertextual connections to the expiring young *erōmenoi* of *Metamorphoses* 10.[61]

Although his death strongly resembles that of Hyacinthus in its densely layered allusions, Parthenopaeus brings grief to more than a single divine lover; his *mors immatura* focuses the pathos of all the tragic young victims of the Theban war. Ultimately, his youth and beauty affect all who see him dying; even his enemies find the sight worthy of tears. David Quint has recently shown that the victors and victims of *Aeneid* 10 replay the deaths of Sarpedon and his killer, Patroclus, both figures who shift between arrogant brutality and pathetic victimhood. This mutability, he argues, serves an equalizing purpose:

> Virgil exploits these likenesses and the interchangeability of victor and victim in the close alternation of models that has the warriors of the *Aeneid* switching between Iliadic roles from one verse to the next. He does so in part to suggest the problem of distinguishing *morally* among his characters once they are engaged in battle, particularly the problem of judging his hero who at times seems only minimally different from the other combatants [...][62]

The Trojan Sarpedon and the Greek Patroclus share essential qualities that are reproduced among the Trojan and Italian combatants of *Aeneid* 10. In a similar manner, the multiple models for youthful beauty and death, culled and distilled as they are from numerous traditional models, authorize and universalize the pathos of a single figure, Parthenopaeus, to Thebans, Argives, and

---

[61] Note especially how the pathetic adjective *lacrimabile* corresponds to the programmatic element of mourning contained in the *Met.* accounts of Cyparissus (*Met.* 10.141–2) and especially Hyacinthus (*Met.* 10.214–6), whose flower bears an inscription of Apollo's grief.

[62] Quint (2001) 62.

Romans alike. By placing an epitaph for the dead Parthenopaeus at the end of the poem, Statius turns this beautiful *puer* into the paradigmatic victim of what Quint calls the "deathtrap" of epics like the *Iliad* and the *Aeneid*.[63] While these earlier epics may have taken the genre as a medium to explore themes of human choice, mortality, and national identity, in the figure of Parthenopaeus, Statius' epic thematizes the affective emotionality of grief.[64]

---

[63] *Th.* 12.805–7: *Arcada quo planctu genetrix Erymanthia clamet, / Arcada, consumpto seruantem sanguine uultus, / Arcada, quem geminae pariter fleuere cohortes.* Quint (2001) 65.

[64] See Fantham (1999) and Henderson (1998).

5

Amphiaraus, Predestined Prophet, Didactic *Vates*

This chapter develops the reading strategies proposed in the previous study of Parthenopaeus. Statius' typical "combinatorial imitation" in characters produces an essentialized figure like the Doomed Ephebe, whose very familiarity contains a strong narrative trajectory. Like exempla, these figures possess their own schematic traits and narrative implications. Whereas in Vergil the Paris figure offers a doppelgänger, an alternative founder who only implicitly casts a shadow on the world outside the poem, every element of this eroticized, glamorous Parthenopaeus contributes to the *mors immatura* pressure upon the narrative—we can't escape the morbid awareness that he is just too beautiful to live. Ovid and Seneca's interpretations of Ovidian topoi are critical to Statius' allusive poetics; just as Apollonius takes the *Homeric Hymns* as an intermediary model for allusion to Homer, Ovid and especially Seneca's wholesale absorption of Ovidian "codes" prove a fundamental intermediary for Statius' tendentious readings of the epic tradition. In the figure of Amphiaraus, the Argive prophet who knew too much, Statius thematizes the preordained nature of his mythological narrative, only to perform extraordinary innovations and reversals. Amphiaraus' characterization is a bait and switch: the conventional elements Statius employs create a roller coaster of narrative and generic expectations raised and subverted. The first half of this chapter will track the pressures Amphiaraus' portrayal places on the narrative; the second half explores Amphiaraus' representation as a didactic *vates* of philosophical epos and how this essentialized *vates* figure interacts with mythological epic.

I. Predestination and Prolepsis

As Elaine Fantham has recently discussed, Statius' Amphiaraus also derives his essential characteristics from a variety of models, some earlier incarnations of himself in the tradition (the *Odyssey*, Aeschylus' *Septem*, Accius' *Eriphyle*), and other vatic figures like Vergil's Calchas or Laocoon.[1] While Fantham analyzes Amphiaraus as figure of "tragic grandeur" who nobly confronts his doom in full foreknowledge, my reading emphasizes the way Amphiaraus' characterization seems to warp the narrative. The prophet's precise visions of his own uncanny fate generate instances of narrative prolepsis: every time Amphiaraus sees his own doom, we are reminded of the abyss that awaits him. While six of the seven Argive leaders must die in the expedition, Amphiaraus is the only warrior whose perspective mirrors that of the narrator and the audience—when he sees the future, the prophet performs a gesture that is doubly "vatic," both prophetic and narratological.[2]

The poem's first mention of Amphiaraus programmatically defines the prophet by his unusual death, the "sudden swallowing up of the garlanded prophet" (*laurigeri subitos an vatis hiatus, Theb.* 1.42). This noun-adjective phrase in synchysis (ABAB) spells out the juxtaposition of prophetic foreknowledge and doom that characterizes Amphiaraus. Note, however, the coy ambiguity in *subitos*—everyone knows that Amphiaraus will be swallowed by the earth—I will discuss below how this mythological end might be considered "sudden" or even "surprising." Early on in the narrative, even before she commits the treachery that will send her husband to war, Amphiaraus' wife Eriphyle is proleptically defined in terms of her husband's mortality as the "wife of the doomed prophet" (*coniunx perituri vatis*, 2.299). Eriphyle's betrayal, however, is portrayed as almost incidental to her husband's end. Statius minimizes her involvement, representing her intervention as secondary to the predetermined requirement of fate (4.187–91):

> iamque et fatidici mens expugnata fatiscit
> auguris; ille quidem casus et dira videbat
> signa, sed ipsa manu cunctanti iniecerat arma
> Atropos obrueratque deum, nec coniugis absunt
> insidiae, vetitoque domus iam fulgurat auro.

> And now the embattled resolve of the fate-telling prophet wavered; he certainly still saw the outcome and the dread indications, but Atropos herself forced the weapons into his wavering grasp and overruled the god, nor were his wife's contrivances lacking, and their home was already glowing with illicit gold.

---

[1] Fantham (2006) 147–53.

[2] On other *vates* figures in Statius, see Lovatt (2007).

Though the details of his wife's bribery and its tragic effects represent a significant part of the tradition around Amphiaraus in the literary tradition, here Statius focuses on the supernatural causation. One of the personified Fates, Atropos, physically forces Amphiaraus into the campaign with the same phrase (and dramatic gesture) that Vergil's Juno uses to open the gates of war in the *Aeneid* (*tum regina deum caelo delapsa morantis / impulit ipsa manu portas, et cardine verso, Aen.* 7.620–1).[3] Amphiaraus' capitulation despite his foreknowledge takes on the momentousness of the Latins' war against Aeneas; in both cases goddesses physically intervene to bring forth the long-delayed hostilities, though as often in Statius, an Olympian's work is performed by a divinity of Hades. The litotes used to denote Eriphyle's betrayal suggests her redundancy (*nec coniugis absunt / insidiae*). By diminishing the human agency involved, Statius heightens the sense of supernatural inevitability surrounding Amphiaraus' end; Atropos, her etymological "speaking name" significantly highlighted in the line initial of 190, is already overrunning Apollo's protection of his prophet, well before the god himself withdraws in book 7.[4]

From the first description of Amphiaraus, his peculiar fate is repeatedly anticipated in the narrative, both in incidental epithets and in larger narrative episodes. The paradigmatic moment of the prophet's self-reflexive foreknowledge occurs in the only celestial divination of the expedition, the augury of Amphiaraus and Melampus.[5] As in Seneca's *Oedipus*, the preponderance of omens and forewarnings reflects the poem's epigonic status. The overdetermined poem must follow an established mythological script and repeatedly anticipates itself on the narrative level. The augury stands as a miniature epic, a *mise en abyme* related by the *vates/augur*, a poet-substitute.[6] In the augury, Amphiaraus and Melampus read the fates of the seven Argive leaders in the birds. After observing and describing six symbolic avian casualties, Amphiaraus cryptically describes the bird that represents himself: "Why do you hide your tears? O revered Melampus, I recognize the one who is falling" (*Quid furtim inlacrimas? Illum, venerande Melampu, qui cadit, agnosco*, 3.539–47). This allusively loaded phrase carries an additional portentous echo from Lucan's frenzied *matrona* at the ominous end of Lucan's first book (*hunc ego,*

---

[3] Thanks to Denis Feeney for this observation.

[4] The etymology of Atropos from Greek *a* (alpha privative) + *trepein*. Maeon etymologizes in book 3, *placitoque ignara moveri / Atropos* (3.67–8); Maeon and Amphiaraus as doubles in the epic will be developed further below.

[5] The subsequent chthonic prophecies follow the grim models of Seneca's tragedies and Lucan's epic. On Lucan's prophecies and the background to the augury, see Fantham (2006); on chthonic forces even in the augury, see Feeney (1991) 346–58.

[6] Lovatt (2005) 31; we will further examine Amphiaraus as a *vates* of didactic poetry in the augury below.

fluminea deformis truncus harena / qui iacet, agnosco, Luc. 1.686).[7] Amphiaraus recognizes his own death prophetically and intertextually in Lucan's apocalyptic words.[8] Amphiaraus' self-knowledge and the futile seclusion he temporarily pursues only emphasize the inevitability of his own death.[9]

Similarly, the funeral games of baby Opheltes in book 6, like Anchises' funeral games in *Aeneid* 5, serve as an accurate *praelusus* of the battle to come.[10] Amphiaraus, the first of the leaders to die, appropriately wins the first event, the chariot race with the very vehicle that will convey him to his end.[11] Apollo's intervention in the race mirrors his actions in Amphiaraus' last moments on earth: in the race, Apollo decides to help Amphiaraus out of pity for his short life, just as he bestows a last honor in battle (6.372–83; cf. 7.692–3). Unheard, Apollo addresses Amphiaraus in an aside (6.381–3):[12]

> [...] tibi nulla supersunt
> gaudia, nam Thebae iuxta et tenebrosa vorago.
> scis miser, et nostrae pridem cecinere volucres.

> No pleasures are left for you, for Thebes is nigh and the murky chasm. You know this to your dismay; my birds prophesied it to you long ago.

Apollo redundantly confirms the omen Amphiaraus only enigmatically noted earlier in the augury. Here the god stresses Amphiaraus' foreknowledge and explicitly mentions the cavern that will swallow him. During the race itself, even the earth seems to hunger in anticipation as the chariot races on its surface: "the earth emits a groan and already savagely menaces" (*dat gemitum tellus et iam tum*

---

[7] Narducci (1973) on Lucan's Vergilian allusion with Hinds (1998) 8–9; on this passage, see also Fantham (2006) 152–3.

[8] Cf. his response to Capaneus' accusations of cowardice; Amphiaraus replies that he knows perfectly well what fate awaits himself, as well as the rest of the Argive princes: *alio mihi debita fato / summa dies, vetitumque dari mortalibus armis* (3.623–4); also later in the same speech: [...] *potui pariter nescire quis armis / casus, ubi atra dies, quae fati exordia cunctis, / quae mihi* (3.635–7).

[9] On the ineffectiveness of this augury and prophecy in general in the *Thebaid*, see Lovatt (2007) 162.

[10] Galinsky (1968); Lovatt (2005) 18 observes, "In the *Thebaid*, each hero has his game, as each hero has his aristeia later on in the poem." As in the augury, however, the order of the games does not correspond exactly to the sequence of Argive deaths.

[11] See also Lovatt (2005) 26–40 on the metapoetic "chariot of song" and Polyneices as Phaethon. Lovatt does not mention Phaethon's reappearance in Amphiaraus' actual descent: Statius reworks the underworld's fear at Phaethon's possible invasion in *Met.* 2.260–1 in *Theb.* 8.18.

[12] Later, Apollo reveals himself to Amphiaraus on the battlefield as he promises him glory, 7.771–7.

saeva minatur, 6.527; cf. 7.690–1). Apollo's intervention in the race also takes the form of prolepsis: the god sends a terrifying chthonic apparition (6.495–500):

> anguicomam monstri effigiem, saevissima visu
> ora, movet sive ille Erebo seu finxit in astus
> temporis, innumera certe formidine cultum
> tollit in astra nefas. non illud ianitor atrae
> impavidus Lethes, non ipsae horrore sine alto
> Eumenides vidisse queant, turbasset euntes
> Solis equos Martisque iugum.

> He sent forth a serpent-tressed apparition of a monster, its face most savage in expression, whether from Erebus, or whether he fashioned it as a contrivance of the moment, he raised a prodigy adorned with countless terrors to the light. Neither the porter of black Lethe nor the Furies themselves could have looked unmoved upon it without profound dread, it would have distressed the racing horses of the Sun and the team of Mars.

The poet's equivocal description of the creature's origins anticipates Amphiaraus' descent. The diction admits two different possibilities: the creature could be from hell itself, or the god of fictions invented an apparition so terrifying that both heaven and the underworld would fear it. The compression of the three realms and the images of boundary violation (*movet ... Erebo, tollit in astra*) parallel the transgressive nature of Amphiaraus' imminent katabasis. Apollo moves heaven and hell to ensure his prophet's victory in the games; his assistance anticipates the chthonic nature of Amphiaraus' end. The pressures of the knowledge of what is to come, both for Amphiaraus and for the audience, seem to draw hell close to the prophet well before his death.

1. Fateful Symbols

Amphiaraus' end is utterly overdetermined, both by the mythological tradition and throughout the narrative itself. Amphiaraus sees his death and its subterranean horror over and over again without any possibility of escape. Statius augments these narrative anticipations and prolepses with talismans, attributes that convey their own doom. Just as Parthenopaeus' winsome coloring and flowing locks practically demand soiling and presage death, Amphiaraus' distinctive attire contains allusive associations. In his descriptions of Amphiaraus' appearance, Statius consistently emphasizes the prophet's ritual garb, the *vitta*, *infula* (properly, the *vitta* is a headband or fillet wrapped around the head worn by women and priests, with which the ritual *infula*—hanks of wool elaborately knotted with loose-hanging ends suspended at the temples—may be entwined), and the olive branch.[13] In Statius, the conventional inviolability these symbols of religious honor embody would seem to invite impious trampling. As in his representation of the Doomed Ephebe, Statius employs the imagery's conventionality to generate certain narrative expectations for the characters. The fillets and branches serve as an iconographic cue to a schematic set of narrative expectations. These symbols guide the audience to anticipate what will (or must) follow, according to the "rules" of the models. In the case of Amphiaraus, the very inviolability and reverence that are attached to these prophetic attributes create an expectation that eventually, the prophet's garb will be desecrated.

The catalogue of Argive leaders in book 4 is an obvious place to look for signs and symbols, given the semiotic emphasis of Aeschylus' choral ode in the *Septem*. As in Aeschylus, Statius describes each of the Seven in terms of his defining attributes or characteristics; contradicting Aeschylus' prophet whose shield bears no insignia (*Septem* 591), Statius emphatically dwells on the incongruity of the symbols that indicate a priest of Apollo at war (4.216–8):[14]

> ... vatem cultu Parnasia monstrant
> vellera: frondenti crinitur cassis oliva,
> albaque puniceas interplicat infula cristas.

> The Parnasian wool in his array declares him to be a prophet:
> his helmet is garlanded with leafy olive, and the white fillets
> entwine with the crimson crests.[15]

---

[13] Festus, *Infulae sunt filamenta lanea, quibus sacerdotes et hostiae templa velantur*, 100L = 113 M; they indicate dedication to the god. See Fantham (2008) 163 and *passim*. The *vitta* is the chaplet or headband that symbolizes purity and chastity, not only for priests and religious figures, but also for brides or maidens, as in Ovid *Ars* 1.31, *este procul vittae tenues, insigne pudoris*. The ritual *infula* is worn by suppliants or priests (Cic. *Verr*. 2.4.50 § 110, *sacerdotes Cereris cum infulis*) and by sacrificial victims (*Georgics* 3.487), Newman (1967) 26–7. In Vergil, *vittae* can also stand for the *infula*, cf. Sinon's account in *Aen*. 2.132–3, *mihi sacra parari et salsae fruges et circum tempora vittae* with Fantham (2008) 165 on the frequent substitution of the metrically convenient *vittae* for the hexametrically impossible *infulae*; see Harrison (1991) *ad Aen*. 10.538 on the ironic presentation of a priest turned victim, a repeated motif in the *Aeneid*; like Haemonides (*Aen*. 10.537–41), Laocoon's death is also portrayed as a perverted "sacrifice" (*Aen*. 2.223–4).

[14] As Zeitlin (1982) 114 explains, Aeschylus' Amphiaraus defies reduction to a visual icon. It is typical of Statius to acknowledge Aeschylus' portrayal in a reversal; Statius, like Aeschylus, also concerns himself with the fundamental ambiguities of the prophet's identity, but he employs physical symbols and iconography to track those ambiguities and reversals.

[15] Micozzi (2007) *ad* 4.216 provides a full list of prophet-warrior models from the *Aeneid*, of which the most significant is the Italian priest of Apollo and Diana, Haemonides (10.537–41). The vocabulary and imagery of Haemonides and his impious slaughter by Aeneas will recur frequently in Statius' depiction of Amphiaraus, especially in book 8.

The priestly attributes themselves take on agency as the subjects of the verbs, *monstrant* and *interplicat*, thus emphasizing their importance as identifying features. Statius adds the detail that his shield bears the Delphic Python (4.222), explicitly indicating Amphiaraus' devotion to the oracular Apollo. At the beginning of the chariot race in book 6, the juxtaposition of woolen fillets and weapons again identifies the prophet (6.630–1).[16] These ritual items serve as a kind of synecdoche for the prophet and his divine craft.

Though Amphiaraus is the only one of the seven heroes who bears these attributes, the sacral items themselves possess a significance that can be transferred from character to character. Other figures also bear priestly attire, and its venerability correspondingly settles on anyone portrayed as a servant of a god. By making these reverential associations transferable, Statius imbues the objects themselves with special power. For example, Laius borrows Teiresias' prophetic authority with his disguise when he rises from the underworld to terrify his grandson, Eteocles (2.94–101):

> tunc senior quae iussus agit; neu falsa videri
> noctis imago queat, longaevi vatis opacos
> Tiresiae vultus vocemque et vellera nota
> induitur. Mansere comae propexaque mento
> canities pallorque suus, sed falsa cucurrit
> infula per crines, glaucaeque innexus olivae
> vittarum provenit honos; dehinc tangere ramo
> pectora et has visus fatorum expromere voces:

Then the old man did what he had been ordered; lest he seem a counterfeit vision of night, he put on the face, voice and familiar fillets of Teiresias. His hair was the same, the white beard combed down from his chin and pale countenance were his own, but a deceitful fillet ran through his locks, and a token, woven of silvery olive and woolen wreaths preceded him; then he appeared to touch his chest with the branch and to utter these words of prophecy:

Why are the *vellera* called *nota*? Here the poet seems to reference the audience's awareness of Teiresias as a mythological and literary figure from tragedy.

---

[16] Cf. also Melampus and Amphiaraus setting out for their bird augury together *hoc gemini vates sanctam canentis olivae / fronde comam et niveis ornati tempora vittis / evadunt pariter* [...] (3.466–8); Teiresias identifies Maeon's ghost in the underworld, *nostra praesignem Maeona lauro* (4.598); the Argives lament the lost Amphiaraus, *heu ubi laurigeri currus sollemniaque arma / et galeae vittatus apex?* (8.174–5), and Thiodamas accepts his post as Amphiaraus' replacement, *atque is ubi intorto signatus vellere crinem* (8.294).

Though *nota* could be seen as a focalization of Eteocles' familiarity with the aged prophet, it is significant that though the audience cannot really imagine *what* Teiresias looks or sounds like (*vultus vocemque*), the visual appearance of the prophet's garb is something that could be successfully imagined. That Laius "puts on" (*induitur*) Teiresias' appearance and attire to create a false impression of authenticity underscores the associations that these physical articles embody—even as part of a costume, the prophet's attire inspires respect. After delivering his message as Teiresias, Laius tears off his disguise in order to reveal his true chthonic origins to his grandson (*ramos ac vellera fronti / deripuit, confessus avum*, 2.121–2); this act powerfully transfers the dreadful origins of the commands from the heavens to hell.

The ritual articles symbolize the prophet's connection to the divine, and are even "activated" when in use. In his *nekuia* for Eteocles, the *vittae* stir as Teiresias abandons the guidance of his daughter, Manto, and recounts his own supernatural vision of Hades (4.579–91):

> talia dum patri canit intemerata sacerdos,
> illius elatis tremefacta adsurgere vittis
> canities tenuisque impelli sanguine vultus.

> Such things the virgin priestess chanted boldly to her father, his quivering white hair rose up from his raised braids, and his withered countenance flushed with blood.

Often the responses of others to the *vittae* and the sacred branches reveal their importance, as when the shades recede before Teiresias' branches (4.602–3). Lycurgus, the king of Corinth who is also a priest of Jupiter, also demonstrates the reverence owed to the sacred symbols when he confronts the Argive leaders as they defend Hypsipyle. Angered by his son's death and the Argives' retaliatory murder of the sacred serpent, Lycurgus appears ready to attack the Argive leaders when Amphiaraus conciliates, "respectful of the bonds of their shared *vittae*" (*sociae veritus commercia vittae / Amphiaraus ait*, 5.668–9). Here as elsewhere, the *vittae* themselves are synecdochic of sacred function and engender a reverence simply from their appearance.[17]

While ritual garb symbolizes the prophet's special relationship to the divine, mistreating these significant emblems can in turn manifest the prophet's rejection of or alienation from the god. Amphiaraus himself reacts to the ill omens

---

[17] Cf. Amphiaraus' own mistaken killing of Lycoreus, a Theban priest of Apollo: [...] *sacrumque Lycorea Phoebo / (invitus: iam fraxineum demiserat hastae/robur, et excussis apparuit infula cristis), Theb.* 7.715–7. The narrator implies that had he noticed the fillets in time, Amphiaraus would have spared him out of reverence.

of the bird augury by removing the priestly accoutrements and withdrawing into his home (3.566–8):

> ergo manu vittas damnataque vertice serta
> deripit abiectaque inhonorus fronde sacerdos
> inviso de monte redit;

> Therefore, with his hand he tore the *vittae* and the doomed wreath from his head and the priest returned from the hateful mountain, stripped of his distinction by the wreath he had discarded.

After having seen his own uncanny death predicted in the bird omens, Amphiaraus expresses his sense of betrayal by the god. Applying the proleptic *damnata* to the wreath strengthens the identification between the prophet and his attributes. In the epic, *deripio* + religious items (cf. Laius 2.121–2, above) becomes almost idiomatic as the expression for this predictable gesture. The priest-king Lycurgus demonstrates his mourning for his son, Opheltes, by removing his *vittae* (*exutus honoro / vittarum nexu*, 6.30–1), a gesture that also communicates his resentment toward his patron god, Jupiter. After tossing his priestly garments on his infant son's funeral pyre (6.193–4) he addresses Jupiter as *"perfide"* (6.197). Here Statius amplifies a father's mourning with a physical gesture that represents divine betrayal. Statius establishes a pattern to show that individuals who abuse their own prophetic garments perform this transgressive deed out of despair at being abandoned by the divine.

These ritual articles demand reverence, but in literature, their sanctity more frequently attracts abuse and mistreatment. These items contain a narrative pattern, in which they are the object mockery and destruction, as when Cassandra, forseeing her own murder, violently mocks Apollo's empty protection. Her speech (*Ag.* 1256–94) articulates her anger at the god's betrayal, and she rejects her service by casting off her *skēptra* and *manteia stephē* (*Ag.* 1265).[18] The conspicuous symbols of her status only enhance the humiliation of her condition (1271).[19] Laocoon, venerable priest of Troy, makes his most iconic appearance in the *Aeneid* soiled in blood (*perfusus sanie uittas atroque ueneno*, *Aen.* 2.221). The *vittae* and *infula* represent the prophet, but these items contain

---

[18] As Fraenkel observes *ad loc.*, "*katagelōmenēn*: this is what she has experienced time and again in the past; because of this experience she has just (1264) felt as *katagelōs* the very fact that she is still wearing the garb of a prophetess." Fraenkel (1950).

[19] That this scene later became paradigmatic of Cassandra may be seen in Euripides' *Troades*. Both Hecuba and Cassandra make reference to destroying Apollo's prophetic garments at *Tro.* 256–9, 451–4. Euripides, like Statius, plays on the audience's familiarity with this famous scene from the *Agamemnon* as the two women mourn Cassandra's doom.

their own narrative that enhances Amphiaraus' status as the Predestined Prophet. By the symbolic logic of the narrative, Amphiaraus' overdetermined end will involve some spectacular, climactic laurel-trampling and/or headband-tearing, just as Parthenopaeus' death requires hair, dust, white flesh, red blood, and floral imagery. Once Statius establishes his rules and activates the audience's expectations, there is greater potential for surprise, precisely because we harbor an intertextually validated sense of what must happen.[20]

2. Costume Drama: "Prophet versus Tyrant"

Ritual dedication to a god in the literary tradition rarely ensures proper treatment or respect. A confrontation between religious and political authority begins the *Iliad*, when Agamemnon refuses to ransom Chryseis, daughter of Chryses, priest of Apollo. This familiar type of confrontation contains certain elements, especially verbal abuse threatening or ridiculing the prophet's appearance. Insulting a priest or prophet's ritual attire is an essential part of this familiar scenario, what we might term a "Prophet versus Tyrant" script. Agamemnon's threats against Chryses establish a paradigm for this abuse: "Old man, let me not come upon you lingering by the curved ships, not now, nor henceforth, lest neither your staff (*skēptron*) nor your fillets (*stemma*) of the god avail you" (*Il.* 1.26–28). The synecdoche is clear: the priest's physical attributes represent the god's patronage, a protection that will grievously punish the Greeks for their leader's impiety in the plague. Tragedy similarly offers a number of examples; in Oedipus' *agōn* with Teiresias, he accuses Teiresias of being not a prophet but a *magos*, a two-bit magician for hire in the pay of Creon (*OT* 386–9 and *passim*).[21] Pentheus' furious tirades against the priest of Bacchus criticize his effeminate attire and threaten bodily harm (Eur. *Ba.* 346–51). Pentheus frequently rails against the priest's flowing hair and the thyrsus, both of which the priest states belong to Dionysus himself (Eur. *Ba.* 493–6). Statius stages a similar conflict between Capaneus and Amphiaraus; Capaneus, the *superum contemptor* (3.602), violently rages against the prophet whose seclusion delays the expedition.[22] The impious Capaneus predictably attacks Amphiaraus' status as prophet by mocking his

---

[20] This is a different kind of "false narrative anticipation" based in "negative allusion" as analyzed in Valerius by Zissos (1999), although the phenomenon relies on a similar poetic referentiality.

[21] Creon himself plays the part of the accuser in the *Antigone*, 1033–63, when he claims that Teiresias has been bribed by the Thebans to frighten him.

[22] Stover (2009) highlights the Apollonian Idas as a model for Capaneus, while Fantham (2006) 158–9 discusses Aeschylus' Capaneus, Vergil's Mezentius, Turnus, and Drances; see also Snijder (1968) *ad* 3.602 on epic models for Capaneus.

clothing (3.655–7; 3.666–7), thus confirming his own characterization as a blasphemer and the narrative's emphasis on the prophet's attributes.[23]

Capaneus taunts Amphiaraus with the impotence of his sacral symbols, and sarcastically suggests that he should try brokering a peace with the Thebans under the auspices of his religious protection (*i Sidonios legatus ad hostes: / haec pacem tibi serta dabunt*, 3.655–7). The subsequent narrative unexpectedly affirms the very religious protection mocked by Capaneus: The only survivor of Eteocles' ambush on Tydeus is the prophet Maeon, spared by Tydeus to announce the tyrant's failure. This minor figure, known to Homer and the Theban tradition, seizes center stage to enact an abbreviated Prophet versus Tyrant episode.[24] Maeon here is a double of Amphiaraus, and his actions are yet another prelude to the main event, Amphiaraus' death. This distinctly self-contained episode functions as a kind of microcosm of many of the epic's themes, but reflects the Amphiaraus narrative most directly. As in so many Roman epics, Statius' characters have doubles who parallel the essential qualities of the main figure; these doubles often distill the referential elements of the poet's models.[25] Maeon's spectacular suicide and the disproportionately effusive *makarismos* offered by the poet (3.99–113) provide some clue as to Statius' epic model here: his framing of the Maeon episode seems to reflect Lucan's repeated, obsessive use of Cato's suicide as an *exemplum libertatis* in his epic.[26] As discussed in chapter 2, Lucan deploys this most exemplary Roman hero as a model for many voluntary deaths in his epic, and he explicitly signals Cato-imitation by appending a narrative judgment in the first person.[27] The uncharacteristically impassioned tone of the apostrophe to Maeon with its praise of *libertas* seems to suggest Lucan's notoriously vehement first-person editorializing.[28] If we regard Maeon as a version of Lucan's Cato, the most "imitable" (and imitated) character of the

---

[23] Apollo protects Amphiaraus from another such blasphemer, Hypseus, on the battlefield, who vows to drown the prophet's armor and "vittae, bereaved of the augur" (*tristesque sine augure vittas*, 7.735) in his paternal waters.

[24] *Il.* 4.382–400; see Gantz (1993) s.v. "Maion, son of Haimon."

[25] See chapter 1 on Aeneas and Paris in the *Aeneid*, chapter 2 on Lucan's Cato, and also chapter 4 on Parthenopaeus and Crenaeus.

[26] Vessey (1973) 112–6 notes the parallels with Cato's exemplary deed, but not Lucan's poetics; McGuire (1989) also sees Maeon as an exemplar of "imperial suicide" but neglects possible imitation of Lucan. Elaine Fantham has generously shared a paper on Maeon presented at University of Toronto in November 2009.

[27] Of Scaeva, Luc. 6.256, cf. Vulteius, a flawed *exemplum*, Luc. 4.574. Lucan himself has his uncle Seneca's obsession with the exemplary Cato and his suicide in mind, as discussed above in chapter 2.

[28] On Lucan's apostrophes, see Asso (2009), D'Alessandro Behr (2007), Faber (2005), Leigh (1997).

De Bello Civili, his function as a double of Amphiaraus comes into focus. Like Amphiaraus, Maeon knows that he is reserved by destiny for a special end, and as in the case of Amphiaraus' futile delay, Maeon's foreknowledge had no practical effect (2.690–5):

> [...] restabat acerbis
> funeribus socioque gregi non sponte superstes
> Haemonides (ille haec praeviderat, omina doctus
> aeris et nulla deceptus ab alite) Maeon,[29]
> nec veritus prohibere ducem, sed fata monentem
> privavere fide. [...]

> The unwilling survivor, Maeon, son of Haemon, was singled out from the cruel deaths of his comrades (he had foreseen these events, being learned in omens of the air and undeceived by any bird), nor had he feared to defy his commander, though destiny had prevented him from being believed.

Maeon's skill in augury anticipates Amphiaraus' and Melampus' dramatic episode in book 3, and he enacts in miniature the Argive augur's predicament: he sees the danger ahead, but is prevented by the Fates from altering the course of events. Maeon's first speech (3.59–77) is full of recrimination and abuse against Eteocles' unjust rule and the ruinous destruction that will ensue.[30] Maeon's bold accusations are founded in his special knowledge of divine sanction; as he states, he was denied death with the others, and is no longer afraid since he realizes that it was destined that he survive the massacre (3.67–9):

> sed mihi iussa deum placitoque ignara moveri
> Atropos atque olim non haec data ianua leti
> eripuere necem. [...]

> But the will of the gods, and Atropos, who does not how to be swayed from her decision, and this entrance to death denied before have deprived me of my end.

Maeon emphasizes the preordained nature of his unwilling survival: the gods and the personified fate Atropos took an active role in Maeon's survival,

---

[29] Cf. the description of Amphiaraus in 7.707–8, *qui doctus in omni / nube salutato volucrem cognoscere Phoebo*.

[30] Dominik (1994) 84–7 emphasizes the conflict between divine authority and tyrannical power, Markus (2003) 67.

much as Atropos is later reported to have forced weapons into Amphiaraus' reluctant hands (4.187–91).[31]

Maeon's defiant speech to Eteocles signals the beginning of a Prophet versus Tyrant scene, but the episode is dramatically abbreviated; Statius does not detract from Amphiaraus' much more elaborated confrontation with Capaneus later in the book (3.598–677). Eteocles, the enraged autocrat, begins promisingly with rage and imminent threats (3.77–81). His henchmen prepare to strike but are thwarted by the sudden self-inflicted blow that interrupts Maeon's impassioned declaration.[32] The rest of the scene follows Lucan's essentialized Stoic script of the Catonian suicide: the gory wound (3.88–91) contrasts with the martyr's beatifically unchanged expression (3.94), the bystanders react to the spectacle (3.92–3), and an editorial assessment of the act follows in an apostrophe (3.99–113):[33]

> Tu tamen egregius fati mentisque nec umquam
> (sic dignum est) passure situm, qui comminus ausus
> vadere contemptum reges, quaque ampla veniret
> libertas, sancire viam: quo carmine dignam,
> quo satis ore tuis famam virtutibus addam,
> augur amate deis? Non te caelestia frustra
> edocuit lauruque sua dignatus Apollo est,
>
> * * * * *
>
> et nemorum Dodona parens Cirrhaeaque virgo
> audebit tacito populos suspendere Phoebo.
> nunc quoque Tartareo multum divisus Averno
> Elysias, i, carpe plagas, ubi manibus axis
> invius Ogygiis nec sontis iniqua tyranni
> iussa valent; durant habitus et membra cruentis
> inviolata feris, nudoque sub axe iacentem
> et nemus et tristis volucrum reverentia servat.

> You, however, outstanding in your end and in your spirit, never to endure oblivion (as is only right), you dared to scorn kings face to face, and to consecrate a way by which abundant freedom might come. With what song shall I honor you, with what lips shall I sufficiently heap up your repute with merits,

---

[31] Maeon's fate is again linked with Atropos in Teiresias' recapitulation of the failed ambush in the necromancy (4.592–601: [...] *hos ferrea neverat annos / Atropos*, 4.601).

[32] The speech is part of the Catonian suicide, as discussed above in chapter 2.

[33] See above, chapter 2.

o augur beloved by the gods? Not in vain did Apollo teach you heavenly skills, and consider you worthy of his own laurel

***

Both Dodona, mother of groves, and the Cirrhaean maiden will be so bold as to mystify their people while Apollo is silent. Now go, remote from Tartarean Avernus, reach the shores of Elysium, where the sky shuns Theban ghosts and the criminal tyrant's hateful commands hold no sway. Your dress and limbs remain untouched by bloodthirsty beasts, and both the grove and the mournful reverence of the birds keep you under the open sky.

Lucan's Catonian template seems to hijack this minor episode: *libertas*, more a preoccupation of Lucan's epic than the *Thebaid*, is asserted as the message of this *mors voluntaria*.[34] Certain details in the *makarismos* underscore the anticipatory mirroring of Amphiaraus' end: Maeon's status as augur merits remention, as does Apollo's special favor, whose interventions for Amphiaraus will be both noteworthy and yet empty, as those of so many of Statius' gods (3.104–5).[35] Hence the deflating comment about Apollo's oracular silence in the (Roman) future, a jab at the exhausted god that Thiodamus will repeat when establishing Amphiaraus' cult at Oropus.[36] While Maeon will travel straight through to Elysium, avoiding Tartarus and removed from earthly tyrants like Eteocles (3.110), Amphiaraus will enact a very full Prophet versus Tyrant scene with a tyrannical Dis himself in the bowels of Tartarus (7.821).

Finally, Maeon worthily receives inviolability for his service to Apollo; in this poem filled with the proleptic dread of unburial, the ultimate mark of divine favor resides in physical preservation in the face of attempted impiety and mutilation (3.97–8). Significantly, Maeon's *habitus* and *membra* are detailed individually (3.111). *Membra* is synecdoche for the corpse itself; therefore *habitus* indicates Maeon's dress as a priest of Apollo. Maeon's special honor consists in preserving his all too vulnerable ritual vestments: the

---

[34] As discussed above, Cato's suicide symbolizes two forms of *libertas* in Seneca, both political freedom (*Const.* 2.3.1) and philosophical freedom (*de Ira* 3.15); see also Ker (2009) 78–85 on Cato in Senecan "scripts" for suicide.

[35] Diana, certainly in the case of Parthenopaeus, and Minerva, though Tydeus' grotesque cannibalism drives the goddess from his side. Statius seems to share Ovid's and Seneca's position on the problematic nature of divine attention to human affairs, even for gods and their favorites. See Feeney (1991) 357–8, who quotes Apollo's own self-recrimination to Diana in book 9, *saevus ego immeritusque coli* (9.657).

[36] *tacito ... Phoebo* (3.107) cf. *Phoebo absente* (8.338), and discussion below.

prophet's body will be preserved from the predations of scavengers, and his clothing will remain unscathed as well.[37]

This self-contained episode, framed by imitation of Lucan's Cato-template, provides yet another preview of Amphiaraus' end. This set piece glorifies a relatively unknown Theban prophet as augur, sketches out the Prophet versus Tyrant scene in miniature, raises the ever-present Theban horror of unburial, and again establishes the sacral garb and implements as the locus of ritual inviolability.

3. *Aristeia*, Exemplarity, Closure

In the next section I propose that these established patterns can actually mislead the audience, who might at this point be feeling smugly secure that they know what will happen. Our sense of allusive familiarity renders us overconfident in our ability to read the narrative of a character like Parthenopaeus or Amphiaraus. As the proleptic narrative and symbolic logic of Amphiaraus' talismans have established, the prophet's doom is predestined and he courageously confronts his fate in full foreknowledge. What then is left to shock or surprise? The only remaining surprise lies in reversing the narrative's carefully engineered expectations—we await Amphiaraus' descent into the abyss, but we do not expect a sequel in the underworld that entails a further trajectory from darkness to enlightenment, from myth to cult.

Amphiaraus' *aristeia* in book 7 (690–823) recapitulates all of the distinctive characteristics established thus far in the epic. There is a paradoxical sense in which the "exceptional" *aristeia* is the most conventional epic moment for any character. In the *aristeia*, the hero surpasses all others on the battlefield and stands out among the roiling mass. Nonetheless, the *aristeia* is also utterly generic: the scene itself is instantly recognizable as an epic set piece that confers glory on a warrior in conventional language and typical scenarios such as supplication and flyting. As in Parthenopaeus' final appearance on the battlefield, Statius uses Amphiaraus' *aristeia* to consolidate themes and motifs established previously: the poet finally maximizes the paradigmatic features of his Predestined Prophet.[38] The long-awaited doom has arrived and Amphiaraus

---

[37] cf. *OLD* 3 s.v. "*habitus*," "Style of dress, toilet, etc. 'Get up' (especially proper to a particular class or occasion)."

[38] Smolenaars (1994) 321–2 thoroughly discusses the influence of Homeric scenes of *aristeia*, especially that of Diomedes in *Iliad* 5, as well as the Vergilian and Valerian imitations of *Iliad* 5 in his introduction to lines 7.690–823. Smolenaars takes the Homeric model as the template from which the later Latin poets incorporated key elements, such as the god granting honor, the list of named victims, substitution of the charioteer, etc., details of which appear in his appendix 9 (pp. 416–23).

dies according to the script, but in the underworld, this overdetermined figure takes an unusual turn.

Amphiaraus' first appearance in battle signals the *aristeia* and recapitulates some distinguishing characteristics in anticipation of his climactic end (7.690–704). The prophet appears "center stage" (*eminet ante alios*, 7.690) and is endowed with the gifts of two gods, glorious appearance from Apollo (7.692) and physical invulnerability from Mars (7.695–8).[39] These cues of *aristeia* are explicitly granted in compensation for Amphiaraus' imminent death, reiterating Apollo's intervention in book 6 (301–3). Like Maeon, the Predestined Prophet (*vatem*, 7.696) will remain inviolate, consecrated to Dis. Statius also mentions Amphiaraus' powers as augur, "and never would his skill in prophecy have been greater, had there been any time" (*et numquam tanta experientia caeli, / si vacet*, 7.701–2). This is no otiose reminder of his prophetic skills; his enhanced vision is channeled into a passionate *devotio*, in which his awareness of imminent death feeds his courage in battle (7.699–70; *morti contermina Virtus*, 703).[40]

Amphiaraus' last earthly moments carefully replicate elements and themes of the many previews seen in the epic. Just as anticipated in the chariot race of book 6, Apollo himself intervenes to aid Amphiaraus, personally guiding his chariot on the battlefield. Apollo promises Amphiaraus fame and freedom from unjust exposure by Creon, "you who will surely not suffer the commands of a Creon or lie exposed, deprived of a monument" (*certe non perpessure Creontis / imperia aut vetito nudus iaciture sepulcro*, 7.776–7). This mention of Creon and the outrage of unburial look back to Maeon in book 3 and take prophetic authority from the literary past: Apollo sees beyond the epic itself to the events of the *Antigone*. But as befits Apollo's own "companion of the tripod and pious protégé of celestial divination" (6.377), Amphiaraus rivals his patron god in vision and prophecy. While Apollo's powers cannot overcome death (7.774–5), Amphiaraus sees into the underworld that awaits him, and declares the vengeance that must follow his disappearance (7.779–88):

> Olim te, Cirrhaee pater, peritura sedentem
> ad iuga (quis tantus miseris honor?) axe trementi
> sensimus; instantes quonam usque morabere manes?
> audio iam rapidae cursum Stygis atraque Ditis
> flumina tergeminosque mali custodis hiatus.
> accipe commissum capiti decus, accipe laurus,

---

[39] Smolenaars (1994) *ad loc.* on imitation of Homer, Apollonius, Vergil, Valerius Flaccus.

[40] The *devotio* is another form of noble *mors voluntaria* also associated by Lucan with Cato, as discussed above in chapter 2; cf. Maeon, *pectora et extremam nihil horrescentia mortem*, 3.70; *quo carmine dignam, / quo satis ore tuis famam virtutibus addam / augur amate deis?* 3.101–2.

> quas Erebo deferre nefas. nunc voce suprema,
> si qua recessuro debetur gratia vati,
> deceptum tibi, Phoebe, larem poenasque nefandae
> coniugis et pulchrum nati commendo furorem.

> Long since, Cirrhaean father, have I felt you resting on this doomed chariot with its shuddering axle (why so great an honor to the damned?); how long will you delay the ghosts that are already here? Already I hear the flow of the swift Styx and the black waters of Dis, and the tripled guardian with his evil maw. Receive the ornament entrusted to this head, take the laurel, which it is forbidden to bear to Erebus. Now, in my last breath, if any gratitude is owed to your prophet who is about to depart, to you, Phoebus, I entrust my betrayed home, and the punishments of my accursed wife, and the noble violence of my son.

Amphiaraus seems to focalize the audience's own weariness with the narrative's relentless foreshadowing, asking Apollo, "What took you so long?" (*Olim te*, 7.779). The prophet's knowing response deflates Apollo's portentous revelation and provides one last proof of Amphiaraus' prophetic vision: nothing is hidden from him, even the expectant underworld itself. In conclusion, Amphiaraus expresses pious concern for his prophetic emblem, the celestial laurel wreath, which must be kept from ultimate desecration in the underworld.[41] His final request for vengeance takes on metaliterary authority by referring to the Attic tragedies about his family.[42] The literary past, as so often in Statius and other Latin poets, confirms the surety of the future. In his final moments above ground, Amphiaraus consistently adheres to his essential characteristics, predestination and prophetic prolepsis.

But can we really trust this consistency? Amphiaraus has already undergone one drastic transformation in the *aristeia* that provokes the narrator's comment (7.705–11):

---

[41] Smolenaars (1994) *ad* 7.787–8 "A's respectful words here allude to and invert Cassandra's coarseness when throwing to the ground her staff and fillet (imitated in *Th.* 3.566f) in Aesch. *Ag.* 1267 *it es phthoron*, as is noted by Canter (Fraenkel's note *ad loc.*), who also points to Eur. *Tro.* 256ff, 451ff."

[42] Apollodorus 3.77, Propertius 2.34.39; Ovid *Met.* 9.406–12, *Tr.* 5.14.12. Sophocles wrote an *Eriphyle*, while he and Aeschylus both treated the subject of the son Alcmaeon's matricide in their homonymous plays, *Epigonoi*. For the earliest reference to Eriphyle and the bribery, *Od.* 11.326–7, also *Od.* 15.246–7. The subject is also popular in vase painting, *LIMC* s.v. "Eriphyle." See also Hutchinson (1985) 132–3.

> Hicne hominum casus lenire et demere Fatis
> iura frequens? quantum subito diversus ab illo
> qui tripodas laurusque sequi, qui doctus in omni
> nube salutato volucrem cognoscere Phoebo!
> innumeram ferro plebem, ceu letifer annus
> aut iubar adversi grave sideris, immolat umbris
> ipse suis: [...]

> Is this the one who lightened the misfortunes of men and curtailed Destiny's due? How suddenly changed he is from that man who cultivated the tripods and the laurel, who was learned in every cloud, recognized the flight of birds, when Phoebus had been greeted! He sacrificed on his sword a countless multitude to his own shade, just like a pestilent year or the baleful gleam of a malign star.

In the interrogative *hicine* (705), the narrator dramatizes the contrast between the figure presented up to this point, the erudite, pious prophet, and the now bloodthirsty killer of the *aristeia*.[43] The prophet is transformed from a benefactor of mankind into the very supernatural blight that he once used to ameliorate, as the simile in 709–10 ironically emphasizes.[44] In this final battle, Amphiaraus is far from the man he was, and this change in representation anticipates a final transformation, his descent into the underworld. An intertextual clue signals Amphiaraus' trajectory: *quantum subito diversus* (7.706) evokes Hector's ghost, bloodied and mutilated, so changed from the victor of Patroclus and proud bearer of Achilles' armor (*quantum mutatus ab illo / Hectore...*, *Aen.* 2.274–5). We too will see Amphiaraus after his death. Statius' overdetermined, proleptic narrative of Amphiaraus has prophesied, foreshadowed, and prefigured—even up to the very moment of his descent—the prophet's mythological end. The story should end there; even Apollo cannot say more. And yet, against all traditional versions, Amphiaraus' narrative continues in Statius' epic.

Certainly the lengthy description of the chasm (794–823) that concludes book 7 gives a definitive sense of closure. The cinematic, slow-motion gaping (*iamque recessurae paulatim horrescere terrae*, 794) carries on climactically, complete with multiple reactions on both sides, a simile of battle at

---

[43] Smolenaars *ad loc.*; through the verb *immolat* (7.710), Statius draws a parallel with the vengeful Aeneas, whose Achillean rage at Pallas' death so transforms him that he kills the priest, Haemonides (*Aen.* 10.537–41; 540–1, *lapsumque superstans / immolat ingentique umbra tegit*).

[44] Vessey (1973) 261 discusses these lines and Amphiaraus' complete transformation on the battlefield when he kills Lycoreus, the priest of Apollo (7.715–6). This killing, though inadvertent, pointedly reverses his reverence for the Corinthian priest-king, Lycurgus in book 5 (668ff.).

sea, and even a miniature natural historical digression on theories of earthquake and its possible significance as an omen (809–16).[45] The book closes satisfyingly with the earth itself, as Amphiaraus watches the rift reseal above him (821–3). In book 8, however, contrary to all expectations, we discover ourselves in hell. Statius thematizes the audience's surprise in the appalled reaction of the underworld. Rather than beguiling the grim denizens like an Orpheus, this intruder into the underworld causes surprise and consternation, even to the startled Parcae, who belatedly confirm Amphiaraus' death by cutting his thread after he arrives (8.11–13).[46] The panic above ground is replicated in the fear below: "Dismay seized them all, and they marveled at the weapons and the horses and the new body on Stygian shores" (*horror habet cunctos, Stygiis mirantur in oris / tela et equos corpusque novum*, 8.4–5).[47] Statius emphasizes the novelty of his account through the focalizing adjective *novum* and continues his surprising turn of events by studiously avoiding hackneyed descriptions of the underworld (already dismissed by Tiresias in book 4 as *vulgata*, 4.536–40), though he later covers the obligatory list of celebrity inhabitants and invaders in Dis' speech.[48]

This contrast between the prophet's corporeality and the shadowy realms signifies the dramatic novelty of this descent. The poet reports that Amphiaraus was swallowed whole by the chasm (7.819–21): just as he was (*sicut erat*, 7.820), Amphiraus enters Hades and counterintuitively terrorizes the dead with his hale and hearty appearance.[49] A divine reward on earth (physical inviolability) is a frightening violation in the underworld. In hell, different rules and

---

[45] Further discussion on this description of the chasm below in the second half of this chapter.

[46] Cf. Apollo's portentous words, *inmites scis nulla revolvere Parcas/stamina* (*Th.* 7.774–5)—though he cannot undo his fated time, Amphiaraus somehow surprises the sisters.

[47] Vessey (1973) 262–3; on the cowardly dead as a favorite Ovidian topos, see *Met.* 5.356–8 and Anderson (1997) *ad loc*.

[48] Tiresias makes his point by echoing Vergil's narrator on hackneyed mythological tropes in *G.* 3.4–5, Feeney (1991) 342–3; Dis' resentful tirade mentions the invaders, Theseus and Pirithous, Hercules, Orpheus, and his own denizens, Tantalus, Ixion, the Giants and the Titans. In *Met.* 10.40–44, Ovid lists Tantalus, Ixion, Tityos, the Danaids, and Sisyphus, already itself an expansion of Orpheus' encounter with Ixion in *Georgics* 4.481–4. Statius' Dis "remembers" the Eumenides weeping at the Ovidian Orpheus' song (*Theb.* 8.58–60; *Met.* 10.45–6).

[49] In this instance, *sicut erat* (*Th.* 7.820) may carry some of the same allusive overtones as the Vergilian phrase *qualis erat* (*Aen.* 2.274). As Van Dam (2006) 187–9 has argued on Statius *Silv.* 2.1.157, this phrase signals the preservation of physical appearance after death: Glaucias, like Hector and Patroclus (*Il.*22.65–8), retains his beauty even in the underworld. Glaucias goes to the underworld inviolate, [...] *manesque subibit / integer et nullo temeratus corpora damno, / qualis erat* (2.1.155–7); the closer parallel, as Van Dam notes, is with Thiodamas' dream vision of Amphiaraus in book 10.202–6, which replicates more of the language from Hector's appearance to Aeneas.

conventions apply, and the inversion of all that is above ground holds sway, as Statius expresses in his emphatic use of negation (8.5–11):⁵⁰

> [...] nec enim ignibus atris
> conditus aut maesta niger adventabat ab urna,
> sed belli sudore calens, clipeumque cruentis
> roribus et scissi respersus pulvere campi.
> necdum illum aut trunca lustraverat obvia taxo
> Eumenis, aut furvo Proserpina poste notarat
> coetibus adsumptum functis; [...]

> For he was not laid to rest with black fires, nor did he arrive, blackened by an urn of mourning, but steaming with the sweat of war, and spattered on his shield with bloody drops and with the dust of the gashed battlefield. Not yet had a Fury encountered and purified him with a branch of yew, nor had Proserpina marked him at the shadowy doorpost as admitted to the ranks of the dead.

Amphiaraus has bypassed all of the burial rituals so crucial to the epic of Thebes. By pedantically listing all the proper rites for admission left incomplete (rites that may well have been invented for this rhetorical purpose), the poet exaggerates the prophet's unnatural appearance.⁵¹ He arrives hot, steaming, dirty, and large as life—in fact alive. His meaty corporeality seems to be the most distressing aspect to the shades. Amphiaraus presents a novel sight— a fresh, intact body—to the inhabitants, and therefore a new cause for fear, all caused by a new occurrence, the *novo* [...] *hiatu* (8.19).⁵²

Despite the insistence on novelty and transgression, however, a familiar scenario emerges, albeit with a new twist. The new context in which Statius deploys the prophet's motifs and type scenes creates novelty and surprise. Amphiaraus, the essentialized super-trope of a prophet, must play his part in one final Prophet versus Tyrant confrontation. Like Eteocles to Maeon, Dis responds to Amphiaraus with suspicion, threats, and disproportionate rage. Dis is portrayed as an autocrat even before Amphiaraus' intrusion; Dis

---

⁵⁰ This description uses the same technique as Lucan's account of Cato's remarriage to Marcia (2.326–91); both poets emphasize the anomalousness of the event by casting it in terms of what was *not* done. See Fantham (1992a) *ad loc.*

⁵¹ Amphiaraus himself uses these negative formations about his burial rites in his explanation to Dis, <u>non</u> *igne miser lacrimisque meorum / productus, toto pariter tibi funere veni* (8.113–4); cf. his descent into the cavern, [...] *non arma manu, non frena remisit: / sicut erat* (7.819–20).

⁵² Cf. Amphiaraus on his own *nova fata* (8.100); see note 389 above; on Aetna's volcanic rumblings, *quid moliretur rerum natura novarum* (*DRN* 6.646).

is *iratus* (8.23) like all tyrants, meting out his own brand of harsh justice to the newly arrived shades. Amphiaraus' sudden arrival is taken as merely the latest in a tiresome series of invasions (*anne profanatum totiens Chaos hospite vivo / perpetiar?* 8.52–3). Even the realm under Thebes is contaminated with fraternal rivalry and paranoia: Dis suspects his brothers of plotting against him, despite his conviction that they have already cheated him out of the best part of the Olympian inheritance (8.36–46).[53] In hasty retaliation, Dis adds his own curses to the already condemned Thebes and promises even more demonic energy to the battle (8.65–79). As usual, the paranoid, vengeful monarch blusters violently, but this time, the tyrant cannot threaten the innocent prophet with death, mutilation, or unburial since he has already moved beyond such possibilities. As the narrative stresses, Amphiaraus is precisely the same figure he has been throughout the poem, but by entering the underworld still alive, he affronts the ruler of Hades. Dis, the angry tyrant, confronts Amphiaraus, but in this case, the usual threats do not really apply. What is Dis going to do, kill him?

Denying that he has come intending harm, Amphiaraus swears that he is no Hercules or Theseus; he rejects "Herculean brigandage" and points to his sacral garb as proof of his innocence (*nec venerem inlicitam (crede his insignibus) ausi / intramus Lethen*, 8.96–7). Everything that his clothing signified above ground has no validity, as his vain attempt to justify himself by his Apolline *insignia* reveals. In an attempt to accommodate himself to the new regime underground, the prophet rejects the guarantor of oaths on earth, Apollo, in favor of the validation of Chaos: "I am the prophet once most beloved to Apollo's altars, Chaos, the void, is my witness, for how can one swear by Apollo here?" (*augur Apollinaeis modo dilectissimus aris, / testor inane Chaos (quid enim hic iurandus Apollo?)*, 8.98–9). Amphiaraus acknowledges that the rules of the underworld dictate that all that is sacred and holy above ground will be inverted. Amphiaraus, the living prophet of a celestial deity, has transgressed an unlawful boundary (*limite . . . non licito*, 8.84–5), and as he anticipated (7.785), Apollo's ritual symbols do not belong here. Merely by being the same (*sicut erat*, 7.820) Amphiaraus offends and violates the realm of the dead.

After all of the threats to the prophet both on earth and in the underworld, his body does remain intact, just as Apollo and Mars promised (7.697–8). Even after his corporeal body vanishes (from head to toe, apparently), Amphiaraus preserves his prophetic insignia (8.86–9):

> iam tenuis visu, iam vanescentibus armis,
> iam pedes: extincto tamen interceptus in ore

---

[53] On the cosmic rivalry and the poem's themes, see McNelis (2007) 129–30.

> augurii perdurat honos, obscuraque fronti
> vitta manet, ramumque tenet morientis olivae.

> Now his aspect shrivels, now the weapons gradually fade, now his feet. And yet, the emblem of his prophetic craft remains fixed on his faded visage, and the blurry fillet remains on his brow, and he holds a branch of wilting olive.

Though the olive branch may be dying, the emblems remain fully visible, identifying markers to the last. Like Maeon, Amphiaraus' shade will be distinguishable as a prophet among the shades of Hades (*nostra praesignem Maeona lauro*, 4.598). We witness the prophet's survival in the underworld, where he even retains his *honos*, a rarity in the messy and contaminated world he left behind. The *vates*' special relationship to prophecy and predestination has prepared us for Amphiaraus' uncanny death, but nothing beyond. The very attributes that represent his prophetic powers have been consistently portrayed as vulnerable targets of threat and assault, and yet they improbably survive to distinguish Amphiaraus, even in Hades. Even a confrontation with the ultimate tyrant, the enraged lord of the underworld, ends in anticlimax as Dis grudgingly ignores Amphiaraus' intrusion (8.122–26). And yet, even this unexpected continuation of the mythical "plot" was itself anticipated and proleptically rehearsed through Maeon's confrontation with Eteocles in book 5. As Tiresias had already stated, the underworld is the ultimate location for hackneyed repetition (4.537, *ne vulgata mihi*, with its metaliterary evocation of *Georgics* 3.4); in Amphiaraus' character-trajectory of predestination and prolepsis, even mythological innovation is anticipated in the narrative.

II. Chthonic Transcendence

While the sudden shift in locale contains some comical elements, the ultimate fate of the *vates* is of vital narrative and metapoetic importance. After the epic's insistent emphasis on Amphiaraus' uncanny End, we are unexpectedly confronted with a narrative continuation: what will become of the *vates*? As we saw in his all too familiar confrontation with the tyrannical Dis, the prophet's characterization qua prophet—comprising the role's ritual emblems and literary associations—contains its own narrative trajectories. In this last section I will argue that Statius utilizes the allusive associations of the *vates* to enact a form of chthonic transcendence, an underworld apotheosis. Here we will trace his trajectory through the epic as a *vates* of philosophical didactic from the augury to his descent into Hades. Why and how does Statius "plot" these allusions to philosophical epos, and what are his models?[54] Allusions to Empedocles, Lucretius, and Ovid's Pythagoras in Amphiaraus' characterization incarnate the prophet as an embodied reading tradition of philosophical epos, signaling his posthumous transcendence into a prophetic divinity.

1. Amphiaraus, Didactic *Vates*

In his prayer to Jupiter during the augury, Amphiaraus seemingly redundantly speculates on the origins of avian portents; his inquiry takes the form of an amphiboly, a opposed set of supernatural and materialist causes (3.482–89):

> […] mirum unde, sed olim
> hic honor alitibus, superae seu conditor aulae
> sic dedit effusum chaos in nova semina texens,
> seu quia mutatae nostraque ab origine versis
> corporibus subiere notos, seu purior axis
> amotumque nefas et rarum insistere terris
> vera docent: tibi, summe sator terraeque deumque,
> scire licet: […]

> Its source is wondrous, but long since have birds held this distinction, whether the founder of the heavenly vault granted it thus, as he was weaving spilt chaos into new seeds, or whether being transformed from our own form they climb the winds in changed bodies, or whether the heightened purity of the pole, and their distance from evil, and the fact that they so rarely land on the earth, teach [them] truths: O highest engenderer of the earth and of the gods, you are allowed to know [this] ….

As Fantham has noted, this speculation on the origins of augury is a significant departure from any prayer formula and stands in contrast to the otherwise conventionally Roman ritual conducted by Amphiaraus and Melampus.[55] This list of multiple explanations evokes Epicurean philosophical practice and the

---

[54] In this section philosophical epos and didactic poetry will be used interchangeably since Statius' target texts are largely poems of natural philosophy and science (cosmogony, astronomy, geology) or parodies of such works (Pythagoras' speech in the *Metamorphoses*). Philip Hardie (2009b) treats some of the Statian passages in his discussion of Lucretian multiple explanation and its reception in nonphilosophical genres, arguing that the Epicurean "habit of indecision" enhances a pessimism about the limits of human knowledge in later Latin epic.

[55] Fantham (2006) 151.

related idioms of post-Lucretian didactic poetry:[56] the first hypothesis of cosmogonic origin (3.483–4) initiates an Empedoclean inquiry on the physical universe. The second suggestion of physical metamorphosis from human to avian form (3.485–6) recalls another famous amphiboly from the *Georgics* in which the poet offers two explanations for the origins of avian weather predictions, one materialist and one mythological (G. 1.415–23).[57]

These first two supernatural explanations are further linked by large-scale imitation of Ovid's *Metamorphoses* proem. Amphiaraus introduces his Lucretian multiple explanations with a familiar series of incipiatory keywords (*Th.* 3.483–6):

> […] superae seu conditor aulae
> sic dedit effusum chaos in nova semina texens,
> seu quia mutatae nostraque ab origine versis
> corporibus subiere notos […]

Compare *Metamorphoses* 1.1–4:

> In nova fert animus mutatas dicere formas
> corpora; di, coeptis (nam vos mutastis et illa)
> aspirate meis primaque ab origine mundi
> ad mea perpetuum deducite tempora carmen.

Stephen Wheeler has recently demonstrated that the incipit of Ovid's *Metamorphoses* was as recognizable in later poetry as Vergil's *arma virumque*, and Statius uses part of the proem in his praise of Lucan as a synecdoche for Ovid (*Silv.* 2.7.78, *et qui corpora prima transfigurat*).[58] Both of these supernatural explanations recall the first episode of the *Metamorphoses*: Amphiaraus' demiurge (*conditor*) grants birds their prophetic power while "knitting up" (*semina texens*) Ovid's "diffuse" Chaos (*Met.* 1.7–9, especially 9: *non bene iunctarum discordia semina rerum*; Ovid's *deus* organizes inchoate Chaos at *Met.* 1.21). This large-scale imitation of the *Metamorphoses* incipit, proem, and cosmogony enhances Amphiaraus' portrayal as didactic *vates* through Statius' characteristic

---

[56] On the reception of Lucretian multiple explanations in his poetic successors and on this passage in particular see Hardie (2009b) 239; Myers (1994) 140 signals Ovid's use of the "Epicurean multiple causation device" in Pythagoras' speech as a parody of didactic poetry.

[57] Introduced by the metamorphic narrative of Nisus and Skylla (G. 1.404–9) retold, inevitably, in *Met.* 8.1–151; note also the nearby mention of the halcyon bird (G. 1.398–9) in this section on weather signs, another irresistible topic of metamorphosis for Ovid at *Met.* 7.401, 11.410–748.

[58] Wheeler (2008) 149–50.

"combinatorial imitation": Amphiaraus' Ovidian Chaos (*Met.* 1.7–14) recalls Lucr. 5.432–5 ~ Empedocles B27 (D-K).[59] Similarly, the second metamorphic explanation that continues the Ovidian proem (*Th.* 3.485–6 with the coy wordplay on **bodies** transformed **in verse**: *ab origine versis / corporibus*) also signals a double reference to Nisus and Skylla's avian transformations in both the *Georgics* and the *Metamorphoses* (*G.* 1.404–9; *Met.* 8.1–151).[60]

Statius invites us to read Amphiaraus' prayer as a pastiche of philosophical epos. While the *Metamorphoses* is not a didactic poem, Statius allusively features the cosmogonic opening that has the most affinity with Empedoclean epos and places this allusion within the structure of an Epicurean multiple explanation. Statius takes his cue from Ovid himself, whose proem plays with the conventions of philosophical epos (*DRN* 5.548 *prima concepta ab origine mundi*), and then recycles the proem in his own miniature didactic parody: as Katharina Volk has shown, Pythagoras' speech may be read formally as a didactic poem *in nuce*, one that concludes with its own reworking of *in nova ... corpora: desinet ante dies ... quam consequar omnia verbis / in species translata novas* (*Met.* 15.418–20).[61] The didactic poets Manilius and the author of the *Aetna* also recast the Ovidian incipit in their scientific epics, subversively appropriating the lofty claims of totalizing, mythological epic to their competing poems of natural philosophy.[62]

The latter two explanations that complete the materialist half of the amphiboly (*Th.* 3.486–88) seem to accord better with Manilius' area of specialty, the sky, although the pseudo-scientific claim that birds are closer to the divine because they live in the purer air of the aether may also derive from Ovid's cosmogony (*Met.* 1.75–81). Is this a parody of philosophical epos? The avian subject matter also contains several suggestive links to the poetic cosmogony in the parabasis of Aristophanes *Birds* (*Av.* 685–722), the avian-centric parody of Hesiodic and Empedoclean epos.[63] Statius provocatively applies the language of scientific causation to the entirely inappropriate topic of avian portents. The

---

[59] Hardie (1995) 209; on "combinatorial imitation" see above chapter 4 note 2 on Smolenaars (1994) and Van Dam (2006).

[60] See also Fantham (2006) 156.

[61] On the scientific/didactic affiliations of Ovid's proem, Myers (1994) 5–6; Volk (2002) 65–7; on the "transformed" incipit in Pythagoras' speech, Wheeler (2008) 156–7; on Ovid's Pythagoras as a singer of "Empedoclean epos," Hardie (1995).

[62] Manilius' "proem in the middle" (3.1–4) begins *in nova surgentem maioraque viribus ausum*; cf. the proem of the *Aetna* lines 1–8, especially 6–8: [...] *tecumque faventes / in nova Pierio properent a fonte sorores/vota* [...]; Wheeler (2008) 152–6. The *Aetna* is an important model for the reception of Lucretian didactic in Amphiaraus' characterization, as I will discuss further below.

[63] Eros as a universal bonding force, *Av.* 700 cf. *philotēs* in Empedocles B35 (D-K) on love and strife as cosmic forces Tarrant (1923); on avian weather signs, *Av.* 709–715; on bird omens as "Ammon, Delphi, Dodona, Phoebus Apollo," *Av.* 716–17 and birds' association with divination generally *Av.* 717–22.

Stoic Manilius who had emptied the sky of gods no less than the Epicurean Lucretius would be appalled at this application of philosophical inquiry into communication with the divine![64] As Hardie articulates, this form of inquiry is explicitly intended to debunk, not foster religious speculation: "For the Epicureans the use of multiple explanations is useful in preventing the temptation to ascribe a supernatural cause to phenomena otherwise inexplicable, in particular astronomical or meteorological events."[65] We will examine a more conventional topic of multiple explanation below in the chasm's opening, but in the augury episode, multiple explanation is provocatively misapplied to a supernatural topic.[66] We see Amphiaraus utilizing the language and practices of philosophical epos in his role as prophetic *vates*.[67] In the augury, the prophet Amphiaraus "speaks didactic" while contradicting the philosophical principles of his poetic predecessors; the cosmogonic opening of the *Metamorphoses* and its self-parody in the didactic speech of Pythagoras is the perfect target text to convey this subversive appropriation of philosophical epos.[68] Amphiaraus' self-contradictory utterance and the augury itself demonstrate the futility of seeking knowledge of the future. Neither Epicurean inquiry nor prophetic insight can provide any clear direction in this pessimistic epic; the augury concludes with the narrator's protest against the human hunger for divination (3.547–65), an insatiable curiosity whose origins are aptly enough expressed through allusion to Lucan's despairing Nigidius and his multiple speculations on the reasons for divination's existence (*DBC* 2.4–15).[69]

2. Seismic Katabasis: Causes of Earthquake

Earlier, we observed the significant placement of the chasm at the end of book 7: the earth's closure seismically signifies the long-anticipated end of

---

[64] See *Georgics* 1.471–2, where Vergil similarly reworks Lucretius to anti-Epicurean ends: the Cyclopean rumblings of Aetna as one of the omens of Caesar's assassination (Lucr. *DRN* 6.681–93), Hardie (2009b) 238.

[65] Hardie (2009b) 234.

[66] Epicurus vehemently rejected divination, as Cicero states in *N.D.* 2.162 *nihil tam inridet Epicurus quam praedictionem rerum futurarum*; for testimonia on Epicurus' statements on the topic see Usener (1887) 261–2.

[67] Amphiaraus is not the only Epicurean-inflected figure of the epic; on Capaneus as an "Epicurean" hero in his atheistic resistance to the gods, see Leigh (2006) 225–33; on Capaneus as an allusive synthesis of Aeschylus' Capaneus, Parthenopaeus, and Tydeus, and Vergil's Mezentius, see Fantham (2006) 159–60.

[68] Segal (2001) on Pythagoras' anti-Lucretian poetics; note also Apollo's own predilictions for philosophical epos at *Th.* 6.360–4.

[69] On multiple causation in the Nigidius episode and the aftermath of the augury, see Hardie (2009b) 250 on Nigidius and 259–60 on the augury; similarity between these two passages briefly noted by Fantham (2006) 156–7.

Amphiaraus' mortal narrative. The startled responses of the Parcae themselves may mirror our own surprise as we witness Amphiaraus' story extend into a mythological sequel. Here we will turn our attention to the chasm itself, its description in multiple explanation, and its affinity with Lucretian accounts of other seismic activity. This climactic episode further develops Amphiaraus' affiliation with heroic figures of philosophical epos and its teacher-heroes, subtly preparing the terms for his chthonic apotheosis in book 8 and beyond.

Statius' description of the chasm has strong affiliations with scientific discourses on the causes of earthquake, as scholars have noted; none, however, have sufficiently refuted Williams' castigation of the passage as an example of "pedantry or mere information for its own sake, without regard for its relevance."[70] I suggest that this instance of multiple explanation coherently maintains Amphiaraus' identification with philosophical epos as demonstrated above and provides a generically appropriate ending for the didactic *vates*, whose Empedoclean similarities will be discussed further in this and the following section. Furthermore, this explicit imitation of Lucretian seismology again uses Lucretian language and scientific topic to an entirely anti-Lucretian end. Like Amphiaraus' speech in the augury and in his final speech to Dis in the underworld (which we will examine below), Amphiaraus' construction as a didactic *vates* involves consistent "correction" of Epicurean atheism and a refutation of philosophical claims to Apolline authority. This pattern of refutation ultimately validates Amphiaraus' reception as a divinity both within the epic and beyond.

While the primary reference seems to be Lucretius' discussion of earthquakes (*DRN* 6.535–607), it has not been noticed that Statius' six explanations are "contaminated" with references to Lucretius' related account of Aetna (*DRN* 6.639–702), as well as other texts on both earthquakes and Aetna, the prime literary subject of volcanology in antiquity.[71] Statius echoes Lucretius' association of seismology with Epicurean multiple explanation: Lucretius concludes this section on earthquakes and volcanoes with a programmatic statement on Epicurean multiple explanation (*DRN* 6.703–11; cf. 5.526–33). Epicurus himself had treated the topic of earthquakes in his *Letter to Pythocles*, and Lucretius' account establishes establishes seismology and volcanology as the paradigmatic topics of Epicurean inquiry, as Vergil's *recusatio* of Lucretian philosophical epos indicates (*G*. 2.479, *unde tremor terris*).[72] In *Thebaid* 7, the

---

[70] Smolenaars (1994) *ad* 7.809ff.; Hardie (2009b) 260; Williams (1978) 262.

[71] Statius' interest in volcanoes was more than merely academic, as his own native city, Naples, had been devastated by Vesuvius' eruption in 79 CE. Statius mentions the eruption only briefly in three of his *Silvae* (3.5, 4.4, 5.3); Newlands (2010) provides a persuasive reading of Statius' poetic accommodation of the tragedy within his slighter poetic works.

[72] On the correspondences between Epicurus' account in the *Ep. ad Pyth.* 105 and Lucretius' earthquake passage, see Bailey (1947) 1633 and notes *ad DRN* 6.535ff.; see Volk (2002) 142–4 for a convincing account of Vergil's rejection of natural philosophy in *G*. 2.475–94.

phenomenon begins unmistakeably as an earthquake as the tremor spreads over the battlefield, sending the warriors and chariots sprawling, and even shaking the walls of Thebes (*Th.* 7.798–80). The panic that ensues quells the hostilities as the enemies face the threat of total destruction, a vignette well expressed in a simile of sea battle halted by storm (*Th.* 7.804–8). In Lucretius, however, a similar depiction of universal dread at the volcano's "fiery maelstrom" (*flammea tempestas, DRN* 6.642; cf. *tempestas, Th.* 7.806) introduces his rationalist explanation of Aetna's activity (*DRN* 6.639–46). Statius seems to treat Lucretius' section on terrestrial events as a complete unit rather than focusing exclusively on the earthquake passage as a model.

Lucretius and subsequent philosophical authors explicitly declare that they will dispel human fear and superstition about divine causation through their materialist accounts of seismic phenomena.[73] Statius' narrative of Amphiaraus' descent, however, reverses this rationalist agenda: by dwelling on and elaborating the potential causes of the earth's motion, the poet maximizes the uncertainty and horror in the Theban portent. The quasi-scientific multiple explanations exhaustively detail possible sources of the earthquake but to distinctly un-philosophical purposes—the sheer plurality of Statius' causes presents an alarming vision of a fragile earth, crumbling with decay, wavering on its axis, or subject to the violent whims of gods and inexorable fates. As in the augury, Statius' multiple causation take the form of amphiboly, combining materialist with supernatural causation (*Th.* 7.809–16):

> sive laborantes concepto flamine terrae
> ventorum rabiem et clausum eiecere furorem,
> exedit seu putre solum carpsitque terendo
> unda latens, sive hac volventis machina caeli
> incubuit, sive omne fretum Neptunia mouit

---

[73] Lucretius *DRN* 6.38–95, *hunc igitur terrorem animi tenebrasque necessest / non radii solis nec lucida tela diei / discutiant, sed naturae species ratioque* [...]: human fear and ignorance can only be countered with *ratio* about the earth and understanding the true nature of the gods. The *Aetna* poet follows his statement of didactic purpose (to explain the eruptions of Aetna 24–8, *fortius ignotas molimur pectore curas, / qui tanto motus opera, vis quanta perennis/explicet in denso flammas* [...] *mens carminis haec est*) with a lengthy condemnation of mythological fancies about Vulcan's forges or a buried Enceladus (29–75, *principio ne quem capiat fallacia vatum ... haec est mendosae vulgata licentia famae./vatibus ingenium est: hinc audit nobile carmen*); cf. *Aetna* 274–9. Seneca presents a Stoic claim to dispel fear in his preface to the the sixth book of the *NQ* on earthquakes (*NQ* 6.2.1, *Quid ago? Solacium adverus pericula rara promiseram. Ecce undique timenda denuntio. Nego quicquam esse quietis aeternae, quod perire possit et perdere. Ego vero hoc ipsum solacii loco pono, et quidem valentissimi, quando quidem sine remedio timor stultis est: ratio terrorem prudentibus excutit; fit ex desperation securitas.*). On Seneca's adaptation of Lucretius' discourse of "necessity" to dispel *religio* and Lucretian influence on Seneca's seismology, see Williams (2006) 125 and *passim*.

> cuspis et extremas gravius mare torsit in oras,
> seu uati datus ille fragor, seu terra minata est
> fratribus: [...]

> Whether the lands were suffering from wind that had been generated and blasted out the compressed force and fury of the gusts, or whether an unseen current eroded and wore away the crumbling earth, or whether the superstructure of the rotating heavens leaned toward Thebes, or whether Neptune's spear shifted the entire sea and torqued the ocean disproportionately onto distant coasts, or whether that roar was granted to the prophet, or whether the earth was warning the brothers....

In this passage, the amphiboly contributes to the epic and even cosmic sense of the earthquake's rupture.[74] Where Lucretius provides three geologic explanations for earthquakes, Statius provides six in total, initially corresponding to Lucretius' causes of wind, water, orientation (subterranean winds, *Th.* 7.809–10, cf. *DRN* 6.577–607; erosion of the earth by water underground, *Th.* 7.811–2, cf. *DRN* 6.552–6; tilt of the cosmos' axis, *Th.* 7.812–3, cf. tilt of the earth's surface, *DRN* 6.557–76) with one additional (quasi-) materialist and two supernatural causes. The first explanation at 809–10 maintains the confusion between volcanology and seismology: subterranean winds are the primary explanation for earthquakes in Lucretius and others, but in describing how the winds burst open the surface of the earth to create the chasm, Statius adopts the language of volcanic explanations. In Lucretius' account of Aetna, air trapped underground heats up through its activity and becomes wind, eventually blasting out of the volcano in an eruption (*DRN* 6.685–9):

> ventus enim fit, ubi est agitando percitus aër.
> hic ubi percaluit calefecitque omnia circum
> saxa furens, qua contingit, terramque et ab ollis
> excussit calidum flammis velocibus ignem,
> tollit se ac rectis ita faucibus eicit alte.

> For air turns into wind when it has been stirred by motion. When as it rages it has heated and warmed all the rocks around and the earth wherever it comes in contact with

---

[74] The pairing of naturalist and supernatural causes to express uncertainty has its epic origins in Homeric character speculation, and the *Aeneid* seems to increase the number of options under the influence of Lucretian multiple explanation, Hardie (2009b) 240–5.

it, and from them strikes hot fire with its swift flames, it rises up and shoots out high straight through the crater.

For his first hypothesis Statius evokes the imagery and language of Lucretius' first explanation of Aetna's eruptions; the idea of subterranean wind (*ventus*, *DRN* 6.685) whose fury (*furens*, *DRN* 6.687) finally results in violent explosion (*eiecit*, *DRN* 6.689) finds close lexical analogues in *Thebaid* 7.809–10: *sive laborantes concepto flamine terrae / ventorum rabiem et clausum eiecere furorem*.[75] While the "pneumatic theory" of subterranean winds was also used to explain seismic movement, Statius describes the chasm as the result of an eruption (*eiecere*); the parallels with the beginning of Lucretius' Aetna account are striking, whereas there is little lexical similarity to the opening of Lucretius' earthquake exposition, either his introduction to the subject (*DRN* 6.535 ff.) or the section on pneumatic theory (*DRN* 6.558ff.).[76] The unusual phrase *laborantes concepto flamine terrae* (*Th.* 7.809) with its medical overtones (Smolenaars *ad loc.* explains *laborare* + ablative of disease) seems to refer to Aristotle's analogy between earthquakes and flatulence, dismissed by Seneca in the *Natural Questions*.[77] The idea of the earth as a living creature was a scientific commonplace, but one explicitly stated in a similar multiple explanation by Ovid's Pythagoras on Aetna's eruptions (*Met.* 15.342–9 *nam sive est animal tellus* [...]), a passage that imitates the Lucretian Aetna passage cited above (*DRN* 6.685–9).[78] The humorous notion of the earth's flatulence may

---

[75] Seneca also provides a similar cause and effect in *NQ* 6.14.4, where wind trapped underground can force its way out by causing fissures in the earth. This section of Seneca's account has several affinities with *Th.* 7.809–10, as will be further discussed below. Williams (2006) 134–5 argues that Seneca prioritizes air as a primary cause of seismic motion to "normalize" earthquake through analogy to a physical body; thus the earth operates as part of the "corporeal" cosmos, animated by Stoic *pneuma*.

[76] In his discussion of earthquake Lucretius does mention the possibility that winds trapped underground might burst through the surface of the earth and create a great chasm, but there is much less lexical similarity (*DRN* 6.577–84). The references to Lucretius' Aetna are not noted by Smolenaars (1994), who does, however, cite parallels to the *Aetna* without comment. My argument considers these Aetna references as more than generic seismic information—Aetna has a special Empedoclean significance for Amphiaraus' katabasis. For pneumatic theories in antiquity see Bailey (1947) *ad DRN* 6.535ff. and Smolenaars (1994) *ad Th.* 7.809.

[77] Aristotle *Mete.* 2.8.366b 15–20, rejected by Seneca *NQ* 5.4.2 on the origins of wind. As *concepto flamine* certainly points to a source (*OLD* 4 s.v. "*concipio*") of wind, Statius may be referring to the Senecan refutation.

[78] Seneca refers again to Aristotle in his account of pneumatic theory on earthquakes, in conjunction with "those who are of the opinion that the earth is a creature," *quibus animal placet esse terram* (*NQ* 6.14.2). The Ovidian Pythagoras' second explanation for Aetna's fire (*sive leves imis venti cohibentur in antris / saxaque cum saxis et habentem semina flammae*, *Met.* 15.346–8) elaborates Lucretius' idea of trapped winds "striking sparks" from the rocks under Aetna (*et ab ollis / excussit calidum flammis velocibus ignem*, *DRN* 6.687–8).

even be suggested by Ovid's extended metaphors on Aetna's limited "food supply," part of his third explanation on volcanic eruption (*Met.* 15.352–5). Statius' first explanation, which initially appears to be a conventional expression of pneumatic earthquake theory, also incorporates allusions to Lucretian volcanology and Ovidian accounts of Aetna's "digestion".

As the explanations continue, they diverge further from the Lucretian model promised by the Epicurean form. The second explanation of subterranean water eroding the earth and causing collapse is not entirely parallel to Lucretius' earthquake account. Statius must explain the earth's opening as well as the earthquake, whereas Lucretius' discussion concentrates on the "reason for motions of the earth" (*ratio terrai motibus, DRN* 6.535). As in Lucretius, Statius' causes progress from subterranean wind to water, but Statius' erosion theory of the earth's collapse (*Th.* 7.811–2) does not correspond exactly to Lucretius, who specifies that tremor arises from shock waves from underground lakes disturbed by falling masses of rocks or earth (*DRN* 6.552–6).[79] Rather, the *unda latens* that erodes and undermines the earth's surface might recall Aetna's famously porous base, the underwater openings carved by waves whose force also drives air into the volcano (*unda* more naturally refers to waves of the sea, *OLD* 1, s.v. *unda*).[80] As the waves strike, seawater forced into the underground passages stirs air trapped underground and can cause seismic activity, either volcanic eruption or earthquake: the *Aetna* poet in a virtuosic (but sadly corrupt) set of similes uses hydraulically forced air devices as analogues for the volcano (a musical Triton blowing a horn and a water organ, 291–9).[81] Seneca cites this "hydraulic" theory of earthquake to explain Neptune's Homeric epithet, "Earth shaker" (*Enosichthon, NQ* 6.23.4), and a similar associative link between water in subterranean caves and the sea is surely operative in the

---

[79] Seneca also follows this progression from wind to water in his investigation into seismic theories in *NQ* book 6: Roughly, Seneca discusses fire, 6.9–11; air, 6.12–9; water, 6.20.1–4, but quickly dismisses water as a primary cause, though it does play a role in some of the earlier pneumatic theories. The erosion theory is much closer to Seneca's citation of Epicurus (*NQ* 6.20.5), *Ergo, ut ait, potest terram movere aqua, si partes aliquas eluit et adrosit, quibus desiit posse extenuatis sustineri quod integris ferebatur.*

[80] *DRN* 6.694–7. While there is little lexical similarity to Lucretius in this section, Aetna was certainly linked to rough seas, as the volcano's close association with Charybdis attests (*Aen.* 3.554–6, *tum procul e fluctu Trinacria cernitur Aetna, / et gemitum ingentem pelagi pulsataque saxa / audimus* [...]). In *Ep.* 79 on Aetna, Seneca opens with queries on the phenomenon of Charybdis (*Ep.* 79.1) before making his request to Lucilius to ascend Aetna and to record his observations in verse; Seneca also assumes that Aetna's base is permeated with openings (*Ep.* 79.2; cf. *DRN* 6.697).

[81] The lines are 291–300 in the Goodyear (1965) edition; 291–2 introduce the hydraulic similes by articulating a general principle of water compressing and therefore moving particles of air, *praecipiti deiecta sono premit unda fugatque / torpentes auras pulsataque corpora denset.*

transition from the second to the fourth explanation in Statius' sequence (*Neptunia movit / cuspis, Th.* 7.813–4).

After proposing two subterranean causes, Statius expands Lucretius' scientific explanations by adding two more theories to complete a triad of earth, sky, and sea: a cosmic "tilt" of the universe's axis (*Th.* 7.812–3) and a lopsided massing of the seas by "Neptune's trident" (*Th.* 7.813–4). These theories are unattested in Lucretius and have proved quite resistant to precise explanation. I suggest that both of these phenomena may be understood more clearly as corresponding to Seneca's discussion of *inclinatio* as a cause of earthquake.[82] Seneca illustrates *inclinatio* by comparing the surface of the earth to a ship leaning from one side to the other (*altera inclinatio, qua in latera nutat alternis navigii more, NQ* 6.21.2). Statius seems to separate this example into two perspectives that encompass a physical and a supernatural causation. The first posits a "clockwork" atheistic universe (*volventis machina caeli, Th.* 7.812) in which a polar axis tilts (*incubuit, Th.* 7.813) like the ship's mast. The supernatural perspective supposes Neptune's trident (*Neptunia . . . cuspis, Th.* 7.813) massing the waters more heavily onto the furthest shores (*extremas gravius mare torsit in oras, Th.* 7.814), namely, unequally on one side, as when a wave swamps one side of a ship. This mini-amphiboly on *inclinatio* marks a boundary between three materialist and three supernatural explanations, the last two being entirely speculative (*Th.* 7.815–6): either the rumbling was granted to commemorate the prophet, or the earth itself was menacing the fratricidal brothers. After all the possibly distracting scientific explanations, these final two supernatural explanations reemphasize the narrative significance of the chasm itself, a topic to which we will now turn.

In both Amphiaraus' prayer at the augury and in his account of the chasm, Statius' multiple explanations, despite their Epicurean form and origin, depart significantly from a Lucretian model, not least in their admission of divine causation. If this elaborate episode of multiple explanation is not a gratuitously virtuosic interlude, how can we understand the complexity of reference, the multiple scientific perspectives and citations, and the peculiar mingling of Lucretius' earthquake and Aetna discussions in book 6?[83] As we saw in the first section of this chapter, Amphiaraus' particular characteristics seem to influence the narrative surrounding him: as the tale of a prophet who sees future events, his narrative includes frequent prolepses and significant portents and even generates secondary doubles like Maeon, whose fate foreshadows his own.

---

[82] Smolenaars (1994) *ad loc.* adduces the parallel to Seneca among various other references, but does not elaborate on the connection.

[83] As Hine (2002) 69 argues, ancient seismology was far more developed than volcanology as a science, and Aetna was a much more literary than scientific topos, therefore combining the two as Statius does here is somewhat unexpected.

Statius also capitalizes on the poetic coincidence he inherits from the mythological tradition: what better fate for an interpreter of omens than to be swallowed up by a monstrous portent? Amphiaraus' end is also appropriate in yet another way that "warps" the narrative: having been identified with the *vates* of cosmogonic philosophical epos in the augury, it is fitting that Amphiaraus' climactic disappearance should be marked by multiple causation, the most Lucretian of literary devices.

The complex constellation of allusions to philosophical (and pseudo-philosophical) epos as well as to prose scientific treatises goes far beyond the narrative needs. Surely if the katabasis merely required some impression of scientific didactic, there would have been no need for the wide variety of allusions Statius incorporates—a perfunctory multiple explanation that referenced the Lucretian earthquake passage would have sufficed to send the prophet to Hades. While there are other instances of multiple explanation in the epic, none are as extensive or allusively rich as the two we have examined thus far.[84] Rather than pointing to any single primary model like Lucretius, these layered, multivalent references to a wide corpus of scientific texts establish a generic affiliation to philosophical epos and thus depict an essentialized philosopher hero, a didactic *vates*. Statius can therefore activate particular details to enhance Amphiaraus' narrative: thus the ominous earthquake that opens the chasm continues Amphiaraus' affiliations to Lucretian and Senecan scientific inquiry, while incorporating unmistakable references to Aetna and volcanic texts generates another powerful comparandum: Empedocles' infamous leap into Aetna's crater. For his followers, Empedocles' volcanic end was taken as proof of his divinity; to the Augustan poets, his suicide also became a byword for outsized ambitions to poetic immortality (Horace *AP* 464–6: [...] *deus immortalis haberi / dum cupit Empedocles, ardentem frigidus Aetnam / insiluit*).[85] Far from representing gratuitous pedantry, the complexity of allusions to scientific accounts of earthquake and volcanology confirms Amphiaraus' characterization as a didactic *vates* by enacting an appropriately volcanic descent. Furthermore, these Empedoclean gestures point forward to Amphiaraus' transformation into a chthonic prophetic deity in the epic and beyond: surely the erudite son of a Neapolitan *grammaticus* would have been familiar with Empedocles' contention that "prophets, singers, and doctors" were at the highest rung of reincarnation and thus nearest to becoming gods (Emped. B126 D-K).[86]

---

[84] Hardie (2009b) 258.

[85] Diogenes Laertius preserves a number of accounts of Empedocles' death, including the Aetna account first found in Hermippus (D. L. 8.67–8), Wright (1981) 15–17.

[86] McNelis (2002); Inwood (2001); an interest in volcanoes seems to run in the family, not surprising considering their proximity to Vesuvius—Statius' father had been planning to write a poem on the eruption of 79 CE (*Sil.* 5.3.205–8).

3. Apotheosis and Afterlife

As discussed in the first half of this chapter, Amphiaraus' seemingly predictable narrative trajectory takes a sharp curve in the katabasis, and yet even this novel underworld scenario follows a familiar script. Having traced Amphiaraus' associations with philosophical epos, we can appreciate yet another source of audience manipulation and surprise: Hades is the last place one would expect to find a didactic *vates*. As Ovid's Pythagoras declares in his best Lucretian mode (*Met.* 15.153–5):

> o genus attonitum gelidae formidine mortis!
> quid Styga, quid manes et nomina vana timetis,
> materiem vatum, falsique pericula mundi?

> O human race, stupefied by terror of chill death! Why do you fear the Styx, the shades, and empty descriptions, the stuff of poets and the threats of a spurious world?[87]

In direct contradiction to such philosophical rejections of Hades as poetic fictions, the descriptive montage of appalled underworld inhabitants and Dis' own long litany of previous incursions (8.1–79, discussed above) establish Amphiaraus' descent into a fully mythological Hades populated by all the expected denizens who are allusively "mindful" of their own literary past. Hence the heightened sense of incongruity when Amphiaraus opens with an address more appropriate to a hymn or Empedoclean philosophical epos (8.90–3):

> si licet et sanctis hic ora resolvere fas est
> manibus, o cunctis finitor maxime rerum
> (at mihi, qui quondam causas elementaque noram,
> et sator) [...]

> If it is permitted and right to speak here among the holy shades, O mightiest End of existence to all (but to me, who once knew its origins and component parts, also its creator) ...

In this last prayer addressed directly to the god in person, Amphiaraus "remembers" his earlier display of cosmogonic knowledge in the augury through the significant temporal adverb *quondam* (8.93).[88] The prophet addresses Dis not

---

[87] Cf. Lucretius' own programmatic rejection of everlasting punishments as the fancies of poets and the realm of *religio*, *DRN* 1.102–35.

[88] *si licet et .... fas est* echoes the conventional prayer formula *si fas est* adapted by Ovid in his address to Germanicus in *Fasti* 1.25, Green (2004) *ad F.* 1.25.

only as king of the underworld, but also as the source of all, *sator*, the divine engenderer, since Dis keeps Chaos in his depths (*Th.* 8.52–3). Here Amphiaraus again recalls Ovid's cosmogony (*Met.* 1.5–9; cf. *Th.* 3.483–4, where Jupiter is addressed as *sator*), but tactfully foregrounds Hesiod's, in which Chaos gives birth to Earth, Tartarus, Love, Erebos, and Nyx at the very beginning of the world (Hes. *Th.* 116–23).[89] Amphiaraus' self-description as one who "once knew *causas elementaque*" aptly summarizes Amphiaraus' didactic persona. The phrase *causas elementaque* combines Pythagoras' initial description as a teacher of natural science (*Met.* 15.60–72), who taught "the origins of the world, and what nature is" (*rerum causas, et, quid natura, docebat, Met.* 15.68) with his disquisition on the elements (*haec quoque non perstant, quae nos elementa vocamus, Met.* 15.237).[90] By framing this moment of self-identification within the highly allusive mode of memory, Statius highlights the palimpsestic quality of his philosopher hero. Like a set of Russian dolls, this philosophical Amphiaraus contains Ovid's Pythagoras (*Met.* 15.60–72), who himself reflects Lucretius' praise of Epicurus (Lucr. 1.62–79), which in turn echoes Empedocles' praise of Pythagoras (Emped. B129 D-K).[91] As in the case of Parthenopaeus, this multiple "window reference" draws out the correspondences between these figures of the didactic tradition, but with an additional large-scale "correction": their rivalrous claims to vatic authority are restored to a true prophet and future divinity.

Ovid's palimpsestic Pythagoras, himself a figure who embodies multiple traditions of philosophical epos,[92] provides the primary model for Amphiaraus' final transformation, one who represents a synthesis of the "dual, and to Lucretius antithetical, associations of the *vates*, as, on the one hand, a figure of supernatural, even sacerdotal, authority, and, on the other hand, as a scientific

---

[89] Cf. the very similar address of Lachesis to Pluto in Claudian *De raptu Proserpinae* 1.55–62, where he is addressed as the source of the "end of all and all the seeds of birth" (1.57–8, *finem cunctis et semina praebes / nascendi*) and responsible for "whatever physical material comes into being" (1.59–60, *quidquid ubique / gignit materies*). Gruzelier (1993) also notes the parallel in Claudian *ad loc.*; I owe this reference to Antony Augoustakis.

[90] This Ovidian formulation (*rerum causas, et, quid natura, docebat, Met.* 15.68) surely confirms Volk's assertion (2002) 142–3 n. 29 contra Thomas (1988) *ad* 2.490 that Verg. G. 2.490–2 must refer to Lucretian didactic, *felix qui potuit rerum cognoscere causas / atque metus omnis et inexorabile fatum/subiecit pedibus strepitumque Acherontis avari.*

[91] Hardie (1995) 208; cf. the narrator's veneration of Amphiaraus' wisdom at *Theb.* 7.705–8 in precisely the terms of an heroic, enlightened benefactor of philosophical didactic:

> Hicne hominum casus lenire et demere Fatis
> iura frequens? quantum subito diversus ab illo
> qui tripodas laurusque sequi, qui doctus in omni
> nube salutato volucrem cognoscere Phoebo!

[92] Myers (1994); Hardie (1995); Segal (2001); Volk (2002) 64–7.

investigator of and knowledgeable authority on philosophical truths."[93] Ovid's Pythagoras and his literary predecessors of the didactic tradition (viz. Empedocles, Lucretius' Epicurus) all make similar claims to Apolline authority, and Statius essentializes their common pretension to prophetic wisdom.[94] By evoking these vatic models in his portrayal of Amphiaraus, Statius seems to "correct" his predecessors' metaphorical appropriations of divine inspiration by restoring their qualities to an actual prophet. Ultimately, Amphiaraus' vatic characterization and his narrative trajectory produce a curious incongruity: the prophet's katabasis humorously contradicts his philosophical models' eschatologies! Statius employs an Ovidian parody of Lucretian didactic to refute Pythagorean and Epicurean doctrines on the afterlife.[95] In his sequel, Amphiaraus confronts the deity Dis and becomes himself the recipient of human worship, the prophetic divinity of an incubation cult.

4. When Delphi Is Silent

As in the Maeon episode, Amphiaraus too receives a double *makarismos* of sorts, in the form of the Argives troops' lament (8.174–207) and Thiodamas' prayer (8.329–38). The Argive eulogy celebrates Amphiaraus' prophetic powers and his remarkable courage in facing a death foreseen (*quanta sacro sub pectore virtus!* 8.183); the troops also speculate on eschatological matters, proposing theories for Amphiaraus' underworld duties and, finally, predicting that all oracles and shrines of prophecy will fall silent this day in his honor and that he himself will someday be worshipped as an oracular divinity: "And soon there will be a day when they will venerate you and your temples that harbor the fates, and your own priest will render prophecy" (*iamque erit ille dies quo te*

---

[93] Myers (1994) 143–4.
[94] *Met.* 15.143–5:

> Et quoniam deus ora movet, sequar ora moventem
> rite deum Delphosque meos ipsumque recludam
> aethera et augustae reserabo oracula mentis.

Myers (1994) 142–3: "By having Pythagoras so pointedly avow a divine inspiration, Ovid subverts the Lucretian claims for the primacy of reason in philosophical investigation. Epicurus was traditionally vehemently opposed to the practice of divination, and Lucretius contrasts both his own philosophic knowledge and that of the Pre-Socratic philosophers with the Pythian oracle, claiming that the philosophers have spoken *multo certa ratione magis quam / Pythia quae tripode a Phoebi lauroque profatur* (*DRN* 1.738–39, 5.111–2). Yet it was claimed even of Epicurus that he had oracular powers and Lucretius' own attitude towards divine inspiration is notoriously ambiguous in the light of his dual posture as poet and philosopher." Segal (2001) 74; the *Suda* (s.v. "Empedocles") claims that Empedocles bore *stemmata Delphika* as an Apolline affectation.

[95] Both Ovid's Pythagoras and Lucretius' Epicurus explicitly deny the existence of Hades and the torments of the afterlife: Lucr. 1.110–35, *Met.* 15.153–9; discussion in Segal (2001) 79.

quoque conscia fatis / templa colant reddatque tuus responsa sacerdos, 8.206–7).[96] Thiodamas explicitly compares Amphiaraus to the god Apollo himself, and his resting place in the underworld to Apollo's sanctuaries (8.335–8):

> [...] tibi sacra feram praesaga, tuique
> numinis interpres te Phoebo absente vocabo.
> ille mihi Delo Cirrhaque potentior omni,
> quo ruis, ille adytis melior locus. [...]

> I shall perform your prophetic duties, and as the conduit of your divinity, I shall call on you when Phoebus is absent. That place to which you descended is more powerful to me than any Delos or Cirrha, greater than temples.

Both of these passages announce the foundation of Amphiaraus' cult on the very spot, *ille . . . locus* where Amphiaraus disappeared. This cult would not have been a mere historical footnote to Statius and his audience, however. Epigraphic evidence from 73 BCE shows that Sulla had granted tax-exempt status to Amphiaraus' cult, and as we know from Cicero (*de Nat. Deorum* 3.49), the cult of Amphiaraus was still active at least as late as the middle of the first century BC, when the older sanctuaries of Dodona and Delphi had already lost much of their status.[97] Thiodamas' phrase *Phoebo absente vocabo* looks forward to Statius' own time, when the decline of the traditional Greek oracles had become something of a commonplace.[98] This anachronistic reference to Apollo's silence confirms Amphiaraus' re-creation as the patron divinity of a cult still active in the Roman period. In a poem where divinities so often fail their human servants, it seems appropriate that the enlightened Amphiaraus will come to replace the great oracles of Delphi and Delos. And indeed, Thiodamas seems to offer an early demonstration of Amphiaraus' incubation cult in book 10 when he recounts a dream vision of Amphiaraus to the Argive leaders and encourages them to battle—although Statius' use of multiple explanation renders the source of the vision uncertain (*sive hanc Saturnia mentem, / sive novum comitem bonus instigabat Apollo*, 10.162–3). The rousing effect on the Argives, however, is as if "the same god was in all their hearts" (*non secus accensi procures quam si omnibus idem / corde deus*, 10.220–1).

---

[96] Does Amphiaraus perform his own etiological sacrifices on the battlefield? *innumeram ferro plebem ... immolat umbris / ipse suis* (7.709–11) takes *Aeneid* 10.538 as its immediate model, but the action seems closer to Hercules in Livy 1.7 performing the originary first sacrifices at the Ara Maxima for himself, of which the killing of Cacus might also be allegorical; cf. *Aen.* 8.268–72.

[97] Sherk 70 = *SIG3* 747 in Sherk and Viereck (1969).

[98] See above on Maeon, 3.107–8; discussion of decline both as a literary topos and the historical evidence in Levin (1989).

Amphiaraus ends his own story in the underworld by becoming an Empedoclean super-*vates* like Ovid's Pythagoras: a philosopher, a prophet, a religious figure of worship, and an embodiment of self-reflexive poetics. Amphiaraus' speech, like that of Pythagoras in *Metamorphoses* 15, serves a closural function by recapitulating the story, in this case, his own.[99] The prophet relates his own biographical eulogy; beginning with a self-identification as Apollo's augur (8.99), Amphiaraus reports on his wife's betrayal, his achievements as a warrior, and then his descent (8.104–9). As a prophet, however, Amphiaraus goes further in the tale, predicting the end of the war and requesting punishment for his treacherous wife (8.121–2). Ovid's Pythagoras, then, is especially useful as a marker of self-reflexive closure, indicating the trajectory that Amphiaraus has progressed through in the poem. Pythagoras' association with metamorphosis too reminds us that the prophet will be transformed into a greater divinity, even as he rejects the Apolline insignia and its celestial affiliations of his earthly life (*Th.* 8.100; 8.116–9). Amphiaraus can thus be read as an *oppositio in imitando* writ large: just as Ovid's Pythagoras mouths Lucretius in refutation of Epicurean philosophical principles, Statius evokes the celestial, Apolline associations of his Empedocles-derived Roman models at the very moment that his *vates* explicitly abandons Apollo's service. Amphiaraus' apotheosis moves him from prophet to oracular divinity, fiction to tangible historicity, as we are left with the etiology of his cult and its continuing worship. The *vates*, far from declining from his Augustan peak in the Flavian period, has come into his own as a divinity to rival Delphic Apollo in the real world.[100]

Tracking Statius' characters through their individual trajectories reveals how patterns of allusion structure the reader's expectations for the characters' outcomes. Allusions make us the "accomplice of the author," they summon up the models and make us part of Roller's discourse of exemplarity: we use the known—phrases, imagery, characters, type scenes—to process the narrative still in progress. Sometimes our comparisons are all too correct, hence the sick dread and exaggerated pathos associated with Parthenopaeus' appearances. The effects can sometimes be excessive, even "inappropriate," at least judged by Vergilian standards: does the *puer* always have to be quite that sexy, alluring, so shampoo commercial-ready? His outsized affect suffuses his every appearance with epikedic lament quite appropriate to Statius' epic of mourning. Amphiaraus is less dependent on individual *loci* than Parthenopaeus, but his trajectory is no less predestined by audience expectations. The symbols

---

[99] On Pythagoras' speech as a microcosm of the poem as a whole, Myers (1994) 133–59, Wheeler (2000) 117, Hardie (1995) 209.

[100] Newman (1967) 124; political interpretations of the *vates* as a figure of "free speech" in Statius in Markus (2003), Lovatt (2007).

and scenarios of literary prophets in epic and tragedy add to our sense of Amphiaraus' overdetermined end: in Statius' representation, his prophetic vision becomes internalized as our literary expectations. The *vittae* and *infulae* become the markers, or "monuments," of earlier literary prophets, and our awareness that these symbols are so often threatened and violated leads us to expect the same for Amphiaraus. But this figure of prediction and predestination instead creates surprise and novelty and even undergoes an apotheosis in an end that refutes philosophical epos' rivalry with Delphic authority, and surpasses that of his generic model, Empedocles. Horizons of expectation can be as misleading as oracular utterance.

Conclusions

> [Tarantino] loves actors' baggage of all sorts. He likes to tell a story about the time Elmore Leonard visited the set of "Joe Kidd," a movie he wrote for Clint Eastwood. At one point, Eastwood put his hand on his gun and his enemy didn't draw his own gun because he was afraid. Eastwood objected that the enemy should not be afraid at that stage in the movie—how would he know that Eastwood was a lightning draw? The enemy wouldn't, Leonard conceded, but that didn't matter: the audience would know, because they'd seen his other movies.
>
> Larissa MacFarquhar on Quentin Tarantino)[1]

The iconic Clint Eastwood embodies the characteristics of his earlier roles. Distilled to his essence—despite some surprisingly successful forays into comedy—he represents the consummate gunslinger. Elmore Leonard can rely on the audience's competence to complete the scene; from cineaste Eastwood aficionado to film novice there may be great variety in sophistication, but bare recognition of Eastwood's archetypal cultural features is all that is required for comprehension. Like this Hollywood anecdote, this study of character in Roman poetry attempts to go behind the scenes. What did the Roman poet, like Leonard, know about his audience? What did the audience know and expect? And how do characters function as part of the poetics of a work?

The introduction outlined a fundamental question of character in Roman poetry: what if we are reading it all wrong? That is to say, how can we reconsider the "shortcomings" in characterization critiqued by scholars in a way that understands characterization as a successful poetic technique rather than a failure of novelistic psychological "roundedness"? To understand the expectations of both authors and audiences in the Roman world, I have adduced the social discourse of exemplarity as defined by Matthew Roller, as a broad habit of Roman thought that inheres in poetry, an important vehicle for exempla, as

---

[1] Larissa MacFarquhar, "The Movie Lover," *New Yorker*, 20 November 2003.

well as in many other areas. Roman literary criticism assumes that characters, like many other elements of Roman poetry, will refer to models. This emphasis on character imitation can be linked to contemporary areas of Roman thought outside of the world of literature. Stoic philosophy (especially as articulated in book 1 of Cicero's *De Officiis*) and Roman rhetoric, both fundamental influences in Roman intellectual life, consider ethical emulation an essential training to self-presentation. I therefore contend that a similar principle holds in the production of fictional characters by authors whose poetic practice privileged imitation as a vital connection to a literary tradition reaching back to Homer. Some models are more important than others, however; a case study on Apollonius' Thetis reveals the importance of the *Argonautica* as a model for characterization to epigonic Roman authors. Apollonius shows how to incorporate and thematize literary genealogy in individual characters by modeling his Thetis on the Demeter of the Homeric hymn, which is figured as an early emulation of the *Iliad*. "Homer" imitates Homer, which authorizes Apollonius and his Roman descendants.

Genealogy, especially maternity, becomes an important metaphor for literary inheritance in Roman epic. Maternal inheritance is a crucial issue in the *Aeneid*, where Aeneas' descent from Venus entails much undesirable literary inheritance along with contemporary dynastic significance. Perhaps Venus' studiedly unmaternal encounters with her son are a distancing strategy to prevent overidentification with her other cherished favorites, especially the infamous Paris? Chapter 1 analyzes how characterization is dramatized in the *Aeneid* as an active process through the workings of *Fama*, a fickle, unreliable double of the poet. *Fama*, both in her guise as Titanic personification and through rumor and speeches, serves up a double of Aeneas, a composite of the literary Paris and the stereotypical eastern effeminate of the Roman invective tradition. This is epic as agonistic forensic rhetoric, where the rhetorical practice of *fictio personae* generates a schematic but believable alternative version of the opponent like the Clodia of the *Pro Caelio*. The ultimate plausibility of this doppelganger Paris, however, reveals *Fama* (or the poet?) talking out of both sides of her mouth: Aeneas and Paris do share many qualities and coincidental features. This poem of national origins and dynastic foundations paints lineage and inheritance in a surprisingly problematic light.

Exemplarity and its limits define Lucan's Cato in chapter 2. Can exemplarity be taken too far? Can imitation of an outstanding figure like the exemplary Cato actually lead to negative consequences and ethical crimes? As in the first chapter, the dynamic process of establishing character occurs programmatically early in the poem, as Cato ambiguously inspires Brutus in a form of possession. The *furor* that accompanies the multiple instances of Cato-imitation (whose essential, exemplary action has been reduced to his courageous self-killing), reveals the failure of models to teach. As an audience, we recognize the paradigm Lucan adapts from rhetorical and philosophical commonplaces, but our recognition also raises concerns: about "mindless" imitation, about specious claims to virtue, about the horrors of absolute virtue itself.

The concept of decorum is crucial to Roman character, both literary and ethical. To be successful, self-presentation must be appropriate in *facta, dicta, corporis motus et status* (Cic. *Off.* 1.126). Chapter 3 explores an Oedipus in the process of harmonizing his persona to his *status*: he acts as the narrative requires, but he seems half-aware of his true *status*, as the doomed Oedipus of a hostile, Ovidian Thebes. We can read Oedipus' neurotic anxiety and proleptic guilt as symptoms of a disjunction in his persona and literary *status*. Only after he begins tearing away at his eyes and truly delving deep (*scrutari*) into himself does he announce satisfaction with himself, *vultus Oedipodam hic decet* (1003). To achieve decorum, his Oedipus must fulfill the Theban narrative prescribed by Ovid, not Sophocles.

Seneca responds directly to Ovid's geopoetic landscape, and Statius too seems to acknowledge Ovid's primacy as a canonical author throughout the *Thebaid*. Canonical in two senses: Ovid seems to be regarded as poetically on par with the venerable Vergil, at least on the basis of frequency and degree of allusion. But even more striking, Ovid is the poet whose "immanent literary histories" become adopted as canonical by Seneca and Statius: his synthesis of the Theban tragic tradition is the basis of Seneca's *Oedipus* and must be carefully cordoned off by Statius in his proem to the *Thebaid*; even fanciful alternative traditions, such as the Phanoclean pederastic Orpheus and his morbid eroticism, are adopted and recanonized into Statius' epic. Statius' readings of Ovidian texts are themselves mediated by Senecan tragedy as the appendix on Hippolytus in the *Heroides* and the *Phaedra* suggests, and this topic deserves greater attention.

Parthenopaeus and Amphiaraus both exhibit literary characterization that closely parallels the construction of exempla. Roller breaks down the process into four parts: (1) a defining action; (2) an audience; (3) commemoration of the deed; (4) imitation.[2] *Action*: Each of the two figures embodies a defining action, that is, a narrative trajectory that is established and intimated throughout the poem. Parthenopaeus will die young, as signaled to the audience with maximum pathos and morbid eroticism. Amphiaraus is set apart from the other characters precisely because he knows that he will be swallowed up into the earth. In their every appearance, Statius rehearses and anticipates their paradigmatic ends. *Audience*: perhaps even more than other Roman poets, Statius depends on his audience's recognition of allusive cues to generate his exemplary

---

[2] Roller (2004) 4–5.

characters. In addition to imitation of individual *loci* in conventional literary allusion, Statius evokes synthetic patterns, such as Ovidian micro-genre, narrative "type scenes" (such as the Prophet versus Tyrant), and even contemporary referents such as the Flavian fashion for *pueri delicati*. Statius' audience becomes the "malicious accomplice of the author," and our assent produces the characters' exemplary effect. *Commemoration*: "monuments include narratives, statues, scars, or other bodily marks, toponyms, cognomina, and even rituals."[3] Statius creates talismanic physical symbols for Parthenopaeus and Amphiaraus: Parthenopaeus' hair, especially the votive lock, serves as the somatic monument of his *mors immatura*; Amphiaraus' *vittae* and *infula* are synecdochic of his prophetic vision and his imminent destruction. Furthermore, both Parthenopaeus and Amphiaraus are commemorated after their deaths, Parthenopaeus in the poem's epilogue, and Amphiaraus through the elaborate aetiology and foundation of his Boeotian cult. *Imitation*: exemplarity requires imitation in order to replicate its meaning to future generations in an "endless loop of social reproduction".[4] The highly allusive quality of these characters, I would argue, implies an endless loop of literary reproduction. The referentiality of Statius' characters builds on the practices of his own antecedents.

[3] Roller (2004) 5.
[4] Roller (2004) 6.

Appendix

SENECA'S HIPPOLYTUS AND FATAL ATTRACTION

While Parthenopaeus' beauty contributes to the effect of his extravagantly pathetic death, Statius never suggests that his appearance is the cause, although one might read it that way from a metanarrative perspective. In Seneca's *Phaedra*, however, Hippolytus' outstanding beauty seems to be the dramatic motive that replaces Aphrodite's wrath in the Euripidean tragedy. Lacking the goddess' prologue, Seneca's play seems to elevate Hippolytus' beauty into the causal element that instigates and drives the tragedy. Phaedra's helpless attraction to her stepson tragically obviates all moral considerations and causes her to focus on Hippolytus' appearance to the exclusion of his other qualities, most significantly, his utter hatred of all women.[1] Phaedra is not the only character who is affected; while Seneca's Phaedra, like Ovid's epistolary Phaedra before her, rhapsodizes Hippolytus in highly visual terms, the chorus and even Theseus himself also repeatedly return to the youth's appearance as his quintessential characteristic.[2] How others see Hippolytus and what they admire defines and dooms him.

In emphasizing Hippolytus' appearance as his defining character trait, Seneca departs from Euripides, who does not dwell upon Hippolytus' attractions.[3] Seneca treats the theme of failed *rites de passage* in a very familiar

---

[1] An attitude he shares with Euripides' Hippolytus, most explicitly stated in his response to the nurse's appeal, especially 559–64, *sed dux malorum femina* [. . .], and the rest of their exchange, 565–79.

[2] Coffey and Mayer (1990) appendix 1 provides an invaluable cross-reference of passages from *Heroides* 4 imitated by Seneca in this section of the *Phaedra*. The overwhelming importance of Ovid's *Heroides* 4 can be seen in the fact that the editors reproduce the poem in its entirety in their second appendix. Tarrant (1978) 262 also notes parallels between *Heroides* 4 and Seneca's *Phaedra*.

[3] On the dangers of taking classical Attic tragedy as a direct model for Seneca's plays see Tarrant (1978); Tarrant (1995). As in the discussion of Seneca's *Oedipus* in chapter 3, I assume that Seneca was familiar with Euripides' *Hippolytus* (perhaps both versions) and that his departures from the Euripidean play represent thoughtful innovation rather than incompetent bungling.

Roman mode. Hippolytus corresponds to the trope of the Doomed Ephebe from *Metamorphoses* 10, and while the *erastēs* in this case may be female, this seems to modify the terms only slightly. In *Heroides* 4, a significant model for Seneca's tragedy, Ovid's Phaedra describes Hippolytus in terms drawn from both pederastic epigram and from his own conventions of heterosexual attraction. Although she praises rugged masculinity, Ovid's Phaedra also emphasizes Hippolytus' youthful beauty (*Her.* 4.71–8):[4]

> candida vestis erat, praecincti flore capilli,
> > flava verecundus tinxerat ora rubor,
> quemque vocant aliae vultum rigidum que trucem que,
> > pro rigido Phaedra iudice fortis erat.
> sint procul a nobis iuvenes ut femina compti!
> > fine coli modico forma virilis amat.
> te tuus iste rigor positique sine arte capilli
> > et levis egregio pulvis in ore decet:

White was your garment, your hair bound with blossom, a modest blush tinged your blonde-framed face, other women described your face as harsh and even cruel, but Phaedra boldly cast her judgment for austerity. Stay away from us, youths dolled up like girls! Manly beauty desires to be cultivated to a moderate degree. The ruggedness you possess, your artlessly tousled hair, even a little dust on your face suits you.

As befits an *erōmenos*, Hippolytus here is reduced to his superficial characteristics. As Amy Richlin has discussed, portraits of the beloved (whether a *puer* or mistress) tend toward the stereotypical; Ovid's Phaedra succumbs to the irresistible ephebic combination of beautiful blonde hair, ruddy cheeks, and, in a somewhat displaced use of color, white garment. The Euripidean Hippolytus' unyielding and almost fanatical purity becomes transformed into a physical characteristic, a sexy scowl that should have warned her off (other women clearly understood what his expression meant, *quemque vocant aliae . . .*, 73).[5] Phaedra makes a virtue of a necessity, expressing herself as a conventional heterosexual woman by approving of Hippolytus' virile lack of grooming (4.75–8), though again, his hair proves an especial point of fascination.[6]

---

[4] *Heroides* text from Showerman and Goold (1977).

[5] Richlin (1983) *passim*.

[6] Cf. Ovid's injunction against male hairdressing, for which Hippolytus and Adonis are mythological exempla (*Ars* 1.507–10):

> Forma viros neclecta decet: Minoida Theseus
> abstulit a nulla tempora comptus acu;

In Phaedra's letter, the female *erastēs* imposes her objectifying gaze upon the young man's body, reducing him to a set of physical traits that all denote his attractiveness.[7] She misreads even his hostile, misogynistic attitude as a symbol of manly *rigor*, which she as a heterosexual woman finds alluring.[8] From Euripides to Ovid, Hippolytus' status as a love object undergoes a development enabled by the shift from the dramatic to the epistolary genre. Once an independent figure on the dramatic stage, Hippolytus becomes observed and inscribed solely through the eyes of a single female lover, whose gender and passion determine his portrayal.

In Seneca's play, Phaedra similarly gives her own account of how she conceived her passion. When asked by her naive stepson whether her torments are surely inspired by uxorious love for the absent Theseus, Phaedra attempts to turn this topic to her advantage (*Ph.* 646–60):[9]

> Ph: Hippolyte, sic est: Thesei vultus amo
> illos priores, quos tulit quondam puer,
> cum prima puras barba signaret genas
> monstrique caecam Gnosii vidit domum
> et longa curva fila collegit via.
> Quis tum ille fulsit! Presserant vittae comam
> et ora flavus tenera tinguebat pudor;
> inerant lacertis mollibus fortes tori,
> tuaeque Phoebes vultus aut Phoebi mei,
> tuusve potius—talis, en talis fuit
> cum placuit hosti, sic tulit celsum caput.
> In te magis refulget incomptus decor:
> est genitor in te totus et torvae tamen
> pars aliqua matris miscet ex aequo decus:
> in ore Graio Scythicus apparet rigor.

Just so, Hippolytus: I love that countenance of Theseus of old,
the face he bore once when he was a youth, when his first beard

---

Hippolytum Phaedra, nec erat bene cultus, amavit;
  cura deae silvis aptus Adonis erat.

The linkage between Hippolytus and Adonis as Doomed Ephebes seems significant, as their tragic ends may well ironically undercut their value as models of masculine grooming.

[7] For further investigation into the lover's "dismembering gaze" and Seneca's Phaedra as a female rapist, see Seo (forthcoming) with some overlap with this appendix.

[8] Pollini (2003) 166 suggests that the long-haired portraits of slightly older male slaves may well have been commissioned by women who enjoyed their sexual services once they matured too much for male pederasts.

[9] *Phaedra* text from Zwierlein (1986).

> was marking his unsullied cheeks and he saw the blind home of the Cretan abomination and gathered up the long thread on his winding way. How he shone then! His fillets held his hair back and a golden modesty set off his tender face; he had strong muscles in his delicate arms, and his face was like your Diana, or my Apollo, or rather, like yours—that's what he was like, just like that, when he seduced his host, he held his head high, in that very manner. That unpolished beauty shines out even more in you: You are entirely your father, and yet some part of your fierce mother tempers your beauty in equal measure: a Scythian hardiness shows in your Greek features.

Under the feeble rhetorical guise of praising his father's erstwhile beauty, Phaedra details Hippolytus' physical attractions. Programmatically, the term *puer* (647) predicts the description to follow; Seneca's Phaedra adopts a more conventionally pederastic aesthetic: the first beard, the blond hair, and the androgynous mystique. The debt to Ovid is clear in her obsessive detailing of his physical appearance, and Seneca's Phaedra still retains her interest in male undergrooming and strong muscles, but every instance of masculine detail is here carefully undercut by a feminizing element. Though Hippolytus may be *incomptus* (657), thus avoiding any charges of effeminate overattention to appearance, his youth and attractions are defined by androgyny. Theseus-Hippolytus has strong muscles in his still delicate arms (*lacertis mollibus*, 53); the adjective *mollis* juxtaposes feminizing implications with heroic strength. This passage features the image much used by Statius in his descriptions of ephebes: the face that blends both male and female.[10] As often in Statius, Phaedra declares that Hippolytus exhibits features of both his father and his mother (658–60).[11] Hippolytus' Amazon mother, Hippolyte, herself contains a transgressive contamination of male and female, and much like Parthenopaeus, his lineage seems to enable his androgyny. Seneca's Phaedra thus goes much further than Ovid's in developing Hippolytus' feminine side. Though Hippolytus may have been put in a passive role as the object of Phaedra's letter in *Heroides* 4, her descriptions correspond to conventional female desires according to Ovid's *Ars*; she emphasizes his masculine appearance and even contrasts him with effeminate youths. Seneca further elaborates the potential androgyny of youth and carefully introduces feminine suggestions that begin to draw a portrait of pathetic ephebic vulnerability, the *mors immatura* conventions of *Metamorphoses* 10 also adopted in Statius' Parthenopaeus.

---

[10] La Penna (1996) 167 also sees a parallel.
[11] Cf. Statius *Th.* 4.335–7, *Ach.* 1.164–5, *necdum prima nova lanugine vertitur aetas, / tranquillaeque faces oculis et plurima vultu/mater inest* [...].

In Seneca's play, boys and their beauty are to blame. The first choral ode has already established the well-known theme of the Hippolytus myth, the destructive power of love (274–356). Using the Ovidian personification of the boyish Cupid, the first ode programmatically describes the powerful god as an irresponsible child (*lascivus puer*, 277), as in the Euripidean ode on the dangers of the young god *erōs*.[12] This first ode on a *puer*'s dangers parallels Hippolytus' vehement self-condemnation after hearing Phaedra's unwelcome plea (*Ph.* 683–6):

> [...] sum nocens, merui mori:
> placui novercae. dignus en stupris ego?
> scelerique tanto visus ego solus tibi
> materia facilis? hoc meus meruit rigor?

> I am guilty, I deserve to die: I have proved pleasing to my stepmother. Look at me, am I fit for debauchery? Do I seem to you singularly appropriate stuff for so heinous a sin? Did my rectitude earn this?

Though his incredulous questions are rhetorical in nature, Hippolytus' language affirms Phaedra's passion. The doubleness of *visus* as both "seem" and "to appear" reflects Phaedra's own obsession with Hippolytus' appearance. Hippolytus is in fact *dignus* since he has been transformed into elegiac *materia* of Phaedra's passion.[13] The final unconsciously ironic note in his protest emerges in his use of *rigor*: his *rigor*, so appreciated by Phaedra in 660, is an essential part of his allure. By stressing his guilt and asking how he deserves these revolting advances, Hippolytus himself establishes the logical connection between his own beauty and his fate that is confirmed in the ode that follows.[14] Like his Oedipus, Seneca's Hippolytus also harkens back to an earlier incarnation of himself: Ovid's.

In the chorus' second ode, a response to the encounter between Phaedra and Hippolytus and the Nurse's opportunistic accusation of rape, the chorus

---

[12] Within this ode, cf. *nulla pax isti puero*, 283, *puer immitis*, 334, cf. Euripides *Hipp.* 525–64. For Cupid as a cruel boy as a particularly Ovidian conceit, see *Am.* 1.1.5 and McKeown (1989) notes *ad loc.* The ode's mythological exempla of the gods in love recalls the *Metamorphoses* (especially Cupid and Apollo, *lascivus puer*, *Met.* 1.456; see Coffey and Mayer [1990] *ad* 295ff.).

[13] On *materia* as the love object in Ovid's elegiac poetry, cf. *Am.* 1.3.20, *te mihi materiam felicem in carmine ... praebe* and McKeown (1989) *ad Am.* 1.1.2.

[14] Littlewood (2004) 262–3 analyzes Hippolytus as an "innocent" who is unknowing of and ultimately betrayed by the intertextual references that import eroticism to his own words and those of others, a phenomenon he terms "deviant intertextuality" after Don Fowler's "deviant focalization." Though he discusses this passage, he does not cite the parallels adduced here. On the *Phaedra*, see Littlewood (2004) 259–301.

does not endorse Hippolytus' anguished declaration of guilt, but they do seem to suggest that his beauty is the cause. The lengthy ode (736–834) divides into roughly four parts, combining lists of mythological exempla with *sententiae*, and bracketed at the introduction and conclusion with descriptions of the stage action. After reporting Hippolytus' horrified flight (736–40), the chorus begins by claiming that Hippolytus' beauty surpasses all others (section 1, 741–60). Hippolytus outshines all other individuals in history (*fama miratrix senioris aevi*, 742) much as the moon, significantly personified as *Phoebe* (747), Hesperus, also identified with Venus by the Romans, and Lucifer, the morning star, eclipse all other lights in the sky. Through these comparisons Hippolytus appears conspicuous, almost excessively visible like the doomed ephebes of Roman epic. Furthermore, this series of figures includes a programmatic combination of male and female; this mingling of male and female comparanda culminates in a direct address to Bacchus, also described in fully androgynous terms (753–60). Ironically, all of these figures taken together give this section an epithalamial tone as they all appear in the ill-fated epithalamial hymn to Jason and his new bride in Seneca's *Medea* (56–115);[15] the inappropriateness of a wedding song after an incestuous approach and the particularly disastrous outcome of the *Medea* hymn both contribute to the uncomfortable sense of doom that this section covertly portends. The themes of androgyny and the surpassing, exceptional nature of his beauty initiate the chorus' argument that Hippolytus' appearance will cause his death.

Having established Hippolytus' conspicuous beauty, the chorus enters into an admonitory protreptic (section 2, 761–94). Two *sententiae* state the case baldly; the first treatment takes on the seductive tone of pederastic epigram (761–3):

> Anceps forma bonum mortalibus,
> exigui donum breve temporis
> ut velox celeri pede laberis!

Beauty is a double-edged boon to mortals, a fleeting gift of short duration, how quickly you slip away on swift tread!

the "gather ye roses" message is elaborated in a second iteration, but concludes on a note of hopelessness (773–6):

> res est forma fugax: quis sapiens bono
> confidat fragili? Dum licet, utere.
> tempus te tacitum subruit, horaque
> semper praeterita deterior subit.

---

[15] I owe this observation to Elaine Fantham.

> Beauty is a fleeting entity: what sensible man would trust in so vulnerable a boon? Use it while it lasts. Time is silently undermining you, and every hour is always worse than the last.

The chorus delivers an exhortation to enjoy his youth and beauty while he can, much as the nurse argued in her appeal (435–82). As the audience knows from Hippolytus' negative response to this carpe diem argument earlier, it is unlikely that he will take this advice now, particularly since he is not even present to hear the appeal (737–40). What, then, might be the point of this section? The fading lilies and roses the chorus uses to illustrate beauty's disappearance (significantly from the cheeks, 768–70) combine the conventions of pederastic epigram with intimations of doom, as in Orpheus' song in *Metamorphoses* 10. This futile protreptic underscores the connection between Hippolytus' beauty and his impending doom.

In this second section the chorus also effectively illustrates their moralizing warning that "beauty is dangerous" with appropriately ephebic examples of untimely death. Hippolytus will never have the opportunity to enjoy the erotic rewards of his youth; like Hylas (777–84), his beauty will destroy him through the lustful pursuit it inspires. Having witnessed Phaedra's aggressive advances, the chorus appropriately adds another example of a youth pursued by a powerful female, Endymion (785–94). Rather than focusing on the boy's obliteration (his end is more peaceful than destructive), the chorus describes their own panicked reaction to the lunar eclipse that Diana's passion creates. This is the second time that the chorus has referred to the cosmic disruption that results from Diana's infatuation with Endymion: in the first choral ode, Apollo has to take the reins of his sister's nocturnal chariot and clumsily guide it through the night sky during her trysts (309–16). This repeated portrait of an uncharacteristically lascivious Diana associates female erotic aggression with cosmic disorder to exaggerate Hippolytus' doom. These concluding exempla emphasize the futility of their erotic protreptic.

In their enthusiasm, the chorus seems almost to invite divine punishment through excessive praise. They first taunt Bacchus directly, informing him that Hippolytus' hair is more beautiful than that of the famously long-haired, adolescent god and then add further insult by referring to the mythological variant that Ariadne eloped with Theseus after her marriage to Bacchus (753–60).[16] In the third section (795–819), devoted to a series of comparisons between Hippolytus and various gods, Apollo, also a prime exemplar of long-haired

---

[16] This variant found in *Odyssey* 11.321 and significantly Euripides *Hippolytus* 339, though it is by no means the primary version of the myth in Latin poetry as established by Catullus 64. *non vinces rigidas Hippolyti comas* (757): this repetition of *rigidas* here attached to hair seems to confirm the "sexy" connotations of *rigor / rigidus* used of Hippolytus both in *Heroides* 4.74 and earlier in *Ph.* 660.

beauty, has his coiffure judged inferior to Hippolytus' tousled locks in a rapturous four-line description (801–4).[17] This attention to hair indicates that both gods appear here as conventional exemplars of long-haired ephebic beauty, as in Tibullus' poem on fickle boys, *solis aeterna est Baccho Phoeboque iuventas/ nam decet intonsus crinis utrumque deum* (1.4.37–8).[18] The hair of Bacchus and Apollo recurs in the description of yet another paradigmatic Doomed Ephebe, Narcissus (*Met.* 3.418–24):

> adstupet ipse sibi vultuque inmotus eodem
> haeret, ut e Pario formatum marmore signum;
> spectat humi positus geminum, sua lumina, sidus
> et dignos Baccho, dignos et Apolline crines
> inpubesque genas et eburnea colla decusque
> oris et in niveo mixtum candore ruborem,
> cunctaque miratur, quibus est mirabilis ipse:

> He gapes at himself, and, frozen by the visage, he is rooted to the spot, like a carving formed of Parian marble. Stretched out on the ground, he gazes at twin stars—his own eyes—and at locks fit for Bacchus, fit for Apollo, adolescent cheeks and an ivory neck, and the radiance of the face, at the blush blended into the snowy gleam. He admires all the attributes for which he himself is admired.

Narcissus plays both parts of the lethal Hippolytus-Phaedra dynamic: his fragmenting, erotic gaze separates the love object into all the requisite Doomed Ephebe parts (hair, cheeks, pink-and-white complexion). This Ovidian passage shapes the Senecan chorus' conventional praise to such an extent that before praising Hippolytus' hair, the chorus speculates contrafactually on his skin's potential marble-like splendor were he less exposed to the elements (*Vexent hanc faciem frigora parcius, / haec sol em facies rarius appetat: / lucebit Pario marmore clarius, Ph.* 795–7).[19] That these two youthful gods, famous for their hairstyles, should be compared with the lovely Hippolytus is not surprising, but as the chorus moves from ephebic to more mature male exempla, the comparisons that follow seem somewhat overreaching. Hippolytus appears as strong as

---

[17] Apollo has already appeared in the first ode in a pederastic context as the chorus mentions his undignified service to Admetus, 296–8.

[18] Cf. Ovid *Am.* 1.14.31–2, regretting the loss of Corinna's tortured hair, *formosae periere comae, quas vellet Apollo, / quas vellet capiti Bacchus inesse suo.*

[19] The parallel to Narcissus is not noted in the commentaries of Coffey and Mayer (1990) or by Boyle (1987). The anomalous attention Ovid places on the youth's *eyes* (*sua lumina*, 3.420) as the first feature surely supports Hardie's suggestion that Ovid's Narcissus is an Oedipus in disguise.

Hercules and as broad-chested as Mars (804–8), but the final regrettable likeness is to Castor, the horseman, as the chorus praises Hippolytus' equestrian skill (809–11).[20] Singling out this particular quality, especially with the violent description of hunting that follows (813–9), ironically anticipates Hippolytus' grisly death in his chariot and the even grimmer "hunt" for his body parts that concludes the play. The excessive and almost hubristic nature of the chorus' admiration in their comparisons to the gods seems to cause Hippolytus' doom in a kind of *klēdōn,* or inadvertent curse.[21]

In the final section (820–8), the chorus concludes with a self-contradictory statement of pessimism tempered with a futile hope that Hippolytus may yet reach maturity, spared by some dramatic metamorphosis that will transform him into an ugly old man (820–3):

> Raris forma viris (saecula perspice)
> impunita fuit. te melior deus
> tutum praetereat formaque nobilis
> deformis senii monstret imaginem.

> Beauty remains unpunished for few among men (look to the ages). May a more favorable god leave you safe and let your noble beauty display the features of a hideous old man.

Just as the chorus' movement from ephebe to heroic male maturity in the previous section proved unconvincing, they undermine the feasibility of their own hope for Hippolytus' survival into old age by declaring that as a rule, "beauty in few men goes unpunished." Their condemnation of Phaedra's perfidious behavior and Theseus' timely return further confirm their pessimistic conclusion (829–34). From this moment Hippolytus' punishment is guaranteed and the chorus' point is more than adequately proved.

Charles Segal in his analysis of this choral ode also notes the thematization of Hippolytus' physical beauty and its association with death. As he explains,

> It is, in fact, ambiguous male beauty (*forma,* 820), not manly strength (*vires,* 805) that sets him apart. Hippolytus' failure to reach manhood

---

[20] Note that Hercules in the first ode (317–24) was depicted in Omphale's service, wearing women's clothes and with his hair tamed, *passus* [...] *dari legem rudibus capillis* (319–20); thus Hercules may be doubly inappropriate as a masculine comparand for Hippolytus, being either too powerful or too effeminate.

[21] Barkan (1986) 89 notes the prominence of the *tanta est fiducia formae* theme in the *Metamorphoses;* he adduces a string of figures punished for their vanity: Semele, Atalanta, Andromeda for her mother Cassiopeia's pride. As he states, "to boast of beauty is to lose one's form." Also cf. Psyche's explicit and entirely correct assessment of her own punishment at Apuleius *Met.* 4.34.6.

leaves him suspended ambiguously between male and female. Hence his *decus* is not the masculine honor or glory of heroic exploits but the physical beauty that is more frequently praised in women than in men and is a dangerous possession for the latter (820ff.). This beauty, singled out for praise by the chorus (*forma*, 761ff.), is the subject of lamentation at the catastrophe. The messenger bewails the ruined "honor of the son's handsome form" (*formae decus*, 1110).[22]

Segal rightly links the earlier and elaborate praise of Hippolytus' beauty with the laments after the youth's death. Beginning with the messenger, all the mourners express shock at the hideous transformation Hippolytus' body undergoes (1093–6):

> Late cruentat arva et inlisum caput
> scopulis resultat; auferunt dumi comas,
> et ora durus pulcra populatur lapis
> peritque multo vulnere infelix decor.

> He bloodies the fields far and wide and his battered head dashes against the cliffs; the thickets tear out his hair and unyielding stone ravages his beautiful visage. His unlucky beauty perishes in a vast multitude of wounds.

The messenger creates an image of beauty systematically dismantled. Just as the living Hippolytus was lovingly assembled, piece by piece, by his admirers in their descriptions, the manner of his death fittingly reproduces their erotic, objectifying gaze. As the messenger explains, his mourners are still in the process of collecting Hippolytus' corpse (1109–10):

> necdum dolentum sedulus potuit labor
> explere corpus—hocine est formae decus?

> The ceaseless effort of the mourners has not yet been able to reassemble his body—is this the glory of his beauty?

Phaedra also naturally bewails the drastic change to Hippolytus' physical form (1168–74)[23]:

---

[22] Segal (1986) 109.
[23] Cf. Theseus' lament while gathering the pieces of his son, *haecne illa facies igne sidereo nitens/ inimica flectens lumina? huc cecidit decor?* (1269–70). Even the father seems overinvested in his son's damaged beauty.

> Hippolyte, tales intuor vultus tuos
> talesque feci? membra quis saevus Sinis
> aut quis Procrustes sparsit aut quis Cresius,
> Daedalea vasto claustra mugitu replens,
> taurus biformis ore cornigero ferox
> divulsit? heu me, quo tuus fugit decor
> oculique nostrum sidus? Exanimis iaces?

> O Hippolytus, do I see your face like this, did I render it thus? What brutal Sinis or Procrustes dismembered you, or what Cretan minotaur, savage in his horned visage who fills the Daedalean enclosure with loud bellowing, tore you apart? Alas, where has your beauty gone, your eyes that were my star? Are you dead?

Phaedra accurately assumes responsibility for this terrible event. More than she realizes, Hippolytus' violent dismemberment fulfills the logic of her own earlier obsession with specific parts of the young man's body.[24] These laments consistently bewail the damage to Hippolytus' appearance even more than the loss of his life.

In his retelling of Hippolytus' tragedy, Seneca fashions his victim into an embodiment of ephebic vulnerability. Hippolytus is certainly the exemplum of *mors immatura* par excellence; we already know in Phaedra's letter and in Seneca's play that Hippolytus will die a horrible, dismembered death. Seneca's use of Doomed Ephebe elements amplifies and overdetermine the expected end. The elegiac and pederastic literary codes Seneca adopts reveal their own logic when placed into this well-known tale: the objectifying and obsessively fragmenting quality of the erotic gaze seems to predict and even cause the mutilation at the end of the play. In lieu of the supernatural intervention of Euripides' *Hippolytus*, Seneca uses the destructive power of a literary tradition to motivate and execute his victim's death.

---

[24] Most (1992) 394–5 also sees a link between the excessive focus on Hippolytus' beauty and his ghastly disfigurement; he takes this scene as evidence for Seneca's larger engagement with the Stoic problem of personal identity and physical unity. See also Seo (forthcoming).

WORKS CITED

Adams, J. N. 1982. *The Latin Sexual Vocabulary*. London.
Ahl, F. 2008. *Two Faces of Oedipus: Sophocles' Oedipus Tyrannus and Seneca's Oedipus*. Ithaca.
Ahl, F. M. 1976. *Lucan: An Introduction*. Ithaca.
Allen, T. W., W. R. Halliday, et al. 1936. *The Homeric Hymns*. Oxford.
Allen, T. W., and E. E. Sikes, eds. 1904. *The Homeric Hymns*. London.
Anderson, M. J. 1997. *The Fall of Troy in Early Greek Poetry and Art*. Oxford.
Anderson, W. S. 1990. "Vergil's Second *Iliad*." In *Oxford Readings in Vergil's Aeneid*. S. J. Harrison, ed. Oxford: 239–52.
Asso, P. 2009. "The Intrusive Trope-Apostrophe in Lucan." *MD* 61: 161–73.
———. 2010. "Queer Consolation: Melior's Dead Boy in Statius' Silvae 2.1." *AJP* 131.4: 663–97.
Auhagen, U. 2007. "Rhetoric and Ovid." In *A Companion to Roman Rhetoric*. W. Dominik and J. Hall, eds. London: 413–24.
Bailey, C., ed. 1947. *Lucretius: De Rerum Natura*. Oxford.
Barchiesi, A. 1998. "Representations of Suffering and Interpretation in the *Aeneid*." In *Virgil: Critical Assessments of Classical Authors*. P. R. Hardie, ed. London: 324–44.
———. 1999. "Ovid and the Homeric Hymns." In *Ovidian Transformations: Essays on Ovid's Metamorphoses and Its Reception*. PCPS supplementary volume 23. P. Hardie, A. Barchiesi, and S. Hinds, eds. Cambridge: 112–26.
———. 2001a. "Genealogie Letterarie nell'Epica Imperiale: Fondamentalismo e Ironia." In *L'Histoire Litteraire Immanente dans la Poesie Latine*. E. A. Schmidt, ed. Geneva: 315–62.
———. 2001b. *Speaking Volumes: Narrative and Intertext in Ovid and Other Latin Poets*. London.
———. 2002. "Narrative Technique and Narratology in the *Metamorphoses*." In *The Cambridge Companion to Ovid*. P. R. Hardie, ed. Cambridge: 180–99.
Barkan, L. 1986. *The Gods Made Flesh: Metamorphosis and the Pursuit of Paganism*. New Haven.
Bartman, E. 2002. "Eros's Flame: Images of Sexy Boys in Roman Ideal Sculpture." In *The Ancient Art of Emulation: Studies in Artistic Originality and Tradition from the Present to Classical Antiquity*. E. K. Gazda, ed. Ann Arbor: 249–72.
Bartsch, S. 1997. *Ideology in Cold Blood: A Reading of Lucan's Civil War*. Cambridge.
———. 2005. "Lucan." In *A Companion to Ancient Epic*. J. M. Foley, ed. Malden: 492–502.
———. 2006. *The Mirror of the Self: Sexuality, Self-Knowledge, and the Gaze in the Early Roman Empire*. Chicago.
Bellandi, F. 1991. "Ganimede, Ascanio, e la Gioventù Troiana." *Studi di Filologia Classica in Onore di Giusto Monaco* 2: 919–30.

Bettini, M. 1997. "Ghosts of Exile: Doubles and Nostalgia in Vergil's 'Parva Troia' ('Aeneid' 3.294ff.)." *CA* 16.1: 8–33.
Bexley, E. 2010. "The Myth of the Republic: Medusa and Cato in Lucan, *Pharsalia* 9." In *Lucan's Bellum Civile: Between Epic Tradition and Aesthetic Innovation*. N. Hömke and C. Reitz, eds. Berlin: 135–53.
Bloomer, M. 1997. "Schooling in Persona." *CA* 16: 57–78.
Bömer, F., ed. 1969–86. *P. Ovidius Naso: Metamorphosen*. Heidelberg.
Bonner, S. F. 1966. "Lucan and the Declamation Schools." *AJP* 87.3: 257–89.
Bowra, C. M. 1990. "Aeneas and the Stoic Ideal." In *Oxford Readings in Vergil's Aeneid*. S. J. Harrison, ed. Oxford: 363–77.
Boyle, A. J., ed. 1987. *Seneca's Phaedra*. Liverpool.
———, ed. 2011. *Seneca: Oedipus*. Oxford.
Braund, S. H. 2006. "A Tale of Two Cities: Statius, Thebes and Rome." *Phoenix* 60: 259–73.
Braund, S. M. 1998. "Speech, Silence and Personality: The Case of Aeneas and Dido." *PVS* 23: 129–47.
Braund, S. M., and C. Gill 1997. *The Passions in Roman Thought and Literature*. Cambridge.
Braund, S. M., and G. W. Most 2003. *Ancient Anger: Perspectives from Homer to Galen*. Cambridge.
Brown, J. 1994. "Into the Woods: Narrative Studies in the Thebaid of Statius." D.Phil., Cambridge.
Bruère, R. 1951. "Lucan's Cornelia." *CP* 46.4: 221–36.
Clauss, J. J. 1993. *The Best of the Argonauts: The Redefinition of the Epic Hero in Book One of Apollonius's Argonautica*. Berkeley.
———. 1997a. "Conquest of the Mephistophelian Nausicaa: Medea's Role in Apollonius' Redefinition of the Epic Hero." In *Medea: Essays on Medea in Myth, Literature, Philosophy, and Art*. J. J. Clauss and S. I. Johnston, eds. Princeton: 149–77.
———. 1997b. "*Domestici hostes*: The Nausicaa in Medea, the Catiline in Hannibal." *MD* 39: 165–86.
Clay, D. 1988. "The Archaeology of the Temple to Juno in Carthage (*Aen.* 1.446–93)." *CP* 83.3: 195–205.
Coffey, M. and R. Mayer, eds. 1990. *Seneca: Phaedra*. Cambridge.
Connolly, J. 1998. "Mastering Corruption: Constructions of Identity in Roman Oratory." In *Women and Slaves in Greco-Roman Culture: Differential Equations*. S. R. Joshel and S. Murnaghan, eds. London: 130–51.
———. 2007. "Virile Tongues: Rhetoric and Masculinity." In *Companion to Roman Rhetoric*. W. Dominik and J. Hall, eds. Malden: 83–97.
Conte, G. B. 1986. *The Rhetoric of Imitation: Genre and Poetic Memory in Virgil and Other Latin Poets*. Ithaca.
———. 1994. *Genres and Readers: Lucretius, Love Elegy, Pliny's Encyclopedia*. Baltimore.
Conte, G. B. 1999. "The Virgilian Paradox." *PCPS* 45: 17–42.
Corbeill, A. 2007. "Rhetorical Education and Social Reproduction in the Republic and Early Empire." In *Companion to Roman Rhetoric*. W. Dominik and J. Hall, eds. Malden: 69–82.
Cornell, T. J. 1975. "Aeneas and the Twins: The Development of the Roman Foundation Legend." *PCPS* 21: 1–32.
———. 1977. "Aeneas' Arrival in Italy." *LCM* 2: 77–83.
D'Alessandro Behr, F. 2007. *Feeling History: Lucan, Stoicism and the Poetics of Passion*. Athens (OH).
de Jongh, I. 1987. "Paris/Alexandros in the *Iliad*." *Mnemosyne* 40.1: 124–8.
Dewar, M., ed. 1991. *P. Papinius Statius: Thebaid IX*. Oxford.
Dickie, M. 1985. "The Speech of Numanus Remulus (*Aeneid* 9, 598–620)." *PLLS* 5: 165–221.
Dinter, M. 2010. "… und es bewegt sich doch! Der Automatismus des abgehackted Gliedes." In *Lucan's Bellum Civile: Between Epic Tradition and Aesthetic Innovation*. N. Hömke and C. Reitz, eds. Berlin: 175–90.

Dominik, W. J. 1994. *The Mythic Voice of Statius: Power and Politics in the Thebaid*. Leiden.
Dyson, J. T. 1999. "Lilies and Violence: Lavinia's Blush in the Song of Orpheus." *CP* 94.3: 281–8.
Eco, U. 1979. *The Role of the Reader*. Bloomington.
Edmunds, L. 2006. *Oedipus*. London.
Edwards, C. 1993. *The Politics of Immorality in Ancient Rome*. New York.
———. 1999. "The Suffering Body: Philosophy and Pain in Seneca's *Letters*." In *Constructions of the Classical Body*. J. I. Porter, ed. Ann Arbor: 252–68.
———. 2007. *Death in Ancient Rome*. New Haven.
Erskine, A. 2001. *Troy between Greece and Rome: Local Tradition and Imperial Power*. Oxford.
Esposito, P. 2001. "Paradosso ed esemplarità nell' episodio di Vultaeio (B.C. IV 402–581)." *Vichiana* 4.3: 39–63.
Faber, A. 2005. "The Adaptation of Apostrophe in Lucan's *Bellum Civile*." In *Studies in Latin Literature and Roman Hisotry*. C. Deroux, ed. Brussels: 334–43.
Fantham, R. E. 1990. "*Nymphas . . . e navibus esse*: Decorum and Poetic Fiction in *Aeneid* 9.77–122 and 10.215–59." *CP* 85.2: 102–19.
———, ed. 1992a. *Lucan: De Bello Civili Book II*. Cambridge.
———. 1992b. "Lucan's Medea Excursus: Its Design and Purpose." *MD* 29: 95–119.
———. 1995. "The Ambiguity of Virtus in Lucan's Civil War and Statius' Thebaid." *Arachnion* 1.3 http://www.cisi.unito.it/arachne/num3/fantham.html.
———. 1999. "Lament in the Growth and Eclipse of Roman Epic." In *Epic Traditions in the Contemporary World: The Poetics of Community*. M. H. Beissinger, J. Tylus, and S. L. Wofford, eds. Berkeley: 221–35.
———. 2006. "The Perils of Prophecy: Statius' Amphiaraus and His Literary Antecedents." In *Flavian Poetry*. R. R. Nauta, H.-J. Van Dam, and J. J. L. Smolenaars, eds. Leiden: 148–62.
———. 2008. "Covering the Head at Rome: Ritual and Gender." In *Roman Dress and the Fabrics of Roman Culture*. J. Edmonson and A. Keith, eds. Toronto: 158–71.
Fantuzzi, M. 1980. "*Ek Dios archomestha*. Arat. Phaen. 1 e Theocr. XVII." *MD* 5: 163–72.
Feeney, D. C. 1990a. "The Taciturnity of Aeneas." In *Oxford Readings in Vergil's Aeneid*. S. J. Harrison, ed. Oxford: 167–90.
———. 1990b. "The Reconciliations of Juno." In *Oxford Readings in Vergil's Aeneid*. S. J. Harrison, ed. Oxford: 339–62.
———. 1991. *The Gods in Epic: Poets and Critics of the Classical Tradition*. Oxford.
———. 2002. "The Odiousness of Comparisons: Horace on Literary History and the Limitations of Synkrisis." *Rethymnon Classical Studies* 1: 7–18.
———. 2005. "The Beginnings of a Literature in Latin." *JRS* 95: 226–40.
Fehrle, R. 1983. *Cato Uticensis*. Darmstadt.
Felson-Rubin, N., and H. M. Deal. 1980. "Some Functions of the Demophoön Episode in the Homeric *Hymn to Demeter*." *QUCC* 34: 7–21.
Fitch, J. G., and S. McElduff. 2002. "Construction of the Self in Senecan Drama." *Mnemosyne* 55.1: 18–40.
Flower, H. 1996. *Ancestor Masks and Aristocratic Power in Roman Culture*. Oxford.
Forster, E. M. 1927. *Aspects of the Novel*. London.
Fowler, D. P. 1987. "Vergil on Killing Virgins." In *Homo Viator: Classical Essays for John Bramble*. M. Whitby, P. Hardie, and M. Whitby, eds. Bristol: 185–98.
———. 1997. "On the Shoulders of Giants: Intertextuality and Classical Studies." *MD* 39: 13–34.
———. 2000. *Roman Constructions: Readings in Postmodern Latin*. Oxford.
Fraenkel, E., ed. 1950. *Agamemnon*. Oxford.
Freudenburg, K. 2010. "*Horatius Anceps*: Persona and Self-Revelation in Satire and Song." In *A Companion to Horace*. G. Davis, ed. Malden: 271–90.
Galinsky, G. K. 1968. "Aeneid V and the *Aeneid*." *AJP* 89: 157–89.
———. 1969. *Aeneas, Sicily, and Rome*. Princeton.

———. 1981. "Vergil's *Romanitas* and His Adaptation of Greek Heroes." In *ANRW* 2.31.2 985–1010.
Ganiban, R. T. 2007. *Statius and Virgil: The Thebaid and the Reinterpretation of the Aeneid*. Cambridge.
Gantz, T. 1993. *Early Greek Myth: A Guide to Literary and Artistic Sources*. Baltimore.
Garthwaite, J. 1984. "Statius, *Silvae* 3.4: On the Fate of Earinus." In *ANRW* 2.32.1. 111–24.
Garton, C. 1959. "The Background to Character-Portrayal in Seneca." *CP* 54.1: 1–9.
Geiger, J. 1979. "Munatius Rufus and Thrasea Paetus on Cato the Younger." *Athenaeum* 57: 48–72.
George, D. B. 1991. "Lucan's Cato and Stoic Attitudes to the Republic." *CA* 10: 237–58.
Gibson, R. K. 2007. *Excess and Restraint: Propertius, Horace and Ovid's Ars Amatoria*. London.
Gibson, R. K., and A. D. Morrison. 2007. "Introduction: What is a Letter?" In *Ancient Letters: Classical and Late Antique Epistolography*. R. Morello and A. D. Morrison, eds. Oxford: 1–16.
Gildenhard, I., and A. Zissos. 2000. "Ovid's Narcissus (*Met*. 3.339–510): Echoes of Oedipus." *AJP* 121: 129–47.
Gill, C. 1984. "The *Ethos/Pathos* Distinction in Rhetorical and Literary Criticism." *CQ* 34: 149–66.
———. 1986. "The Question of Character and Personality in Greek Tragedy." *Poetics Today* 7.2: 251–73.
———. 1988. "Personhood and Personality: The Four-*Personae* Theory in Cicero, *De Officiis* I." In *Oxford Studies in Ancient Philosophy*. J. Annas, ed. Oxford: 169–99.
———. 1990. "The Character-Personality Distinction." In *Characterization and Individuality in Greek Literature*. C. B. R. Pelling, ed. Oxford: 1–31.
———. 2004. "Character and Passion in Virgil's Aeneid." *PVS* 25: 111–24.
———. 2006. *The Structured Self in Hellenistic and Roman Thought*. Oxford.
Ginsberg, W. 1983. *The Cast of Character: The Representation of Personality in Ancient and Medieval Literature*. Toronto.
Gleason, M. W. 1995. *Making Men: Sophists and Self-Presentation in Ancient Rome*. Princeton.
Goar, R. J. 1987. *The Legend of Cato Uticensis from the First Century B.C. to the Fifth Century A.D.* Bruxelles.
Goldhill, S. 1991. *The Poet's Voice: Essays on Poetics and Greek Literature*. Cambridge.
Gombrich, E. H. 1969. *Art and Illusion: A Study in the Psychology of Pictorial Representation*. Princeton.
Goodyear, F. R. D., ed. 1965. *Incerti auctoris Aetna*. Cambridge.
Gowing, A. M. 2005. *Empire and Memory: The Representation of the Roman Republic in Imperial Culture*. Cambridge.
Gransden, K. W. 1984. *Virgil's Iliad: An Essay on Epic Narrative*. Cambridge.
Green, S. J. 2004. *Ovid, Fasti 1: A Commentary*. Leiden.
Grene, D. 1953. "Seven against Thebes." In *Aeschylus II*. D. Grene and R. Lattimore, eds. Chicago.
Griessmair, E. 1966. *Das Motiv der Mors immatura in den griechischen metrischen Grabinschriften*. Innsbruck.
Griffin, J. 1986. "The Creation of Characters in the *Aeneid*." In *Latin Poets and Roman Life*. Chapel Hill: 183–97.
Griffin, M. T. 1968. "Seneca on Cato's Politics: *Epistle* 14. 12–13." *CQ* 18.2: 373–5.
———. 1986a. "Philosophy, Cato, and Roman Suicide: I." *G&R* 33.1: 64–77.
———. 1986b. "Philosophy, Cato, and Roman Suicide: II." *G&R* 33.2: 192–202.
Griffin, M. T., and E. M. Atkins, eds. 1991. *Cicero: On Duties*. Cambridge.
Griffith, M. 1985. "What Does Aeneas Look Like?" *CP* 80.4: 309–19.
Gruzelier, C. 1993. *Claudian: De Raptu Proserpinae*. Oxford.
Gunderson, E. 2000. *Staging Masculinity: The Rhetoric of Performance in the Roman World*. Ann Arbor.

———. 2003. *Declamation, Paternity, and Roman Identity: Authority and the Rhetorical Self.* Cambridge.
Gurval, R. A. 1995. *Actium and Augustus: The Politics and Emotions of Civil War.* Ann Arbor.
Gutting, E. 2009. "Venus' Maternity and Divinity in the *Aeneid*." *MD* 61: 41–56.
Hall, E. 1988. "When Did the Trojans Turn into Phrygians? Alcaeus 42.15." *ZPE* 74: 15–18.
———. 1989. *Inventing the Barbarian: Greek Self-Definition through Tragedy.* Oxford.
Halliwell, S. 1990. "Traditional Greek Concepts of Character." In *Characterization and Individuality in Greek Literature.* C. B. R. Pelling, ed. Oxford: 32–59.
Hardie, A. 1990. "Juvenal and the Condition of Letters: The Seventh Satire." *PLLS*: 145–209.
Hardie, P. R. 1986. *Virgil's Aeneid: Cosmos and Imperium.* Oxford.
———. 1988. "Lucretius and the Delusions of Narcissus." *MD* 20–21: 71–89.
———. 1990a. "Ovid's Theban History: The First Anti-*Aeneid*?" *CQ* 40.1: 224–35.
———. 1990b. "Flavian Epicists on Virgil's Epic Technique." In *The Imperial Muse: Flavian Epicist to Claudian.* A. J. Boyle, ed. Bendigo: 3–20.
———. 1993. *The Epic Successors of Virgil: A Study in the Dynamics of a Tradition.* Cambridge.
———, ed. 1994. *Aeneis IX.* Cambridge.
———. 1995. "The Speech of Pythagoras in Ovid *Metamorphoses* 15: Empedoclean Epos." *CQ NS* 45.1: 204–14.
———. 1998. "Fame and Defamation in the *Aeneid* (*Aen.* 11.225–467)." In *Vergil's Aeneid: Augustan Epic and Political Context.* H.-P. Stahl, ed. London: 243–70.
———. 2002a. "Another Look at Virgil's Ganymede." In *Classics in Progress: Essays on Ancient Greece and Rome.* T. P. Wiseman, ed. Oxford: 333–61.
———. 2002b. *Ovid's Poetics of Illusion.* Cambridge.
———. 2009a. "The Word Personified: Fame and Envy in Virgil, Ovid, Spenser." *MD* 61: 101–15.
———. 2009b. *Lucretian Receptions: History, the Sublime, Knowledge.* Cambridge.
Harrison, E. L. 1995. "The Metamorphosis of the Ships (*Aeneid* 9.77–122)." *PLLS* 8: 143–64.
Harrison, S. 2002. "Ovid and Genre: Evolutions of an Elegist." In *The Cambridge Companion to Ovid.* P. Hardie, ed. Cambridge: 79–94.
Harrison, S. J., ed. 1991. *Vergil, Aeneid 10.* Oxford.
Heinze, R. 1919. "Ovids elegische Erzählung." *Sitzb. Akad. Leipzig.* Rpt. in *Vom Geist des Römertums* (Stuttgart, 1960) 308–403.
Henderson, J. G. W. 1998. "Statius' *Thebaid*: Form (p)re-Made." In *Fighting for Rome: Poets and Caesars, History and Civil War.* Cambridge: 212–57.
Henry, D., and B. Walker 1983. "The *Oedipus* of Seneca: An Imperial Tragedy." In *Seneca Tragicus: Ramus Essays on Senecan Drama.* A. J. Boyle, ed. Berwick: 128–39.
Henry, E. 1989. *The Vigour of Prophecy: A Study of Virgil's Aeneid.* Carbondale.
Hershkowitz, D. 1998. *The Madness of Epic: Reading Insanity from Homer to Statius.* Oxford.
Heslin, P. J. 2005. *The Transvestite Achilles: Gender and Genre in Statius' Achilleid.* Cambridge.
Hexter, R. 1992. "Sidonian Dido." In *Innovations of Antiquity.* R. Hexter and D. Selden, eds. New York: 332–84.
Higham, T. F. 1958. "Ovid and Rhetoric." In *Ovidiana.* N. I. Herescu, ed. Paris: 32–48.
Highet, G. 1972. *The Speeches in Vergil's Aeneid.* Princeton.
Hill, T. 2004. *Ambitiosa mors: Suicide and the Self in Roman Thought and Literature.* New York.
Hinds, S. E. 1987. *The Metamorphosis of Persephone: Ovid and the Self-Conscious Muse.* Cambridge.
———. 1988. "Generalising about Ovid." *Ramus* 16: 4–31.
———. 1993. "Medea in Ovid: Scenes from the Life of an Intertextual Heroine." *MD* 30: 9–47.
———. 1997. "Essential Epic: Genre and Gender from Macer to Statius." In *Matrices of Genre: Authors, Canons and Society.* M. Depew and D. Obbink, eds. Cambridge: 221–44.
———. 1998. *Allusion and Intertext: Dynamics of Appropriation in Roman Poetry.* Cambridge.
———. 2001. "Cinna, Statius, and 'Immanent Literary History' in the Cultural Economy." In *L'Histoire littéraire immanente dans la poesie latine.* E. A. Schmidt, ed. Geneva: 221–57.

———. 2011. "Seneca's Ovidian Loci." *SIFC* 104: 5–63.
Hine, H. M. 2002. "Seismology and Vulcanology in Antiquity?" In *Science and Mathematics in Ancient Greek Culture*. C. J. Tuplin and T. E. Rihll, eds. Oxford: 56–75.
Hömke, N. 2010. "Bit by Bit Towards Death—Lucan's Scaeva and the Aestheticization of Dying." In *Lucan's Bellum Civile: Between Epic Tradition and Aesthetic Innovation*. N. Hömke and C. Reitz, eds. Berlin: 91–104.
Horsfall, N. M. 1986. "The Aeneas-Legend and the *Aeneid*." *Vergilius* 32: 8–17.
———. 1989. "I Pantaloni di Cloreo." *RFIC* 117: 57–61.
———. 1990a. "Dido in the Light of History." In *Oxford Readings in Virgil's Aeneid*. S. J. Harrison, ed. Oxford: 127–44.
———. 1990b. "Numanus Remulus: Ethnography and Propaganda in 9.598ff." In *Oxford Readings in Virgil's Aeneid*. S. J. Harrison, ed. Oxford: 305–15.
———. 2000. *A Companion to the Study of Virgil*. Leiden.
Housman, A. E., ed. 1927. *M. Annaei Lucani Belli civilis libri decem*. Oxford.
Hunter, R. L. 1985. *The New Comedy of Greece and Rome*. Cambridge.
———, ed. 1989. *Argonautica Book III*. Cambridge.
———. 1993. *The Argonautica of Apollonius: Literary Studies*. Cambridge.
———. 2004. "Roman Epilogue." In *Tradition and Innovation in Hellenistic Poetry*. M. Fantuzzi and R. L. Hunter, eds. Cambridge: 477–85.
———. 2006. *Studies in the Reception of Hellenistic Poetry at Rome*. Cambridge.
Hutchinson, G. O., ed. 1985. *Septem contra Thebas*. Oxford.
Innes, D. C. 1979. "Gigantomachy and Natural Philosophy." *CQ* 29: 165–71.
Inwood, B. 2001. *The Poem of Empedocles: A Text and Translation with an Introduction*. Toronto.
Jacobson, H. 1974. *Ovid's Heroides*. Princeton.
Jakobi, R. 1988. *Der Einfluss Ovids auf den Tragiker Seneca*. Berlin.
Janan, M. 1988. "The Book of Good Love? Design versus Desire in *Met.* 10." *Ramus* 17: 110–37.
Johnson, W. R. 1987. *Momentary Monsters: Lucan and His Heroes*. Ithaca.
Kaster, R. A. 2005a. *Emotion, Restraint, and Community in Ancient Rome*. Oxford.
———. 2005b. "The Passions." In *A Companion to Latin Literature*. S. Harrison, ed. Malden: 318–30.
Keith, A. M. 2000. *Engendering Rome: Women in Latin Epic*. Cambridge.
———. 2002. "Ovidian Personae in Statius' *Thebaid*." *Arethusa* 35.3: 381–402.
Kenney, E. J. 2002. "Ovid's Language and Style." In *Brill's Companion to Ovid*. B. W. Boyd, ed. Leiden: 27–90.
Ker, J. 2009. *The Deaths of Seneca*. Oxford.
Knight, V. H. 1995. *The Renewal of Epic: Responses to Homer in the Argonautica of Apollonius*. Leiden.
La Penna, A. 1996. "Modelli efebici nella poesia di Stazio." In *Epicedion: Hommage à P. Papinius Statius*. F. Delarue, S. Georgacopoulou, P. Laurens, and A.-M. Taisne, eds. Poitiers: 161–84.
Laird, A. 1997. "Approaching Characterisation in Virgil." In *The Cambridge Companion to Virgil*. C. Martindale, ed. Cambridge: 282–93.
Leach, E. W. 1974. "Ekphrasis and the Theme of Artistic Failure in Ovid's *Metamorphoses*." *Ramus* 3: 102–42.
Leigh, M. 1997. *Lucan: Spectacle and Engagement*. Oxford.
———. 2000. "Lucan and the Libyan Tale." *JRS* 90: 96–109.
———. 2006. "Statius and the Sublimity of Capaneus." In *Epic Interactions: Perspectives on Homer, Virgil, and the Epic Tradition Presented to Jasper Griffin by Former Pupils*. M. J. Clarke, B. G. F. Currie, and R. O. A. M. Lyne, eds. Oxford: 217–41.
Levene, D. S. 2010. *Livy on the Hannibalic War*. Oxford.
Levin, S. 1989. "The Old Greek Oracles in Decline." In *ANRW* 2.18.2. 1599–1649.
Littlewood, C. A. J. 2004. *Self-Representation and Illusion in Senecan Tragedy*. Oxford.

Long, A. A. 2009. "Seneca on the Self: Why Now?" In *Seneca and the Self.* S. Bartsch and D. Wray, eds. Cambridge: 20–36.
Lord, M. L. 1967. "Withdrawal and Return: An Epic Story Pattern in the Homeric Hymn to Demeter." *CJ* 62: 241–8.
———. 1969. "Dido as an Example of Chastity: The Influence of Example Literature." *HLB* 17: 22–44.
Lounsbury, R. C. 1975. "The Death of Domitius in the *Pharsalia*." *TAPA* 105: 209–12.
Lovatt, H. 2005. *Statius and Epic Games.* Cambridge.
———. 2007. "Statius, Orpheus, and the Post-Augustan *Vates*." *Arethusa* 40: 145–63.
Luck, G. 1975. "Panaetius and Menander." *AJP* 96.3: 256–68.
Malamud, M. 2003. "Pompey's Head and Cato's Snakes." *CP* 98.1: 31–44.
Markus, D. D. 2003. "The Politics of Epic Performance in Statius." In *Flavian Rome: Image, Culture, Text.* A. J. Boyle and W. J. Dominik, eds. Leiden: 431–67.
Marti, B. M. 1945. "The Meaning of the Pharsalia." *AJP* 66.4: 352–76.
———. 1966. "Cassius Scaeva and Lucan's *Inventio*." In *The Classical Tradition: Literary and Historical Studies in Honor of Harry Caplan.* L. Wallach, ed. Ithaca: 239–57.
Mastronarde, D. J. 1970. "Seneca's Oedipus: The Drama in the Word." *TAPA* 101: 291–315.
McGuire, D. T. 1989. "Textual Strategies and Political Suicide in Flavian Epic." *Ramus* 18: 21–45.
McKeown, J. C., ed. 1989. *Ovid: Amores. Text, Prolegomena and Commentary.* Leeds.
McNelis, C. 2002. "Greek Grammarians and Roman Society during the Early Empire: Statius' Father and His Contemporaries." *CA* 21.1: 67–94.
———. 2007. *Statius' Thebaid and the Poetics of Civil War.* Cambridge.
Micozzi, L. 2007. *Il catalogo degli eroi: Saggio di commento a Stazio, Tebaide 4, 1–344.* Pisa.
Momigliano, A. 1982. "How to Reconcile Greeks and Trojans." *Mededelingen der Koninklijke Nederlandse Akademie van Wetenschappen, Afd. Letterkunde N.R.* 45: 231–45.
———. 1987. *On Pagans, Jews, and Christians.* Middletown.
Morford, M. P. O. 1967. "The Purpose of Lucan's Ninth Book." *Latomus* 26: 123–9.
Morgan, L. 1997. "*Achilleae comae*: Hair and Heroism According to Domitian." *CQ* 47.1: 209–14.
Moseley, N. 1926. *Characters and Epithets: A Study in Vergil's Aeneid.* New Haven.
Most, G. M. 1992. "*disiecti membra poetae*: The Rhetoric of Dismemberment in Neronian Poetry." In *Innovations of Antiquity.* R. Hexter and D. Selden, eds. New York: 391–419.
Myers, K. S. 1994. *Ovid's Causes: Cosmogony and Aetiology in the Metamorphoses.* Ann Arbor.
Nagy, G. 1999. *The Best of the Achaeans: Concepts of the Hero in Archaic Greek Poetry.* Baltimore.
Narducci, E. 1973. "Il tronco di Pompeo." *Maia* 25: 317–25.
———. 1979. *La provvidenza crudele: Lucano e la distruzione dei miti augustei.* Pisa.
———. 1985. "Ideologia e Tecnica Allusiva nella *Pharsalia*." *ANRW* 2.32.3: 1538–64.
———. 2002. *Lucano: Un'Epica contro l'Impero. Interpretazione della "Pharsalia".* Roma.
Nelis, D. 2001. *Vergil's Aeneid and the Argonautica of Apollonius Rhodius.* Leeds.
Newlands, C. 1997. "The Metamorphosis of Ovid's Medea." In *Medea.* J. J. Clauss and S. I. Johnston, eds. Princeton: 178–210.
———. 2010. "The Eruption of Vesuvius in Statius and Pliny." In *Latin Historiography and Poetry in the Early Empire: Generic Interactions.* A. J. Woodman and J. F. Miller, eds. Leiden: 106–33.
———, ed. 2011. *Statius: Silvae Book II.* Cambridge.
Newman, J. K. 1967. *The Concept of Vates in Augustan Poetry.* Brussels.
Nisbet, R. G. M. 1961. *M. Tulli Ciceronis: In L. Calpurnium Pisonem, oratio.* Oxford.
Nisbet, R. G. M., and M. Hubbard. 1980. *A Commentary on Horace: Odes, Book 1.* Oxford.
Nisbet, R. G. M., and N. Rudd. 2004. *A Commentary on Horace: Odes, Book 3.* Oxford.
Nussbaum, M. C. 1994. *The Therapy of Desire: Theory and Practice in Hellenistic Ethics.* Princeton.

Oliensis, E. 1997. "Sons and Lovers: Sexuality and Gender in Virgil's Poetry." In *The Cambridge Companion to Virgil*. C. Martindale, ed. Cambridge: 294–311.
———. 1998. *Horace and the Rhetoric of Authority*. Cambridge.
———. 2009. *Freud's Rome: Psychoanalysis and Latin Poetry*. Cambridge.
Olson, S. D. 2012. *The Homeric Hymn to Aphrodite and Related Texts*. Berlin.
Panoussi, V. 2002. "Vergil's Ajax: Allusion, Tragedy, and Heroic Identity in the Aeneid." *CA* 21.1: 95–134.
Pavlock, B. 2009. *The Image of the Poet in Ovid's Metamorphoses*. Madison.
Pease, A. S., ed. 1935. *Aeneidos liber quartus*. Cambridge.
Pecchiura, P. 1965. *La figura di Catone Uticense nella letteratura latina*. Turin.
Peek, W. 1955. *Griechische Vers-Inschriften*. Berlin.
Pelling, C. B. R. 1990. *Characterization and Individuality in Greek Literature*. Oxford.
Poe, J. P. 1983. "The Sinful Nature of the Protagonist of Seneca's Oedipus." In *Seneca Tragicus: Ramus Essays on Senecan Drama*. A. J. Boyle, ed. Berwick: 140–58.
Pollini, J. 2003. "Slave-Boys for Sexual and Religious Service: Images of Pleasure and Devotion." In *Flavian Rome: Culture, Image, Text*. A. J. Boyle and W. J. Dominik, eds. Leiden: 149–66.
Putnam, M. C. J. 1998a. "Dido's Murals and Virgilian Ekphrasis." *HSCP* 98: 243–75.
———. 1998b. *Virgil's Epic Designs: Ekphrasis in the Aeneid*. New Haven.
Quint, D. 1993. *Epic and Empire: Politics and Generic Form from Virgil to Milton*. Princeton.
———. 2001. "Patterns of Homeric Imitation in *Aeneid* 10." *MD* 47: 35–66.
Reckford, K. 1996. "Aeneas Meets His Mother (I)." *Arion* 3.2: 1–42.
Reed, J. D. 2007. *Virgil's Gaze: Nation and Poetry in the Aeneid*. Princeton.
Richardson, N. J. 1974. *The Homeric Hymn to Demeter*. Oxford.
Richlin, A. 1983. *The Garden of Priapus: Sexuality and Aggression in Roman Humor*. New Haven.
———. 1997. "Gender and Rhetoric: Producing Manhood in the Schools." In *Roman Eloquence: Rhetoric in Society and Literature*. W. J. Dominik, ed. London: 90–110.
Riggsby, A. M. 1995. "Pliny on Cicero and Oratory: Self-Fashioning in the Public Eye." *AJP* 116.1: 123–35.
Rimell, V. 2006. *Ovid's Lovers: Desire, Difference, and the Poetic Imagination*. Cambridge.
Roller, L. E. 1997. "The Ideology of the Eunuch Priest." In *Gender and the Body in the Ancient Mediterranean*. M. Wyke, ed. Oxford: 118–35.
———. 1999. *In Search of God the Mother: The Cult of Anatolian Cybele*. Berkeley.
Roller, M. 2004. "Exemplarity in Roman Culture: The Cases of Horatius Cocles and Cloelia." *CP* 99: 1–56.
Rosati, G. 1983. *Narcisso e Pygmalione: Illusione e spettacolo nelle Metamorfosi di Ovidio*. Florence.
Rose, C. B. 1998. "Troy and the Historical Imagination." *CW* 91.5: 405–13.
———. 2003. "Re-evaluating Troy's Links to Rome." *JRA*: 479–81.
Rosenmeyer, T. G. 1989. *Senecan Drama and Stoic Cosmology*. Berkeley.
Russell, D., ed. and trans. 2001. *Quintilian: The Orator's Education, Books 9–10*. Cambridge (MA).
Rutz, W. 1960. "Amor Mortis bei Lucan." *Hermes* 88.4: 462–75.
Sanna, L. 2004. "Partenopeo e Podeto: Due pueri dell'epoca Flavia e l'ossimoro *arma-puer*." *Prometheus* 30: 261–8.
———. 2008. "Dust, Water, and Sweat: The Statian Puer." In *The Poetry of Statius*. J. J. L. Smolenaars, H.-J. Van Dam, and R. R. Nauta, eds. Leiden: 196–214.
Saylor, C. 1986. "Some Stock Characteristics of the Roman Lover in Vergil, *Aeneid IV*." *Vergilius* 32: 73–7.
Schiesaro, A. 1992. "Forms of Senecan Intertextuality." *Vergilius* 38: 56–63.
———. 2002. "Ovid and the Professional Discourses of Scholarship, Religion, Rhetoric." In *The Cambridge Companion to Ovid*. P. Hardie, ed. Cambridge: 62–75.
———. 2003. *The Passions in Play: Thyestes and the Dynamics of Senecan Drama*. Cambridge.

Segal, C. 1986. "Boundary Violation and the Landscape of the Self in Senecan Tragedy." In *Interpreting Greek Tragedy: Myth, Poetry, Text*. Ithaca: 315–36.
———. 2001. "Intertextuality and Immortality: Ovid, Pythagoras and Lucretius in *Metamorphoses* 15." *MD* 46: 63–101.
Seo, J. M. 2011. "Lucan's Cato and the Poetics of Exemplarity." In *Brill's Companion to Lucan*. P. Asso, ed. Leiden: 199–222.
———. Forthcoming. "Senecan Tragedy, Neronian Violence."
Shackleton Bailey, D. R. 2003a. *Statius: Thebaid, Books 8–12; Achilleid*. Cambridge (MA)–
———. 2003b. *Statius: Thebaid, Books 1–7*. Cambridge (MA).
———, ed. 2003c. *Statius: Silvae*. Cambridge.
Sherk, R. K., and P. Viereck. 1969. *Roman Documents from the Greek East: Senatus Consulta and Epistulae to the Age of Augustus*. Baltimore.
Showerman, G., and G. P. Goold, eds. 1977. *Ovid: Heroides and Amores*. Cambridge (MA).
Sklenár, R. 2003. *The Taste for Nothingness: A Study of Virtus and Related Themes in Lucan's Bellum Civile*. Ann Arbor.
Slatkin, L. M. 1986. "The Wrath of Thetis." *TAPA* 116: 1–24.
———. 1991. *The Power of Thetis: Allusion and Interpretation in the Iliad*. Berkeley.
Smolenaars, J. J. L. 1994. *Statius Thebaid VII: A Commentary*. Leiden.
Snijder, H.M. 1968. *P. Papinius Statius Thebaid: a Commentary on Book III*. Amsterdam.
Sorabji, R. 2000. *Emotion and Peace of Mind: From Stoic Agitation to Christian Temptation*. Oxford.
Soubiran, J., ed. 2002. *Cicero, Aratea: Fragments poétiques*. Paris.
Stahl, H.-P. 1981. "Aeneas—an 'Unheroic' Hero.'" *Arethusa* 14: 157–78.
Stinton, T. C. W. 1965. *Euripides and the Judgement of Paris*. London.
Stover, T. 2008. "Cato and the Intended Scope of Lucan's *Bellum Civile*." *CQ* 58.2: 571–80.
———. 2009. "Apollonius, Valerius Flaccus, and Statius: Argonautic Elements in Thebaid 3.499–647." *AJP* 130.3: 439–55.
Suter, A. C. 1984. *Paris/Alexandros: A Study in Homeric Techniques of Characterization*. Princeton.
———. 1993. "Paris and Dionysos: *Iambos* in the *Iliad*." *Arethusa* 26.1: 1–18.
Tandoi, V. 1965. "*Morituri Verba Catonis*." *Maia* 17: 315–39.
Tarán, L. 1985. "ΕΙΣΙ ΤΡΙΧΕΣ: An Erotic Motif in the *Greek Anthology*." *JHS* 105: 90–107.
Tarrant, D. 1923. "Aristophanes *Birds* 700." *CR* 37.5–6: 113.
Tarrant, R. J. 1978. "Senecan Drama and Its Antecedents." *HSCP* 82: 213–63.
———. 1995. "Greek and Roman in Seneca's Tragedies." *HSCP* 97: 215–30.
Thomann, T. 1961. *Lucius Annaeus Seneca: Sämtliche Tragödien*. Zurich.
Thomas, R. F. 1982. *Lands and Peoples in Roman Poetry: The Ethnographical Tradition*. Cambridge.
———. 1986. "Virgil's *Georgics* and the Art of Reference." *HSCP* 90: 171–98.
———. 1988. *Virgil Georgics*. Cambridge.
Tipping, B. 2010. *Exemplary Epic: Silius Italicus' Punica*. Oxford.
Töchterle, K. 1994. *Seneca, Lucius Annaeus, Oedipus*. Heidelberg.
Toll, K. 1997. "Making Roman-ness and the *Aeneid*." *CA* 16.1: 34–56.
Toohey, P. 1984. "Politics, Prejudice and Trojan Genealogies: Varro, Hyginus and Horace." *Arethusa* 17.5: 5–28.
Usener, H., ed. 1887. *Epicurea*. Leipzig.
Van Dam, H.-J., ed. 1984. *P. Papinius Statius, Silvae, Book II: A Commentary*. Leiden.
———. 2006. "Multiple Imitation of Epic Models in the *Silvae*." In *Flavian Poetry*. R. R. Nauta, H.-J. Van Dam, and J. J. L. Smolenaars, eds. Leiden: 184–205.
Vernant, J.-P. 2001. "A 'Beautiful Death' and the Disfigured Corpse in Homeric Epic." In *Oxford Readings in Homer's Iliad*. D. L. Cairns, ed. Oxford: 311–41.
Vessey, D. 1973. *Statius and the Thebaid*. Cambridge.
———. 1986. "Transience Preserved: Style and Theme in Statius' Silvae." *ANRW* 2.32.5: 2754–2802.

Vian, F., ed. 1996. *Apollonius de Rhodes: Argonautiques chant III*. Paris.
Vinchesi, M. A. 2004. "La vicenda di Trasimeno (Silio Italico 5, 7–23) e la fortuna del mito di Ila in età imperiale." *Percorsi della Memoria* 2: 103–11.
Volk, K. 2002. *The Poetics of Latin Didactic: Lucretius, Vergil, Ovid, Manilius*. Oxford.
———. 2010. *Ovid*. London.
Watkins, C. 1986. "The Language of the Trojans." In *Troy and the Trojan War: A Symposium Held at Bryn Mawr College, October 1984*. M. J. Mellink, ed. Bryn Mawr: 45–62.
Webster, T. B. L. 1967. *The Tragedies of Euripides*. London.
Wheeler, S. M. 2000. *Narrative Dynamics in Ovid's Metamorphoses*. Tübingen.
———. 2008. "The Incipit of Ovid's Metamorphosis as Intertext." *MD* 61: 148–60.
Williams, B. 1993. *Shame and Necessity*. Berkeley.
Williams, G. W. 1978. *Change and Decline: Roman Literature in the Early Empire*. Berkeley.
Williams, G.D. 2006. "Greco-Roman Seismology and Seneca on Earthquakes in 'Natural Questions 6'." *JRS* 96: 124–46.
Williams, R. D. 1998. *Virgil: Aeneid I–VI*. London.
Wills, J. 1996. *Repetition in Latin Poetry: Figures of Allusion*. Oxford.
Wilson, R. 1975. "On Character: A Reply to Martin Price." *Critical Inquiry* 2: 191–8.
Woodman, A. J. 1966. "Some Implications of Otium in Catullus 51.13–15." *Latomus* 25: 219–23.
Wright, M. R., ed. 1981. *Empedocles: The Extant Fragments*. New Haven.
Zeitlin, F. I. 1982. *Under the Sign of the Shield: Semiotics and Aeschylus' Seven against Thebes*. Rome.
———. 1986. "Thebes: Theater of Self and Society in Athenian Drama." In *Nothing to Do with Dionysus? Athenian Drama in Its Social Context*. J. J. Winkler and F. I. Zeitlin, eds. Princeton: 137–67.
Zissos, A. 1999. "Allusion and Narrative Possibility in the *Argonautica* of Valerius Flaccus." *CP* 94.3: 289–301.
———. 2009. "Shades of Virgil: Seneca's Troades." *MD* 61: 192–210.
Zwierlein, O., ed. 1986. *L. Annaei Senecae: Tragoediae*. Oxford.

INDEX LOCORUM

Aeschylus
  Ag.
    1256-94: 154
  Sept.
    532-7: 133-4
    591: 151
Apollonius
  Argon.
    4.792: 25
    4.807: 25
    4.811-5: 24
    4.816: 27
    4.817: 26
    4.858-9: 27
    4.863-4: 27
    4.864: 28
    4.866: 27
    4.868: 27, 28
Aristophanes
  Av.
    685-722: 170

Bellum Africanum
  88.4: 75

Catullus
  Carm.
    63.12-22: 55, 81-2
    63.14: 56
    63.15: 56
    63.32: 56
    63.34: 56
Cicero
  Att.
    1.18.3: 49

De Off.
    1.93-151: 13
    1.97: 14-5
    1.105-25: 14

    1.126: 14, 187
  Nat. D.
    3.49: 182
  Pis.
    25: 53

Empedocles
  DK 27 B: 170
  DK 126 B: 178
  DK 129 B: 180
Euripides
  Andr.
    295: 61
  Bacch.
    346-51: 155
    439-6: 155
  IA
    1283-6: 61
  Tro.
    987-96: 53

Hesiod
  Theog.
    27-8: 49
    116-23: 180
    1008-10: 61
Homer
  h. Cer.
    212-55: 27
    235-41: 29
    246: 27
    251: 27
    258: 27
    263: 29
  h. Ven.
    38-52: 62
    54: 61
    177: 43
    202-17: 62
    256-8: 43, 61

Homer (cont'd)
Il.
    1.8: 55
    1.26-8: 155
    2.820-1: 61
    3.39: 52
    3.51: 52
    3.54-5: 52, 53
    3.380-2: 57
    3.390-4: 56
    5.260-72: 62
    5.311-7: 57, 61
    5.449-53: 57
    6.321ff: 68
    9.413: 29
    18.56-7: 29
    18.434-5: 25
    20.89-92: 62
    23.140-51: 137, 139
    23.144: 139
Od.
    13.248-9: 37
    16.172-6: 40
Horace
  Ars P.
    121-2: 49
    464-6: 178
  Odes
    1.5.4-5: 137
    1.7: 46
    1.15: 52, 59
    1.15.13-20: 52, 54, 56
    4.9.13-5: 52, 53
    4.9.19-20: 54

Lucan
    1.128: 86
    1.686: 149
    2.4-15: 171
    2.234: 75
    2.241: 83
    2.242-4: 69
    2.247: 71
    2.266-73: 69-70
    2.285: 75
    2.287: 84
    2.297-303: 70
    2.306-19: 71, 74, 79, 82
    2.323-5: 71, 77
    2.350-91: 91
    4.474-5: 75
    4.476-521: 75-7
    4.488-502: 76-7
    4.539-44: 77
    4.544-5: 77
    4.549-56: 77
    4.560-2: 78
    4.566-8: 78
    4.572-9: 78-9
    6.144-8: 79
    6.150-65: 79
    6.189-92: 80
    6.212-3: 80
    6.214-9: 80
    6.224-5: 87
    6.234-5: 81
    6.250-1: 80
    6.253-62: 81
    7.599-616: 82-3
    7.680-9: 84-5
    7.706: 85
    7.709-11: 85
    8.568-71: 83-4
    8.575-6: 84
    8.579-82: 86
    8.584-9: 86
    8.613-22: 86
    8.622-35: 86
    8.639-61: 86
    8.666: 86
    8.667-8: 86
    8.673-4: 87
    9.1-18: 88
    9.190: 88
    9.283-93: 89
    9.302: 90
    9.379-81: 90
    9.390-402: 90
    9.402-3: 90
    9.406: 90
    9.409-10: 83, 90
    9.563: 91
    9.564: 81
    9.601-4: 81
    9.733: 91
    9.759-60: 92
    9.761-2: 92
    9.803-4: 92
    9.832-3: 92
    9.848-80: 91
    9.881-9: 91
Lucretius
    1.62-79: 180
    5.432-5: 170
    5.526-33: 172
    5.548: 170
    6.535-607: 172-3, 175, 176
    6.639-702: 172, 173, 174, 175
    6.685-9: 174
    6.703-11: 172

Martial
  Epigrams
    9.11: 142
    9.12: 142
    9.16: 142

9.17: 142
9.36: 142

Ovid
  Her.
    4.71-8: 190
    12.212: 100
  Met.
    1.1-4: 169
    1.7-9: 169
    1.7-14: 170
    1.21: 169
    1.75-81: 170
    2.833-75: 104
    3.1-130: 104, 105, 113
    3.111-2: 77
    3.138: 113, 114
    3.253-5: 114
    3.418-24: 196
    3.511-732: 105
    4.1-415: 105
    4.416-542: 105
    4.545-50: 114
    4.564: 104
    6.146-312: 108-9, 114
    6.280-1: 115
    7.523: 103
    8.1-151: 170
    10.83-5: 127, 129
    10.141-2: 127
    10.148-55: 127-8, 130
    10.155-61: 128
    10.164-6: 128-9
    10.167: 130
    10.182-5: 130
    10.190-5: 129
    10.210-3: 133
    10.215-9: 130
    15.60-72: 180
    15.153-5: 179
    15.237: 180
    15.342-9: 175
    15.352-5: 176
    15.418-20: 170

Proclus
  Chr.
    1: 61
Propertius
  2.34.66: 99
Seneca
  Ep.
    11.9.1: 91
    11.10.5: 91
    24.8: 74, 75, 80
    67.13: 75
    70.17: 75
    70.19: 75

    88.45: 119
    104.30.1: 87
  Const.
    2.2: 67
  De Ira
    1.7: 71
    3.6.1: 70
    3.15.4: 79
    3.19.3: 91
  Med.
    56-115: 194
    910: 117
    1021: 117
  Oed.
    12-36: 97-100
    31: 101
    75: 102
    86-102: 100
    110-200: 102, 103-4, 113
    124-32: 103
    197-201: 102, 115
    215-6: 100
    257-63: 118
    299-402: 95
    403-508: 106-7
    530-658: 95
    586-8: 107
    589: 107, 115
    598: 113
    609-18: 107-8
    709-63: 109-14
    764: 115
    925-6: 116
    931-3: 116
    943-7: 116
    960-70: 117
    974-7: 119
    998-1003: 119, 187
    1032-3: 120
    1042-5: 120
    1051: 121
  Phaed.
    274-356: 193, 195
    435-82: 195
    646-60: 191-2, 193
    683-6: 193
    736-834: 194, 195, 196, 197, 198
    820-3: 197
    1109-10: 198
    1168-74: 198-9
    1093-6: 198

  Q Nat.
    6.21.2: 177
    6.23.4: 176
Seneca the Elder
  Suas.
    6.2.1: 72

INDEX LOCORUM

Servius
  Aen.
    1.87: 46
    1.198: 35
    4.215: 51
    4.216: 51
Sophocles
  OT
    31-9: 98
    386-9: 155
Statius
  Achil.
    1.161-2: 133, 135
  Silv.
    2.1.34-45: 135
    2.1.41: 133
    2.1.52-4: 138
    2.1.112: 133
    2.6.38-47: 136-7
    2.7.78: 169
    3.4: 142
    3.4.12-24: 142
    3.4.78-82: 142
    3.4.84-5: 143
  Theb.
    1.4-17: 104
    1.41-2: 124, 147
    2.94-101: 152
    2.121-2: 153, 154
    2.299: 147
    2.690-5: 157
    3.59-77: 157
    3.67-9: 157
    3.77-81: 158
    3.88-91: 158
    3.92-3: 158
    3.94: 158
    3.97-8: 159
    3.99-113: 156, 158-9
    3.482-9: 168-71
    3.483-6: 169
    3.539-47: 148
    3.547-65: 171
    3.566-8: 154
    3.598-677: 158
    3.602: 155
    3.665-7: 156
    4.187-91: 147, 158
    4.216-8: 151
    4.222: 152
    4.251-3: 130-1
    4.260-3: 134
    4.275: 132
    4.536-40: 164, 167
    4.579-91: 153
    4.598: 167
    4.602-3: 153
    5.668-9: 153
    6.30-1: 154
    6.193-4: 154
    6.197: 154
    6.301-3: 161
    6.372-83: 149, 161
    6.495-500: 150
    6.527: 150
    6.583-6: 139
    6.607-10: 138
    6.630-1: 152
    6.633-4: 139
    7.690-823: 149, 150, 159, 160-4
    7.705-11: 162-3
    7.779-88: 161
    7.809-16: 173-7
    8.4-5: 164
    8.5-11: 165
    8.11-3: 164
    8.19: 165
    8.23: 166
    8.36-46: 166
    8.52-3: 166, 180
    8.65-79: 166
    8.84-5: 166
    8.86-9: 166
    8.90-3: 179
    8.96-7: 166
    8.98-9: 166, 183
    8.100: 183
    8.104-9: 183
    8.116-9: 183
    8.121-2: 183
    8.122-6: 167
    8.174-207: 181
    8.329-38: 181
    8.335-8: 182
    9.701-3: 132, 135
    9.855-6: 139
    9.877-9: 140
    9.880-3: 143-4
    9.900-907: 140
    10.162-3: 182
    10.220-1: 182
    11.614-5: 101
    12.805-7: 124

Tibullus
  1.1.45-8: 48-9
  1.4.37-8: 196

Vergil
  Aen.
    1.2: 102
    1.4: 102
    1.11: 102
    1.26-8: 62
    1.171-9: 58, 63
    1.197ff: 46

Index Locorum

1.198: 35
1.26-8: 62
1.257-96: 37, 64
1.325: 37
1.335-70: 38, 42
1.372-85: 36-7
1.387: 37
1.407-9: 44
1.411-2: 57
1.439-40: 39-40
1.455-7: 38
1.463: 38
1.475: 139
1.479-82: 39
1.483-7: 38, 39
1.488: 39, 40
1.489: 38
1.490-3: 39
1.544-9: 42
1.565-6: 42
1.588-93: 40
1.605-6: 43
1.607-10: 43
1.618-9: 43, 50, 58, 61
1.619-26: 44-5, 46
1.661: 44
1.677-8: 63
1.680-1: 58
1.691-4: 58, 63
1.717-9: 58, 63
1.720-2: 58
2.221: 154
2.274-5: 163
2.604-7: 57
3.5-6: 60
4.188-94: 48, 58
4.203: 50
4.215-7: 50, 53

4.218: 56
4.221: 49
4.266: 49
4.271: 49
4.305: 59
4.309-11: 59
4.366: 59
5.122-3: 64
5.249-57: 62-3
5.295: 131, 132
6.93-4: 58
6.473-4: 58
7.319-22: 32, 33, 50
7.358-64: 58-9
7.461: 71
7.620-1: 148
9.80-7: 60-1, 62
9.88-9: 61
9.117: 62
9.136-42: 60
9.300: 137
9.435-7: 129
9.598-620: 54-5, 56
10.81-93: 56-7, 58, 61
10.252: 62
10.831-2: 135
11.68-70: 129
12.97-100: 53, 135

G.
1.404-9: 170
1.415-23: 169
2.479: 172
3.4: 17, 167
4.51-66: 89

INDEX

Achilles, 19, 23–4, 38, 39, 61, 136
  in *Achilleid*, 125, 135
  as infant, 25, 27
  lock of, 137–8, 143
  as symbol of ephebic death, 28, 133 n34, 139–40
  wrath as characteristic of Iliadic, 28, 29–30, 49 (*see also mēnis*)
Actaeon, 105, 111–2, 112 n40, 113–4, 114 n45
Aeneas, 2, 7, 18, 19–20, 32–65, 66, 69, 102, 135 n45, 138, 148, 151 n15, 163 n43, 186 (*see also* Mt. Ida, Paris, Trojan inheritance)
  in epic tradition, 35–42 (*see also* epic cycle, *Iliad*)
  as founder, 20, 21, 34, 35, 39, 47, 65 (*See also ktistēs*)
  indistinct physical appearance of, 39–40 (*see also* ecphrasis)
  and maternal inheritance 19, 43–4, 47 (*see also Homeric Hymn to Aphrodite*, Venus)
Aetna, 165 n52, 171–8 (*see also* seismology)
Aetna poem, 170, 170 n62, 176
  in Lucretius, 172, 173–175, 177
  in *Metamorphoses*, 175, 175 n78, 176
  as Empedoclean signifier for *katabasis*, 175–6, 178
  in Seneca 176 n80
allusion *See* intertextuality
amor mortis. *See mors voluntaria*
Amphiaraus, 21, 121, 123, 124, 146–84 (*see also* prophetic garb)
  incubation cult of, 181–3
  predetermined tradition, 147–50
  as Predestined Prophet, 155, 160, 162
  as super-*vates*, 183 (*see also* super-trope)
amphiboly, 168–9, 170
  in avian weather prediction, 169 n 57
  in earthquake, 173–4, 177

androgynous eroticism, 132, 135, 137, 141–2, 192, 194 (*see also* ephebic beauty)
Aphrodite. *See* Venus
Apollo, 57, 111, 120, 128, 151, 195
  as *erastēs*, 127, 128–9
  long-haired, 192, 195–6, 196 n18 (*see also* hair)
  oracular silence of, 159, 163, 181–2
  as patron, 148–9, 158–9, 161–2, 183
  symbols of, 150, 151–2, 154, 155, 166 (*see also* prophetic garb)
aristeia, 125, 139
  as exemplary moment, 160–3
Ascanius, 58, 63, 64 n83, 131, 137–8
Atropos, 147–8, 157–8
audience expectations, 4–8, 10–11, 16, 25, 34, 67–8, 100, 122–3, 183, 185,
  contributing to narrative effects, 18–21, 88, 121, 130, 151, 155, 160, 164, 188
  derived from visual culture, 51, 141
  of mythological character, 15, 99, 152
  prescribed by genre, 6–7
augury, 148, 154, 157, 167–71 (*see also* amphiboly)
  as miniature epic, 148

Bacchus, 195
  androgynous, 194 (*see also* ephebic beauty)
  long-haired, 155, 195–6 (*see also* Apollo)
  as patron god of Thebes, 106–7
beautiful death, 125, 129
botanical motifs, 126, 129–131, 144 (*see also mors immatura*)

carpe diem motif in erotic protreptic, 126, 194–195
Carthage as homeland, 37, 39, 40–1
Cassandra, 154–5, 154 n19

217

Cato, 7, 19, 20, 66–93, 186, 100
  as *exemplum libertatis*, 72, 74, 87–8, 156, 158–9
  as *exemplum virtutis*, 20, 67, 69, 72, 78–9, 80–1, 89–92, 181–2
  as paradigm of suicide, 73, 90, 158–60
  as Republican martyr, 67, 72, 83, 87–8
  as rhetorical exemplum, 18, 67, 68 n6, 72–3, 86, 88 (*see also* declamation schools)
  in Stoic hagiography, 20, 71
Cato's wound, 74–5, 80, 83, 87, 158
Catullus, 4,
  Attis of, 54–5,
  epithalamia of, 129–30
Chaos, 166, 168–70, 180
characterization, 1–5, 14–5, 185
  allusive, 4, 15, 16, 21–2, 23, 34, 99, 125, 187–8
  essentialized, 49–50, 66, 95–6, 125, 146–7, 171, 180
  in Livy, 2 n4, 5
  and narrative effects, 123–4, 125, 147, 167–7, 181
chasm, 149, 163, 171–9
Cicero, *De officiis*, 9, 12–15, 186 (*see also* Panaetius)
combinatorial imitation, 122 n2, 146, 170, 179
cosmogony, 170
  in Aristophanes *Birds*, 170
  in *Metamorphoses*, 169–70, 180
  Hesiodic, 180
Crastinus, 82–3

Dardanius, 43, 57–58, 61 (*see also* epithets)
decorum, 12–15, 34, 42, 94, 116, 119, 187
  language of, 12–3
  in Senecan characters, 117 n48, 119–120
devotio, 71, 74, 77, 79, 82, 87, 161 n40
didactic poetry *see also* philosophical epos, 169, 179
Dido, 4 n9, 46–7, 48, 50, 58–9, 64 n83
  in historiographical tradition, 41–3
  as interstitial figure, 44–5
divination, origins of 168–9, 170 n63, 171, (*see also* augury)
divine cruelty. See *saeva*
Domitian 4, 21, 142
  and baldness, 136 (*see also* Earinus)
Domitius Ahenobarbus, 82–3
Doomed Ephebe, 123, 125, 143, 146, 151, 190 n6, 194, 196, (*see also* super-trope, Parthenopaeus)

Earinus, 136, 141–3
  and castration, 142

ecphrasis, 38
  of Juno's temple, 38–41, 46 n38
  of Ganymede, 63
Elmore Leonard, 185
Empedocles, 168, 169, 170, 180, 181 n94, 184
  and Aetna, 178
ephebic beauty, 21, 63 n80, 125, 130–3, 142, 190, 196 (*see also* androgynous eroticism)
  of Hippolytus, 189, 191–2, 197–8
  pink cheeks, 132, 195
  roses, 132 n32, 195 (*see also* botanical motifs)
  associated with untimely death, 192
epic cycle, 38–9, 44
epic epitaph, 124, 145
Epicurean multiple explanation, 169 n 56, 174 n74
  in augury, 168–9, 171 n69
  in earthquake, 172, 173–7
  in Thiodamas' prayer, 182
epithets (*see also* Dardanius) 49, 62–63, 83, 131 n29, 138 n50, 148
Euripidean prologues, 99, 189
Euryalus, 131, 132, 137, 139
exemplarity, 1, 12, 14, 18, 65, 67, 72–5, 77–8 n41, 79, 82, 89–93, 183, 185, 187–8
  relation to literary practice, 10, 15
  Roman discourse of, 9–10

fama, 36–8, 41–3, 45 n34, 50–52
  mechanisms of, 19, 33–34, 64, 186
  as rumor, 34, 50,
Fama, personification of, 19, 33, 48, 61 n71, 186
  as double of epic poet, 48 n40, 48–9, 126,
  Allecto as agent of,
forensic rhetoric see invective
funeral games, 124
  of Anchises, 49, 149
  of Opheltes, 138–9, 149
furor, 69, 78, 79 n42, 186

Ganymede, 62, 128, 142
genre, 3 n7, 4, 7–8, 16, 19, 49, 109, 125–6, 127, 130, 168 n54, 191
  as code, 6, 6 n15, 21
  Ovidian micro-, 126, 128, 143, 188,
Glaucias, 133, 135, 138–9, 143, 165 n49

hair, 34, 40, 52–53, 126 n14, 132, 133–6, 143–4, 152, 153, 155, 188, 196 n18, 197 n20, (*see also* ephebic beauty)
  in dedicatory locks, 137–41, 142–3
  fouled with dust, 54, 134 n39, 134–5
  long, 141, 191 n8, 195–6,
  masculine neglect of, 136–137, 190, 191–2
  as signifier of effeminacy, 50–51, 52, 135, 155
  simplex applied to, 137

Index

Hera, 22–5, 26, 27, 29–31
  as Juno, 32, 34, 38, 42, 50, 55, 56–9, 62, 103 n17, 105, 106, 114–5, 148
Heroides, 7, 16, 17, 26, 99, 117 n48, 187, 189 n2, 190–1, 192, 195 n16
hiatus see chasm
Homeric Hymn to Aphrodite, 35 n10, 37, 43–44, 47, 61, 62
Homeric Hymn to Demeter 19, 23–30, 186
  Demeter of, 23–8
  Demophoön in, 27, 28–9
  as an *Iliad*, 26–7, 28–9, 30
Hyacinthus, 128–130, 133, 144

Iliad, 22, 23–5, 26, 28–30, 39, 52, 57, 99, 125, 129, 139, 143–5, 155, 160 n38, 186 (*see also Homeric Hymn to Demeter*)
  Paris of, 34, 37, 49, 52, 55, 57
interiority, 5–7, 15
intertextuality 3–4, 3 n7, 15, 16–18, 103, 128, 146, 188 (*see also* referentiality)
  characterization as, 4–5, 15, 16, 19, 20–4, 34, 121, 125, 167, 168–71, 180, 187–8
invective, 19, 49 n43, 50, 186

katabasis, 21, 107–8, 150, 171–8, 181 (*see also* Aetna, chasm)
kleos. See *fama*
ktistēs, 35, 46–7 (*see also* Aeneas)

libertas, 70, 72, 74, 87, 88, 156, 158–159 (*see also* Cato, Maeon)
literary genealogy, 10, 21, 22, 30, 34, 44, 47, 100, 186
  as heredity, 30, 44, 47
literary ghosts, 32, 94, 100, 107–9
love elegy, 6, 19, 48–9
  objectifying gaze of, 193, 199 (*see also* Phaedra)

Maeon, 148 n4, 152 n16, 156–9, 161, 165, 181
  as double of Amphiaraus, 152, 156, 177
  and Cato imitation, 156–159
maius, 99 n12, 99–100, 116, 120
makarismos, 81, 156, 181
Manilius, 170, 171
Manto, 107–9, 109 n31, 153
Medea, 16 n42, 22, 24, 30, 96, 194
  in *Heroides* 12, 99–100
  in Senecan *Medea*, 117 n48, 194
Melampus, 148, 152 n16, 157, 168, (*see also* augury)
mēnis as family trait, 29–30
Metamorphoses incipit, 169–70
mist as tool of Venus/Aphrodite, 38, 39–40, 57
modello esemplare (model text) and *modello codice*, 3 n7, 23, 82 n53

Mt. Ida, 43, 50, 51 n48, 54, 59 n67, 60–63
mutilation, 197–8

Narcissus, 95 n3, 96, 105, 106 n22, 108, 196 (*see also* Doomed Ephebe)
narrative surprise, 21, 99, 121, 123, 155, 184 (*see also* audience expectations)
  novelty in underworld as, 164–5, 172, 179
necromancy as repetition, 107–8
  described as *vulgata*, 17, 164, 167

Odysseus as model, 35 n12, 37, 40–1, 44, 67, 88, 89, 92
Oedipus, 20, 74, 94–121, 155, 187
  self-awareness of literary tradition, 100–101, 117 n 48
  blinding as self-discovery, 117–8
oppositio in imitando, 44, 81, 183
Ovid code, 16–18, 187
Ovidian Niobe "corrected", 109
Ovidian Orpheus, 125–30, 133, 141, 143, 195
  Phanoclean pederastic poetics of, 128, 187
Ovidian Pythagoras, 168, 170–1, 175–6, 179–81, 181 n94

Panaetius, 9, 12–15 (*see also* Cicero *de Officiis*)
  four *persona* theory, 13
Paris, 18, 19, 32–4, 47–65
  defined through multiple association, 49–50
  as negative exemplum, 19, 34, 66
  physical characteristics described, 50–4 (*see also* hair)
Parthenopaeus, 21, 122–45, 150, 155, 183, 187–8, 192, (*see also* Doomed Ephebe)
  in Aeschylus, 133–4
Peleus, 22–30, 138
Phaedra, 189–200 (*see also Heroides*, love elegy)
  as *erastēs*, 190–1
Philetos, 136–7
philosopher hero. See didactic *vates*
philosophical *epos*, 168, 171, 180 (*see also* didactic poetry)
poetic memory, 45 n34
Pompey, 83–87
possession, 69–71, 77, 186
prolepsis, 146–62, 167
Propertius, 6, 12, 99 (*see also* love elegy)
Prophet versus Tyrant, 155–60, 165–7, 188
  Agamemnon and Chryses, 155
  Amphiaraus and Capaneus, 155–6
  Amphiaraus and Dis, 165–7
  defined, 155
  Maeon and Eteocles, 156–60

prophetic garb, 150–5, 188
    defiling of, 154–5 (*see also* Cassandra)
    habitus preserved, 159
    vitta and *infula*, 150–1, 153, 162, 167, 188
    olive branch, 151
    narrative expectations of, 151 (*see also* audience expectations, narrative surprise)
    symbolism of, 153–4
    transferability of, 152
psychological "roundness". *See* interiority
puer delicatus, 63, 133, 137 n48, 141, 188 (*see also* Earinus, Ganymede, Philetos)

Quintilian, 11, 15,

red blood on white skin, 133, 143–4, 190 (*see also* ephebic beauty)
referentiality, 3, 15, 6, 18, 34, 54, 66, 68, 102–3, 121, 128, 156, 188 (*see also* intertextuality)
rhetoric, 2, 9, 10–12, 15, 53, 66–7, 69, 88, 123 n4, 186–7 (*see also* invective)
    in declamation schools, 11, 67, 68 n6, 72–4 (*see also* Cato)
    as "technology of the self", 11, 14
    persona in, 11–12 (*see also* Panaetius)
    as Ovidian quality, 16–18
Roller, Matthew. *See* exemplarity

saeva, 102, 103 n17, 114–5, 159 n35 (*see also* divine cruelty)
sage, 13, 67, 68–71, 83–4, 86
    perverted, 80, 92
sapiens. *See* sage
Scaeva as Cato, 79–82
securus, 83, 84–5,
seismology, 171–8 (*see also* Aetna, philosophical *epos*)

series as marker of Ovid's Theban narrative, 104–5
Servius, 35, 46, 51
"sexy boy" sculpture, 141–2 (*see also* Earinus)
super *topos*. *See* super-trope
super-trope, 17, 52, 117 n48, 123, 143, 165, 183 (*see also* Doomed Ephebe, combinatorial imitation)

Teiresias, 152–3, 155
Teucer, 45–7
Theban plague, 102–3
Thebes, 20, 77, 94–121, 126, 165, 166, 173,
    "geopoetics" of Ovidian Thebes, 95–6, 96 n5, 187
    as *locus tragicus*, 105–6, 123
Thetis, 22–31
Thiodamas, 181–3
Tibullus, 48, 196
Trojan inheritance, 47, 62, 63–5, 186 (*see also* literary genealogy)

vates as poet, didactic *vates*, 172, 178, 179
    Apolline associations of, 178, 180–1, 183
    inviolability of, 160, 161, 164, 166
Venus, 32–3, 37, 38, 42–4, 47, 50, 52, 56, 62, 63 (*see also* Aeneas, Paris)
    as Aphrodite 23, 43–4, 47, 52, 61, 189, (*see also* Homeric Hymn to Aphrodite)
"Vergil Killing Virgins", 129–30
virtus, 9, 71, 72, 76–81, 89, 90, 91, 92
    false imitations of, 78–82
voyeurism, 132–3
Vulteius, 20, 67, 74, 75–9, 81, 82, 89, 91, 156 n27

window allusion, 23, 180